75

WITHDRAWN

SO LONG AS MEN CAN BREATHE

SO LONG
AS
MEN
CAN
BREATHE

The Untold Story of Shakespeare's Sonnets

CLINTON HEYLIN

Da Capo Press

A Member of the Perseus Books Group

Copyright © 2009 by Clinton Heylin

All rights reserved. No part of this publication may be reproduced, stored
in a retrieval system, or transmitted, in any form or by any means,
electronic, mechanical, photocopying, recording, or otherwise, without
the prior written permission of the publisher. Printed in the United
States of America.

Designed by Timm Bryson
Set in 11 point Arno Pro by the Perseus Books Group

Library of Congress Cataloging-in-Publication Data
Heylin, Clinton.
   So long as men can breathe : the untold story of Shakespeare's
Sonnets / Clinton Heylin. — 1st Da Capo Press ed.
      p. cm.
   Includes bibliographical references and index.
   ISBN 978-0-306-81805-9 (alk. paper)
   1. Shakespeare, William, 1564-1616. Sonnets. 2. Sonnets, English—
History and criticism. 3. Poetry—Publishing—Great Britain—History.
4. Literature publishing—Great Britain—History. I. Title.
   PR2848.H49 2009
   821'.3—dc22

                              2009008999

First Da Capo Press edition 2009
ISBN 978-0-306-81805-9
Published by Da Capo Press
A Member of the Perseus Books Group
www.dacapopress.com

Da Capo Press books are available at special discounts for bulk purchases
in the U.S. by corporations, institutions, and other organizations. For more
information, please contact the Special Markets Department at the Perseus
Books Group, 2300 Chestnut Street, Suite 200, Philadelphia PA 19103, or
call (800) 810-4145, or e-mail special.markets@perseusbooks.com.

10 9 8 7 6 5 4 3 2 1

TO. THE ABLE BEGETTER . OF.
EVERY BOOK ON THE. SONNETS.
MR. S.S. ALL .HAPPINESSE.
AND .THAT. CAFÉ LATTE.
PROMISED.
BY.
THIS. EVERLIVING. SCRIBE.
WISHETH.
THE . WELLWORN.
CHRONICLER . NOW.
RUFFLING.
FEATHERS.

—C.H.

CONTENTS

SECTION TWO (1709–2009)

"This Key . . . Unlocked His Heart"

ABBREVIATIONS

The following abbreviations appear in the main text, enclosed in brackets, to identify specific sources. A full list of sources appears in the Bibliography at the end of the book.

AM   Arthur F. Marotti, "Shakespeare's Sonnets as Literary Property," in *Soliciting Interpretation,* ed. E. D. Harvey and K. E. Maus (Chicago University Press, 1990).

BDC   Ben Crystal and David Crystal, *The Shakespeare Miscellany* (Overlook Press, 2005).

BV   Brian Vickers, *Shakespeare, A Lover's Complaint & John Davies of Hereford* (Cambridge University Press, 2007).

CAB   Charles Armitage Brown, *Shakespeare's Autobiographical Poems* (James Bohn, 1838).

EKC   E. K. Chambers, *Shakespearean Gleanings* (Oxford University Press, 1943).

GT   Gary Taylor, *Reinventing Shakespeare* (Hogarth Press, 1990).

HCB   H. C. Beeching, *Shakespeare's Sonnets* (Athenaeum Press, 1904).

HL   Harold Love, *The Culture and Commerce of Texts: Scribal Publication in 17th Century England* (University of Massachusetts Press, 1998).

HR　　Hyder Edward Rollins, *The Sonnets: A New Variorum Edition,*
　　　　2 vols. (Lippincott, 1944).

HRW　　H. R. Woudhuysen, *Sir Philip Sidney and the Circulation of*
　　　　Manuscripts, 1558–1640 (Oxford University Press, 1996).

JWB　　J. W. Bennett, "The Alleged Piracy of Shakespeare's Sonnets
　　　　and of Some of Jonson's Works," *Studies in Bibliography*
　　　　(1973).

KDJ　　Katherine Duncan-Jones, "Was the 1609 *Shake-Speares*
　　　　Sonnets Really Unauthorized?" *Review of English Studies* 34,
　　　　no. 134 (1983).

KW　　Katharine M. Wilson, *Shakespeare's Sugared Sonnets* (Allen
　　　　and Unwin, 1974).

MSS　　Martin Seymour-Smith, "Shakespeare's Sonnets 1–42: A
　　　　Psychological Reading," in *New Essays on Shakespeare's*
　　　　Sonnets, ed. Hilton Landry (AMS Publishing, 1976).

Q　　Quarto; refers to *Shakes-speares Sonnets* (London, 1609).

SB　　Samuel Butler, *Shakespeare's Sonnets* (London, 1898).

SL　　Sidney Lee, *A Life of William Shakespeare* (John Murray,
　　　　1916).

SL-F　　Sidney Lee, *Shake-speares Sonnets* [Facsimile edition of Q]
　　　　(London, 1905).

WA　　William Archer, "Shakespeare's Sonnets: The Case against
　　　　Southampton," *Fortnightly Review* 78, December 1, 1897.

A BOOKLEG, OR NOT A BOOKLEG?
THAT IS THE QUESTION . . .

This is the story of a "bookleg."

The most famous "bookleg" of them all: *Shake-speares Sonnets.*

What, you may well ask, is a "bookleg"?

Well, it is a book that is also a bootleg, an unauthorized collection of previously unavailable material that has been published, usually surreptitiously, without the author's permission.

In the case of the *Sonnets,* the centuries-old presumption, that it was another example of the "divers stolen and surreptitious copies" that plagued Shakespeare's professional life, has recently been under assault.

In the past twenty-five years, academic opinion has shifted toward viewing the 1609 text as, in some way, approved. But, as I aim to show, once a bookleg, always a bookleg . . .

—C.H.

THE

DARLING

BUDS

OF

MAY

CHAPTER ONE

1609

"THE ONLIE BEGETTER"

The greatest advantage of Shakespearean studies
seems to be that questions may be asked over and
over again, and that almost nobody pays attention to
the answers—unless he borrows them for his own use
in an article or a book.

—HYDER E. ROLLINS, 1944

May 20, 2009, represents the 400th anniversary of the "publication" of one of the most famous books in the world. It was on that day that Thomas Thorpe, a publisher and "procurer of manuscripts," registered "a booke called Shakespeares sonnettes" with the Stationers' Company, a requirement for all publications under a Marian statute. The book, a thin quarto volume, contained a thirty-word dedication by Thorpe, alias "T.T."—not Shakespeare—154 sonnets, and a long poem, "A Lover's Complaint," that has never been definitively assigned to the Bard.

In the intervening four centuries, there have been enough volumes on the subject of the sonnets—and editions thereof—to fill a small public library. At least two entire books exist for the sole purpose of supplying bibliographies of editions of the sonnets. At the same time, the poems have become inextricably linked to a perceived biographical element for which there is still no independent evidence. As such, one would have to say that Shakespeare's several boasts in the sonnets—of which "So long as men can breathe or eyes can see / So long lives this" (18.13–14) is the most brazen—have been fully vindicated.

So how did it come to pass that the most (in)famous English love-poems of all time—written by the most revered writer the English world has known—remained a secret subtext to the man's plays for almost 200 years? And what were the circumstances that originally brought it notoriety, then obscurity, and finally the recognition that fulfilled Shakespeare's own prophecy that they would endure "so long as men can breathe"?

Despite recent assaults on a centuries-old perception, the suspicion remains that we are wholly beholden to Thomas Thorpe for their publication and enduring existence; and that Shakespeare himself, for all his protestations concerning posterity, had long ago washed his hands of these microcosmic masterpieces by the time they appeared in print in the twilight of his career.

Which prompts an altogether different question: What sort of poet would produce such a sustained, endlessly intertwining *sequence* of poems, only to then forget all about them? The answer may well be a popular poet no longer certain where his true strengths lay. For, like a certain song-poet of the twentieth century who exercises a similar fascination, it seems this Elizabethan bard produced his most personally revealing collection when recuperating from some great personal trauma, and on the brink of more mature work.

In Bob Dylan's case (fie! compare ye not), his song-poems were recorded in some friends' basement in the summer of 1967, then cut on acetates and circulated, first as publishing demos, and then, for many years, on bootleg records (which almost single-handedly created the modern bootleg industry). They are the fabled Basement Tapes, Dylan's most quixotic work. Shakespeare's sonnets, on the other hand, were circulated in manuscript form for a decade or more, and when they finally did appear in print it was as a "bookleg" quarto, courtesy of Thorpe.

I do not think that in either case the author set out with any greater intention than "killing time"; the inevitable expansion of poetic range being a fortuitous by-product. The intent was to produce a collection that was private, in every sense of the word. But, somehow, both sonnets and songs slipped out.

There was nothing at all unusual about this process in bygone days. Manuscripts were the bootleg tapes of their day; and there was a small but thriving business in manuscript-copies. They were used both by the acting companies, which needed "scribal copies" in order to put on their plays, and by those who preferred to keep their latest work out of the hands of the Stationers' Company, at least for a time. The scriveners of Shakespeare's day were not unlike the small pressing-plants that fueled the bootleg vinyl industry in the 1970s and 1980s, while also keeping official record companies supplied: They had an incestuous relationship with the printers and were prone to indiscretion. In such a climate, "an enterprising publisher had many opportunities of becoming the owner of a popular book without the author's sanction or knowledge" [SL].

In the here and now of the twenty-first century, barely a week goes by without somebody predicting the death of the publishing, music, or movie industries (take your pick), as a result of a flagrant disregard for the rights of artists, whose copyrights no longer confer the requisite protection in cyberspace. The Internet has transformed the nature of all businesses, but none quite as directly as those who trade in the creative media. In such an environment, pity the man trying to discreetly circulate a set of love poems among his bookish friends. Especially if his should be a name that, when "Googled," generates more than 8 million "hits."

Modern doom-mongers would like everyone to believe that copyright constitutes some inalienable right, not a manmade invention. They'd prefer us to overlook the fact that it was unquestionably created to protect the rights of publishers, not authors. The latter's rights still generally remain subsidiary to the former. Even in the wake of a prolonged writers' strike over "digital rights" in Hollywood, the writer of a TV or film screenplay in the land of the free does not own the primary copyright on his work—or the absolute moral right to be designated its creator. In fact, the studio can have your work rewritten by a.n.other without your input or approval.

So, really not so different from Shakespeare's time. Back then, the popular playwright—yesterday's screenwriter—was a man for hire, working for actors' guilds, for whom he produced new plays for a fee. After he did his job, all rights passed to the company, which jealously guarded these rights, along with the script itself, copies of which remained few and far between. So paranoid were these companies that even the actors would never see the whole play on the page. Instead, their parts "would be written out on a long roll of parchment wrapped round a piece of wood . . . with around three cue words preceding each speech, so he would know when to enter or speak" [BDC]. These scrolls were known as "cue scripts."

Such ruses were considered necessary because, if a play script ended up in the wrong hands, it could be copied and published, and there was nothing the playwright or the acting company could do about it. Copyright, as we know it, simply did not exist. Nor was there a great deal of honor among the Stationers' own brand of thief. Publishers would happily breach each other's rights, republishing books and ballads with new titles whenever the opportunity arose.

And whatever the case when he wrote this private set of lyrics, by 1609 William Shakespeare was undoubtedly the most successful playwright in London. Smart enough to have a financial stake in his own company of players (with a royal warrant), thus controlling the very means of production and any revenue generated, he now knew that publishing was a mug's game. It had been a useful way to get his name known back in the early 1590s, when his long poems, *Venus & Adonis* and *The Rape of Lucrece,* had brought him patronage and fame. But the fortune those poems made was reserved for someone else—the publisher—a fact of literary life that Elizabethan poet Thomas Churchyard bemoaned the year *Venus* appeared, referring to an "infinite number of other Songes and Sonets, given where they cannot be recovered, nor purchase any favour when they are craved"—i.e., published.

Shakespeare no longer craved such recognition. He had long ago decided that he would stake his future—and his commercial concerns—not on his poetry, but on his plays. A steady flow of piratical versions of his plays had been appearing in cheap quarto editions since 1594—i.e., directly after these two poems made publishers aware of his literary worth—proving to be a constant thorn in Shakespeare's side (hence, John Heminge and Henry Condell's sideswipe at "stolen and surreptitious copies" in the preface to their "authorized" folio of the plays). Yet he could do very little to stop the steady dissemination of the more popular plays in print. By 1609 he had already seen at least fifteen of them appear in unauthorized quarto editions—with several of the poorer editions not even deigning to name him on the title page.

Nor did he have to write them to see his name in print. (Plays like *The Yorkshire Tragedy* and *Sir John Oldcastle* went into second [and third] editions with Shakespeare's name on them, even though it is highly debatable whether he had any hand in the former, and pretty certain he had no hand in the latter.) No one, though, would have made a mistake like that in 1609. William had the stamp of royal approval, and his name—however one spelled it—was a selling point for any quarto, be it a play or a series of poems.

Even when the Stratford squire had created a tight company of players, and given them a financial interest in the success of the King's Men, the quarto booklegs just kept coming. As recently as January 28, 1609, a quarto edition of *Troilus & Cressida* had been registered by the publishers Richard Bonian and Henry Whalley—a full six years after another publisher, James Roberts, had registered his own right to publish *The book of Troilus and Cressida, as it is acted by my Lord Chamberlain's men.* The 1609 edition was printed by the same printer as *Shake-speares Sonnets,* George Eld; and, unlike the *Sonnets,* was popular enough to warrant a second edition inside a year. As for Roberts's edition, it would appear he had been bought off, or otherwise persuaded by the King's Men not to proceed.

It was in this anarchic climate that Thomas Thorpe, a little known publisher with just thirteen books to his name after almost fifteen years at the trade, registered this "booke called Shakespeares sonnettes" in the spring of that very year. The book, which probably appeared a matter of weeks after registration, was the only volume Thorpe published in 1609. Presumably, he hoped it would establish his name and relieve him of some of the financial hardships he had endured to date.

So sure was Thorpe of the clout the name Shakespeare held that he felt just two words, "SHAKE-SPEARE" and "SONNETS," would suffice to sell the initial print run, which he evenly divided between two respected London booksellers, William Aspley and John Wright. As he undoubtedly knew, both the playwright's two long poems, first published in 1593 and 1594, respectively, were still "in print," the former in its fifth edition, the latter in its fourth.

And yet, not only is the 1609 edition of *Shake-speares Sonnets* one of the world's most famous volumes, it is also one of the most valuable. Just thirteen copies have survived the centuries (as opposed to almost 300 copies of the 1623 "First Folio"), which has led to the suggestion that the book itself was suppressed, either as a result of its contentious contents, or because it was issued against the wishes of all concerned— i.e., author and dedicatee, the enigmatic "Mr W.H. "(who may well have had the political clout to do something about it). One thing it certainly was not, was a publishing phenomenon.

In some ways, the book might as well have stayed in manuscript. There are as many seventeenth-century manuscript copies of the second sonnet in Thorpe's collection (now thought to have circulated independently in this form) as there are surviving copies of the 1609 edition, known almost universally as "Q" (a moniker it shares, ironically, with the fabled—and long lost—Aramaic source of the first-century Synoptic gospels). Something, it would appear, went badly wrong. Yet, if the failure of *Shake-speares Sonnets* signaled the beginning of the end for Thorpe's personal ambitions as a serious publisher of literary works, it was just the start of the sonnets' own journey through the centuries.

So, what do we know about the elusive "T.T."(as he signed himself here), surely the most scrutinized booklegger in literary history? The short answer is, Not a lot. While other members of the Stationers' Company flourished, directly benefiting from the era's extraordinary literary outpouring, Thorpe never found a secure footing in a business for which he seems to have been singularly unsuited. Sidney Lee starkly portrays him as someone whom "fortune rarely favoured, [but who] held his own with difficulty for some thirty years in the lowest ranks of the London publishing trade . . . never enjoy[ing] in permanence the profits or dignity of printing his 'copy' at a press of his own, or selling books on premises of his own . . . [while he] pursued the well-understood profession of procurer of 'dispersed transcripts' for a longer period than any other known member of the Stationers' Company."

Apprenticed in 1583 at the age of fourteen, to a reputable stationer, Richard Watkins, Thorpe was finally granted the "freedom" of the Stationers' Company in 1594, which allowed him the legal right to publish and be damned. Yet it was a full six years—part of which he spent in Spain—before he was in a position to publish his first title, whether because of the "lack of capital or of family connections among those already in the trade" that Lee speculates hindered him, or because he had ideas above his station when it came to the type of book on which he wished to put his name.

The first book Thorpe did publish, at the turn of the century, set its own pattern of sorts. Featuring Christopher Marlowe's translation of the first book of Lucan's *Pharsalia,* it was a title replete with real literary credentials, if hardly containing the "wow" factor, commercially speaking. He had seemingly acquired the manuscript from fellow-stationer Edward Blount, to whom he dedicated the volume. But without his own printing press, he was obliged to have the book printed by another stationer—another practice that was always eating into a hard-up publisher's profits.

Between those upfront costs he paid the printer and the cut taken by the bookseller, it is highly unlikely Thorpe made any money out of this "niche book." He probably just hoped it would establish his credentials as a publisher of literary remains. That he had become infected with a dose of pretentiousness is evident from his long-winded dedication, full of self-serving allusions to someone struggling to make his way in the world of publishing:

> Blount: I propose to be blunt with you. . . . This spirit [presumably
> Marlowe] was sometimes a familiar of your own, Lucan's first

book translated, which (in regard of your old right in it) I have raised in the circle of your Patronage. But stay now, Edward, (if I mistake you not) you are to accomodate yourself with some few instructions touching the property of a Patron that you are not yet possessed of, and to study them for your better grace as our Gallants fashion. . . . One special virtue in our Patrons of these days I have promised myself you shall fit excellently, which is to give nothing. . . . Farewell, I affect not the world should measure my thoughts to thee by a scale of this Nature: Leave to think good of me when I fall from thee.

Thine in all rites of perfect friendship,

THOM. THORPE.

In such a way did Thorpe establish his credentials as a man with an ostentatious love of the literary, but too little appreciation for language itself. This effusive dedication also demonstrates a man finding it hard to attract patronage, and reliant on the good graces of his fellow stationer, Blount, who seems to have been something of a "procurer of manuscripts" himself. In the preface to a later volume of his own, Blount informed readers of how he learned about some interesting papers, and, "curious to see and reade them over[,] . . . supposed if I could get the copie, they would be welcome abroad," though "the author of this booke I knowe not." Such was the lot of the Jacobethan stationer, ever on the prowl for material he could purloin.

One recent reinterpretation of Thorpe's dedication has suggested that his bitterness may have been at least partly directed at Blount, for claiming ownership of every remnant Marlowe left behind. Obliged to make his own way in the cutthroat world of Jacobethan publishing, Blount had not provided Thorpe with quite the prize his friend may have hoped for, as he probably knew all along. But their association endured well into the first decade of the seventeenth century, with Thorpe invariably turning to Blount whenever he needed a literary leg up.

As it appears he often did. It was Blount who gave Thorpe the opportunity to publish Ben Jonson five years later, relinquishing his original copyright in Jonson's *Sejanus,* and assigning the rights to Thorpe in August 1605, surely another rite of this "perfect friendship." And far from claiming ownership of everything Marlowe left unpublished, Blount gave Thorpe an interest in *Hero and Leander.* (Thorpe subsequently sold his share of said copyright to another publisher, Samuel Vicars, when his own publishing career came to an end.)[1]

Before that, in late May 1603, Thorpe and Blount embarked on a second venture together. Unfortunately, this entry into the Stationers' Register coincided with them running foul not only of the rules, but of the unwritten code, of the company, by registering "a panegyric or congratulation" to James I that had already been registered to another publisher, Gregory Seton. They were duly obliged to cancel the registration. As Colin Burrow recently observed, Thorpe thus violated "one of the key principles of the Stationers' company," a respect for other printers' copyrights, and probably alienated a couple of his fellow stationers into the bargain.

Nor was this Thorpe's only breach of Stationers' etiquette that summer. Another fortuitous association with a fellow stationer, William Aspley—which seems to have been largely responsible for the improvement in Thorpe's publishing prospects in the years preceding the publication of *Shake-speares Sonnets*—commenced in June 1603 with a joint attempt to license for publication another Stationer's copyright. Their claim to "A letter written to ye governors . . . of ye East Indian Merchants" was duly "cancelled owing to the official recognition of another publisher's claim to the copy concerned" [SL-F]. So much for the recent suggestion that "Thorpe was a publisher of some deserved status and prestige" [KDJ].

After this rocky start, things steadily improved, and through the remainder of that difficult decade Thorpe began to make some headway in his chosen vocation. Producing between one and three books a year, he would be responsible for a surprisingly high number of enduring literary works: translations by John Healey and plays by Ben Jonson and George Chapman, as well as the poems of Shakespeare he bequeathed to posterity.

Thorpe's joint registration (with Aspley again) of John Marston's *The Malcontent,* assigned to the pair in July 1604, suggests he had now begun to develop some literary connections of his own. It was perhaps an interest in literature that he shared with Aspley, who had already—in partnership with Andrew Wise—acquired copyrights to both *Henry IV Part Two* and *Much Ado about Nothing.* Aspley, like Thorpe, never owned his own press, but unlike Thorpe, he had his own means of distribution—a shop in St. Paul's.

Meanwhile, Thorpe continued to call in favors from his former fellow-apprentice Blount. In 1605, he had managed to persuade Blount to let him publish Ben Jonson's *Sejanus,* transferring the copyright as part of whatever bargain was struck. Perhaps Blount was concerned that Jonson might prove to be the kind of demanding publishing-bedfellow who made it hard to make an honest shilling. And it must be said that the 1605 quarto of *Sejanus* made quite a contrast to contemporary "bad" Shakespeare quartos, "with its severe columns of verse flanked by marginal scholia and with the proclamations set in the style of a Roman lapidary inscription with medial stops between each word" [HL]. Jonson, who evidently oversaw its publication, was pleased enough with the outcome to let Thorpe publish his next offering, an altogether chancier venture.

Eastward Ho, coauthored with George Chapman (and probably John Marston), fully tested the new monarch's willingness to be lampooned.

But then, Thorpe took risks. He had already chanced his arm back in 1604, publishing an eighteen-page pamphlet by the former Jesuit and Catholic priest, Thomas Wright, on "the nature of Clymactericall yeeres, occasioned by the death of Queen Elizabeth," a book as contentious as anything he ever published, and one which highlighted his Catholic connections. Perhaps it was this reckless nature which ultimately resulted in Shakespeare's sonnets being thrust into his sweaty palms.

While *Eastward Ho* appears to have brought Jonson and Chapman a degree of notoriety—resulting in the temporary incarceration of its caustic coauthors, not so much for expressing overtly anti-Scot sentiments as for making a number of sarcastic references to James I—it perhaps put Thorpe's business on a temporarily sounder footing. It also cemented his relationship with Aspley, who again acquired joint copyright in the provocative play (though, according to its title page, it was published by Thorpe alone—as per the *Sonnets*).

By the end of 1608, when Thorpe probably acquired the precious manuscript of sonnets, he had reached the high tide of his fortunes. That year he had managed to publish three books for the first time, and had even occupied a shop, The Tiger's Head, in St. Paul's Churchyard. Those three books included George Chapman's *Byron* and Ben Jonson's *Masques of Blackness and Beauty,* the third of Chapman's and the fourth of Jonson's works that Thorpe had put into the world.

Thorpe's association with the likes of Jonson and Chapman—a strong candidate for the so-called "Rival Poet" of sonnets 78–86—undoubtedly reinforced his own literary pretensions, and probably convinced him to take a chance on *Shake-speares Sonnets.* That he knew he was taking a chance is borne out by his famous dedication at the front of that volume, which includes a description of himself as a "well-wishing adventurer" for "setting forth" these sonnets. Had he paid too much for the precious "scribal copy," or was he merely concerned that the sonnet fad was largely spent? Or did he recognize a potentially scurrilous sub-text underlying the majority of these lovelorn sonnets?

Whatever his concerns, it seems clear Thorpe was staking much of his meager finances and reputation on a single roll of the dice—and the publishing value of this singular poet's name. But he still couldn't do it by himself. Or didn't want to. When it came to the sonnets, he was still reliant on a printer-friend and two booksellers, one of whom was Asp-ley, to make it happen.

Even in 1609, Thorpe would have needed Aspley more than Aspley needed Thorpe. Having entered into his part-time partnership with Thorpe five years earlier, when he was just another struggling stationer, Aspley was now an altogether more prestigious name than either the sonnets' printer or their publisher. Indeed, he would later become Mas-ter of the Stationers' Company, the most esteemed position in Jaco-bethan publishing, as well as being a member of the syndicate responsible for the 1623 First Folio, and eventually acquiring the rights to publish *Venus & Adonis*.

All of which could well suggest that his appreciation of Shakespeare's work transcended mere commercial interest. And the fact that Aspley was given his own "edition" of the *Sonnets*, credited as seller of the book on the title page, implies that he provided upfront capital, while Thorpe again fulfilled his familiar role as "procurer of manuscripts." (Of the two title pages Thorpe printed, Aspley's is significantly rarer—just four copies of "his" edition have survived.)

This convoluted alliance also involved George Eld, printer of most of Thorpe's Jacobean titles, as well as John Wright, the second "distributor" of *Shake-speares Sonnets*. Wright, who "was largely concerned with chap-books and ballads" [SL], may have been Eld's suggestion, given that Eld also published the 1611 edition of Marlowe's *Faustus* for Wright, which "bore the same imprint as his impression of Shakespeare's sonnets" [SL-F]. The copyright, though, remained with Thorpe, suggesting he considered it a commodity worth hanging on to, even when allying himself with others who shared a history of disregard for the rules of the Stationers' and an interest, commercial and/or literary, in the works of William. Of these comrades, Eld would prove the most "loyal."

George Eld had already published his own contribution to that ever-expanding canon of Shakespearean Apocrypha—a 1607 edition of *The Puritan*, a.k.a. *The Widow of Watling Street*, initially credited to "W.S.," but now considered to be the work of Thomas Middleton. Eld enjoyed a similarly checkered career as a publisher-printer, being fined by the company in 1606 and 1610 for printing ballads without license, a common enough practice. In fact, something like a third of the books published were never entered at all—for reasons hard to comprehend, given that the four or six pence it cost to register a broadside or a book conferred the company's protection and copyright (though, according to J.W. Bennett, "the custom of the trade" meant "copyright was assumed and enjoyed by many who did not trouble to enter their copies").

That Eld was fined twice suggests he was producing, at least for a short time, such broadsheets on a brazen scale. Most such piracy was carried out by the company's members—just as in the present day most audio piracy is conducted by members of the "official" phonographic industry (and is equally tacitly condoned). And Eld, like Thorpe, was fully prepared to violate another printer's copyright, for which he was fined by the company in 1619, by which time he was no longer an associate of Aspley, who had gone on to greater things, or Thorpe, whose days as a publisher were nearing an end.

During the first decade of the new century, though, Eld shared Thorpe's desire to become more than just a printer and/or procurer of works, having in 1604 married a widow of two previous master-printers. As David Frost points out in *The School of Shakespeare* (1968), Eld was doing his utmost in 1606–8 "to break out on his own as a publisher." Having previously published just two books of his own, in these three years "he entered a large number of works in the Stationers' Register, printed fine editions of histories in translation, and acquired the copyright" on some four plays, all of which he published himself.

With partners like these, Thorpe must have acquired the manuscript for the sonnets independent of Eld and/or Aspley. Otherwise, I doubt they would have had any reason to make him a part of the venture. Unlike Thorpe, Eld had his own printing presses, and Aspley had vital means of distribution. Thorpe probably felt the *Sonnets* provided a God-sent opportunity to demonstrate his literary taste, and contacts, and show his fellow stationers that he had what it took. And so it was probably with some bravado, and not a little trepidation, that he penned the most famous dedication in literary history, sometime early in 1609:

TO. THE .ONLIE . BEGETTER . OF.

THESE . INSVING . SONNETS.

MR. W.H. ALL .HAPPINESSE.

AND .THAT. ETERNITIE.

PROMISED.

BY.

OVR. EVERLIVING. POET.

WISHETH.

THE . WELLWISHING.

ADVENTVRER . IN .

SETTING.

FORTH .

—T.T.

According to Sidney Lee, just the act of writing the dedication "on behalf of the author" was a clear indication that "the stationer owned a copyright and controlled the publication," while "the exceptionally brusque and commercial description of the poems" provided further "evidence that the author was no party to the transaction." Poet George Wither articulated the general practice in a 1595 volume of his own, "It is a usuall manner . . . for all those that goe about to publish any work or writing of theirs, to dedicate it to some one or other."

Thorpe had not, however, presumed to provide one of his own inimitable dedications to any of the volumes he published for Jonson or Chapman. Indeed, *Shake-speares Sonnets* seem to have provided a first opportunity to exercise his own penmanship since that garrulous dedication to Blount, back in 1600. And though he pruned the length to which he went this time to sing the "inspirer" or procurer's praise, he managed in the space of thirty words to create quite enough conundrums for the centuries. The meaning of "onlie begetter"; the identity of "Mr W.H."; the import of "well-wishing adventurer"; the kind of "eternitie" which he here promises, are issues that have taxed some of history's finer minds, all of whom have ultimately admitted defeat. Thorpe's dedication has become the literary equivalent of the Sphinx's riddle.

The most contentious, and least resolvable, of the many disputes occasioned by these few words undoubtedly revolves around the meaning of the expression Thorpe coined at its outset, "To The Onlie Begetter." Professor Hyder Rollins displays not the slightest propensity for exaggeration when claiming, in his indispensable variorum edition of the *Sonnets,* "An entire library has been written on [just] the[se] four opening words."

Many a tree has been wasted on the etymology of the expression "onlie begetter" itself, with various authors hoping to demonstrate that "begetter" must mean "inspirer"; or that, all things considered, it could just mean "procurer." A few brave souls have even had the temerity to suggest that it means both—i.e., that the "inspiration" behind the sonnets might have passed them to Thorpe, directly or indirectly.

Most anyone arguing that he meant merely "procurer" has tended to avoid highlighting one contemporary use certainly known to both poet and publisher. Samuel Daniel, dedicating his 1592 *Delia* sequence to the Countess of Pembroke, described his own sonnets as "begotten by thy hand and my desire." Such folk have generally taken their lead from James Boswell, who, in his 1821 "Malone" edition of *The Plays & Poems,* "wished to relieve the poet from the imputation of having written the sonnets to any particular person, or as anything but a play of fancy." But, as Edwardian scholar H. C. Beeching was obliged to point out, "[Even] allowing it to be conceivable that a piratical publisher should inscribe a book of sonnets to the thief who brought him the manuscript, why should he lay stress on the fact that 'alone he did it'?"

In fact, anyone attempting to explicate the reasoning underlying Thorpe's dedication is obliged to take account of the fact that the publisher rarely expressed what he meant, and rarer still, managed to do so with the requisite lucidity or economy of phrasing. As R. G. White observed, a century and a half ago, "This dedication is not written in the common phraseology of its period; it is throughout a piece of affectation and elaborate quaintness."

The sheer convolutedness of the dedication should at least remove any possibility that it was really Shakespeare's own, published, as it were, by proxy. And yet, Katherine Duncan-Jones, in her 1997 Arden edition of the sonnets, refused to let Thorpe stand as the only begetter of his tortuous dedication, suggesting instead that, "though the initials of 'T.T.' are at the bottom, and the over-rhetorical wording is evidently Thorpe's, the dedication, like the text itself, had Shakespeare's authority." The basis for her novel suggestion is a house of cards theory that presupposes Shakespeare not only wanted to see his poems published, but gave them to Thorpe for that purpose.

An altogether more plausible explanation for the cryptic dedication— and one which would still have "Shakespeare's authority"—had been made as far back as 1897. This generally attractive theory, first espoused by William Archer in an article in *The Fortnightly Review,* in which he presented "The Case against Southampton" as the Fair Youth of the sonnets, suggested that the words "To Mr W.H." had been "prefixed to sonnet one" all along:

> The overwhelming probability is that Thorpe did not know the secret history of the Sonnets, and, reading them either carelessly or not at all, supposed them all addressed to the dedicatee whose initials no doubt figured at the head of the Ms. . . . There is no difficulty in supposing that Thorpe did not quite know the history of the poems he was publishing; whereas it is very difficult to conceive his using so common a word [as 'begetter'] in so quaint, affected and archaic a sense [as 'procurer'].

Archer's theory resolves so many of the issues which have plagued sonnet-detectives that it is slightly surprising it has gone largely unadopted—even though Beeching refined it further in his 1904 edition, suggesting that Thorpe may have "found his manuscript of the *Sonnets* headed 'To W.H.' and, being ignorant who W.H. was, supplied the ordinary title of respect." (Beeching was seeking to explain away how a noble, as he supposed, came to be addressed as a mere gentleman.)

The two twentieth-century commentators who have taken Archer's suggestion to their bosoms—E.K. Chambers in the forties and J. Dover-Wilson in the sixties—are also the two most astute literary historians to have tackled the many thorny issues thrown up by these lyrics. In Chambers' case, it took him a while to come round to the view that "Thomas Thorpe in 1609 . . . had [no]thing before him but 'To W.H.' on a manuscript"; he adopted it thirteen years after completing his monumental two-volume magnum opus, *William Shakespeare: A*

Study of Facts and Problems (1930), in a supplementary essay on "'The Youth' of the Sonnets." Dover-Wilson, meanwhile, drawing on Chambers, modified the view to fit his own supposition "that Thorpe procured his collection from a person or persons he had discovered possessed them and that he found 'To W.H.' at the head of the portfolio or chief manuscript."

However, like Chambers and Archer before him, Dover-Wilson found his suggestion fell on stony ground when it came to fellow academics. He was arguing against a rising tide of opinion—in academia, at least—that preferred an ordered, authorized Q text. In suggesting that Thorpe, as the "procurer of the manuscript," had no clue as to the identity of W.H., he was a man out of time.

Yet a private inscription would in an instance remove the demands of social propriety which convinced so many Victorians that "Mr W.H." could never be a man of title. For anyone like the 1855 correspondent to *Fraser's Magazine* who insisted that "if 'Mr W.H.' had been a man of rank and importance . . . 'T.T.' would have given his name in full, with all [his] titles and additions," the possibility that the initialed dedication was a private one—perhaps written when the Fair Youth (i.e., Master W.H.) was still not in his majority—had not even been entertained.

Thorpe's failure to attach any significance to these initials would certainly help "explain" his adoption of such a clumsy expression as "onlie begetter." He was surely making a very bad, if archetypally Elizabethan, pun on "only begotten," a familiar phrase even then, and one with a very specific sense that directly relates to the subject of the first seventeen sonnets—an heir. Indeed, it could have been these sonnets—and these alone—that were dedicated "in ms." to "Mr W.H."

It would be rather fitting if "T.T." did, in the words of Louis Gillet, render these "few lines of gibberish [that] have accounted for more commentaries than the Apocalypse," while wholly unaware of their import.

After all, such dedications on manuscript copies were hardly unknown in the Elizabethan era. A manuscript copy of Robert Southwell's *Four-fold Meditation,* published by another "W.H." in 1606, contains an "epistel dedicatorie" by Peter Mowle on the first page that, according to Lee, expressed "the conventional greeting of happiness here and hereafter"; while so-called presentation copies of Jonson's and Chapman's assorted works invariably contained their fair share of self-conscious inscriptions.

If Thorpe was faced with a similar "epistel dedicatorie," and had no way of checking with the author without alerting him to the publisher's acquisition of said poems, then Duncan-Jones is entitled to suggest that "the over-rhetorical wording is . . . Thorpe's, [whereas] the dedication, like the text itself, had Shakespeare's authority." However, such a dedication would date from the time the manuscript copy was made, not when it was acquired by Thorpe—i.e., at the turn of the century, and not 1608–9, when "T.T." overelaborated what little he had to go on.

For surely, if Shakespeare did agree to the 1609 publication, and "Mr W.H." was a reference to either "lovely boy" who in the interim became Earl of Pembroke or the already-titled Earl of Southampton—and that is a can of worms we shall open soon enough—the playwright-poet himself would never have allowed the original dedication to stand, whatever the earl's feelings about the matter. Circa 1600, when the sonnets remained a private matter, he would have had no such concerns. Whatever the case, methinks some fuel has now been added to the fire of doubt swirling around Thorpe's credentials as a publisher "of some deserved status and prestige."

CHAPTER TWO

1590–1603

"THE SWEETE WITTIE
SOULE OF OVID"

*If [the sonnets] descend to what they descend, they
[also] ascend to what they ascend, and who knows
quite what the body of them is; as, for instance, if
these or those are not [just] exercises on a rainy after-
noon in a country-house?*
                                    —J. A. CHAPMAN, *Essays,* 1943

I t is not just the cryptic dedication to that precious first edition of
Shake-speares Sonnets which provides compelling evidence for its
unauthorized, nay piratical, status. We also have to consider the
existence of some, if not all, of its contents in manuscript form in Lon-
don literary circles more than a decade earlier, at the height of what
might be termed the Elizabethan sonnet fad.

For once, thanks to a reliable paper trail, we have something more
than speculation with which to work. Perhaps the most fabled, and in-
dubitably the most important, contemporary published reference to
Shakespeare as both playwright and poet, comes in Francis Meres's

Palladis Tamia: Wits Treasury (1598). Aside from naming (and therefore helping to date) twelve of the plays, Meres refers to how "the sweete wittie soule of Ovid lives in mellifluous and hony-tongued Shakespeare, witness his Venus & Adonis, his Lucrece, [and] his sugred Sonnets among his private friends, &c."

How literally Meres intended to convey the idea that Shakespeare was an English reincarnation of Ovid, this solitary sentence fails to reveal. There is certainly no shortage of Ovidian sentiment, or reasoning, in these poems, but it was a large part of Meres's general thesis that his English contemporaries had as much to offer as classical authors.

Nor is Meres done with making comparisons. In a later paragraph from the same section of his treasury, comparing (near) contemporary English poets with those from a more exotic past, he elected to place Shakespeare in exalted company—alongside the Earl of Surrey, Sir Thomas Wyatt, Sir Philip Sidney, Sir Walter Raleigh, and fellow sonneteer Samuel Daniel—as one of those "most passionate among us to bewail and bemoan the perplexities of Love." Such a tantalizing description sounds particularly apposite if Meres had in mind the so-called Dark Lady sonnets (Q127–52), which appear to portray a love triangle riddled with guilt, lust, and betrayal—the "perplexities of Love" writ large.

Sadly, Meres does not provide any example of these "sugred Sonnets," just as he fails to reveal the identity of the "lost" Shakespeare play he name-checks, *Love Labours Won* (for which my personal candidate would be *As You Like It*). He also fails to reveal whether he arrived at any of his knowledge of Shakespeare's poetic output firsthand—i.e., if he was "among [the poet's] private friends" honored with a copy or loan thereof. But he was assuredly moving in London literary circles in the period 1597–98, before retiring to the country and the life of a rector-schoolmaster by 1602. He may even have had Shakespeare's blessing when he inserted the reference to these unpublished poems in his own book, in order to engender interest from a publisher or demand from lovers of *Venus* and *Lucrece* for their eventual publication in a form as exact and as popular as those more formal poems.

(It doesn't seem to have occurred to anyone in the past four centuries that Thorpe might have approached Meres directly, at a later date, to see if he had retained a copy of the very sonnets he describes, and would be willing to part with them for a consideration. Thorpe already had a reputation as a "procurer of manuscripts" by the time he acquired the *Sonnets*. If he actively acquired, as opposed to merely chanced upon, these prized specimens of the sonnet-form, Meres would have been a logical starting-point, provided his whereabouts were known. As a literary man, he could have been known to a number of London booksellers even from his remote Rutland rectorship. And as we know, Thorpe was both a collector and a publisher with strong literary interests, albeit unaligned to any real business acumen.)

But, again, mere speculation. Suffice to say, Francis Meres's mention must have excited some interest in a set of unpublished poems from the author of two highly successful epic poems published earlier in the decade. Indeed, at least one London publisher who now went in search of Shakespearean sonnets came up trumps in a matter of months, publishing a collection that purported to contain some twenty of Shakespeare's lyrics—of which nine are in conventional sonnet-form—the following year.

The slim volume, entitled *The Passionate Pilgrim,* "printed for W[illiam] Jaggard . . . to be sold . . . at the Greyhound in [St.] Paules Churchyard," was unambiguously credited to "W. Shakespeare"—and him alone—on the title page. It proved popular enough to undergo two editions in or around 1599, before being republished in revised form in 1612, three years after two of its poems had reappeared in Thorpe's collection (Q138, 144).

Once again, we are back in the murky world of Elizabethan book-publishing, in which any member of the Stationers' Company could publish without "permission" the literary output of any writer careless with his "foul papers"; and even, if he saw fit, to attribute the work of one writer to another, without any real recompense or recourse available to the writers involved. A publisher called Richard Jones, hoping to cash in on the ongoing popularity of *Tottel's Miscellany,* had presented another poetical miscellany as a single-author collection, *Britton's Bowre of Delights,* back in 1592, and though the wronged Nicholas Breton complained loud and long in *The Pilgrimage to Paradise,* the following year, he failed to have the book recalled.

So Shakespeare had hardly been singled out when someone like William Jaggard attributed *The Passionate Pilgrim* to him without establishing whether he, as a "name" author, was actually responsible for the majority—let alone the entirety—of its contents. Of the twenty poems contained therein, just five can be attributed to Shakespeare with any degree of certainty; and of those, three were "manufactured" sonnets, transposed from their true context, in *Love's Labours Lost.* Yet Shakespeare decided not to go down the Breton route—at least, not for a while. Perhaps he was relieved to find Jaggard had accessed so few "sugred sonnets." Or took the forward-thinking view that there was no such thing as bad publicity.

Among these ditties of dubious provenance can be found "drafts" of sonnets 138 and 144 (as they appear in the 1609 quarto), providing much-needed evidence that at least some of the sonnets Thorpe published in 1609 relate to those alluded to back in 1598. Though both sonnets are from the so-called "Dark Lady" section of Q, in the case of Sonnet 144, Shakespeare contrasts the female demon that taunts him with a male guiding light who, within the wider context provided by Thorpe, has been presumed to be the same figure frequenting so many of the "earlier" sonnets:

Two loves I have, of Comfort and Despaire,
That like two Spirits, do suggest me still:
My better Angell, is a Man (right faire)
My worser spirit a Woman (colour'd ill).
To win me soone to hell, my Female evill
Tempteth my better Angell from my side:
And would corrupt my Saint to be a Divell,
Wooing his puritie with her faire pride.
And whether that my Angell be turnde feend,
Suspect I may (yet not directly tell:)
For being both to me: both, to each friend,
I guess one Angell in anothers hell:
The truth I shall not know, but live in dout,
Till my bad Angell fire my good one out.

The implication, adopted wholesale by advocates of at least one earl—
though not one borne out by any credible chronology of composition—
is that both sequences were fully realized by the time Jaggard found his
hoard. Certainly, as of 1599, elements of at least one Shakespearean
sonnet-sequence were in a form that suggests they had been reworked,
before or after being passed "among . . . private friends." The other Q
sonnet, as published by Jaggard, runs as follows:

When my Love sweares that she is made of truth,
I do beleeve her (though I know she lies)
That she might thinke me some untuter'd youth,
Unskilful in the worlds false forgeries.
Thus vainly thinking that she thinkes me young,
Although I know my yeares be past the best:
I smiling, credite her false speaking toung,
Outfacing faults in love, with loves ill rest.

> *But wherefore sayes my love that she is young?*
> *And wherefore say not I, that I am old:*
> *O, Loves best habit's in a soothing toung,*
> *And Age in love, loves not to have yeares told.*
> *Therefore I'le lye with Love, and love with me,*
> *Since that our faultes in love thus smother'd be.*

(The versions in *The Passionate Pilgrim* of Q138 and 144 are marginally clearer than those preferred by Thorpe, though Paul Kerrigan and Katherine Duncan-Jones, in their 1986 and 1997 editions, respectively, seem convinced that they come from memorized transcripts. In the case of 144, two typos in Q—"sight" for "side" [144.6] and "finde" for "fiend" [144.9]—are given correctly in *P.P.*, which makes it unlikely that the differences are solely down to being "transmitted through memorization.")

Yet one should be wary of leaping to the conclusion that "the Q sequence" was complete by the date Jaggard acquired his poetic prize, just because these numerically late sonnets were circulating in the 1590s. For the idea that the 154 sonnets constitute one sustained sonnet-sequence is essentially an invention of posterity, beholden to the order in which Thorpe published them, which may or may not represent the order in which Shakespeare conceived of them.

In fact, there is some evidence that any sequence (and attendant conceit) imposed on the sonnets may have been an authorial afterthought. As Gary Taylor observed, in his 1983 study of the extant seventeenth-century manuscripts of specific sonnets, "*The Passionate Pilgrim* . . . contains only two sonnets present in the 1609 sequence. Since the compiler of *The Passionate Pilgrim* obviously wished to capitalize on Shakespeare's reputation, he had every reason to reproduce as many sonnets as he could acquire, and it therefore seems obvious that

138 and 144 were circulating separately from any other sonnets yet composed. Cumulatively, the testimony of the extant [seventeenth-century] manuscripts and *The Passionate Pilgrim* strongly encourages the conclusion that the sonnets circulated in manuscript individually, not as a sequence."

Taylor overstates his case. He was subsequently challenged by Arthur Marotti, who, "while agreeing with [his] contention that the sonnets circulated in manuscript in a form other than that of the whole collection found in the 1609 Quarto, [thought] it unlikely that single poems were passed about, given . . . the ways that paper was used in this period. . . . [Rather] the uncollected sonnets were either circulated in small sets or groups of poems, passed about in commonplace-book collections, or transmitted through memorization." Marotti has a point, especially as the price of a quire (approximately two dozen sheets) of writing paper at the beginning of the seventeenth century was between 4d. and 5d., with ruled paper double that price, such paper invariably being acquired in quires, not in single leaves.

Taylor himself was aiming to demonstrate that a particular sonnet from the "first" sequence (Q2) circulated "individually, not as [part of] a sequence." Not surprisingly, he preferred to overlook the possibility that Jaggard may have acquired other sonnets from the same sequence, but chose not to publish them because they were unduly concerned with the perversities of love. After all, his compendium wholly comprises light, breezy dispositions on the "perplexities" of heterosexual love.

What evidence has survived argues against the entire Shakespearean sonnet-sequence(s) "circulating" in manuscript form during the 1590s, leaving us unable to definitively place the contents of Q in the decade when such sonnet-sequences ruled the Elizabethan literary landscape. Yet the themes that dominate 152 of the 154 sonnets in Q were surely established within this specific conflux of opportunity and interest.

And it would seem that at least one of the so-called "marriage" son-nets quickly passed into discreet circulation, as Taylor has ably demon-strated, using thirteen surviving manuscript copies of Q2 ("When fortie Winters shall beseige thy brow") dating from the first half of the seven-teenth century. Making a textual comparison of all thirteen manuscripts, he showed that eleven of these versions almost certainly derived from a single copy, which was significantly different from the version Thorpe published. And, in Taylor's opinion, this manuscript version was itself a pre-Q source:

SPES ALTERA

> When forty winters shall beseige thy brow
> And trench deepe furrowes in yt lovely feild
> Thy youthes faire Liu'rie so accounted now
> Shall bee like rotten weeds of no worth held
> Then beeing askt where all thy bewty lyes
> Where all ye lustre of thy youthfull dayes
> To say within these hollow suncken eyes
> Were an all-eaten truth, & worthless prayse
> O how much better were thy bewtyes vse
> If thou coudst say this pretty child of mine
> Saues my account & makes my old excuse
> Making this bewty by succession thin
> This were to bee new borne when thou art old
> And see thy bloud warme when thou feelst it cold.

Q2

> When fortie Winters shall beseige thy brow,
> And digge deep trenches in thy beauties field,
> Thy youthes proud liuery so gaz'd on now,

Wil be a totter'd weed of smal worth held:
Then being askt, where all thy beautie lies,
Where all the treasure of thy lusty daies;
To say within thine owne deepe sunken eyes,
Were an all-eating shame, and thriftless praise.
How much more praise deseru'd thy beauties vse,
If thou couldst answere this faire child of mine
Shall sum my count, and make my old excuse
Proouing his beautie by succession thine.
This were to be new made when thou art ould,
And see thy blood warme when thou feel'st it could.

Taylor's extrapolated version from eleven manuscripts appears to confirm that even a sonnet from the marriage sequence (1–17), the only part of Q that is self-evidently an integrated unit, probably circulated independently. And it had a title, as well. "Spes Altera"—a reference to the line in Virgil's *Aeneid* in which Ascanius is called *magnae spes altera Romae* ("second hope of great Rome")—appears in four codependent manuscripts, and, as Taylor observes, "A copyist is most unlikely to invent a title like 'Spes Altera,' which . . . to my knowledge is not used elsewhere as an epigraph or motto or title in this period." But it was precisely the kind of reference a young literary figure still making his way in the cutthroat world of London, and with a slight inferiority complex, might introduce to demonstrate that his grammar-school education had not been entirely wasted, and that he knew more than "a little Latin."

Q2 appears to have been singled out for a particular type of discreet circulation. No other marriage sonnet achieved a similarly robust second life, being passed from hand to hand in manuscript until finding its way into Jacobean and Caroline commonplace books—though a single seventeenth-century manuscript of another resides at the British Library: Sonnet 8, "Musick to heare . . . "—which may have enjoyed a similar private dissemination but struck far less of a chord with contemporary compilers of manuscript miscellanies.

The "procreation" theme explored in Q2 (and Q8) was one familiar to Elizabethans, and evidently a popular one. Thomas Wilson's familiar textbook, *The Arte of Rhetorique,* revised in 1560, translated an epistle from Erasmus "to perswade a young gentleman to Mariage," providing a direct source for the second sonnet that the literary-minded would have readily recognized: "What man can be greeved that he is old, when he seeth his owne countenance . . . to appeare lively in his sonne? You shall have a pretie little boie, running up and doune your house, soche a one as shall express your loke, and your wives look . . . by whom you shall seme to bee newe borne."

Such a theme would have been especially poignant to a poet still grieving for his dead son, as Shakespeare would have been if—as I am about to suggest—the sonnet dates from shortly after Hannet Shakespeare, just eleven years old, was buried in August 1596. Yet the fact that these sonnets did not appear in *Passionate Pilgrim* suggests that they did not feature in any miscellany or commonplace book that entered Jaggard's clutches, which rather suggests they circulated independent of Q138 and 144 (and/or that any scribal replication occurred after Jaggard had committed himself to publishing the poems he had chanced upon).

Perhaps they were among a set of poems earmarked for a collection cryptically registered for publication in January 1600, as "A booke called *Amours* by J.D. with certain other sonnetes by W.S." Katherine Duncan-Jones argues, in her Arden edition, that "J.D." was probably Sir John Davies. In which case, the sonneteer "W.S." is just as likely to have been Shakespeare as Sidney Lee's preferred candidate, William Smith (offered by Lee even though he considered one of Davies' "gulling sonnets" a parody of Shakespeare's legal phraseology in Q26).

All of which—as and when possibilities revert to probabilities, and perchance becomes an absolute—could well suggest there were other

Shakespearean sonnets waiting to be harvested. Coming from someone in whom "the sweete wittie soule of Ovid lives," these could have complemented some of Davies' own satirical sonnets, or even a new translation of Ovid's *Amores*. Duncan-Jones overstretches, though, when she goes on to suggest that Shakespeare might have "prepared some sonnets for publication early in 1600 motivated by a desire to put right Jaggard's damaging misappropriation and misidentification of his work." There is absolutely no evidence that Jaggard's book "damaged" Shakespeare's reputation (the fact there were two editions close together tends to suggest the reverse).

It seems more likely that these "certain other sonnetes"—if they were Shakespeare's, and not some other W.S.'s—were among those that ultimately appeared in Q. As to why they were not published "authoritatively" at this time, the reason cannot have been a purely commercial one. A collection of sonnets from the author of *Venus & Adonis* and *Lucrece* would, on the face of it, have been a valuable commodity; a fact Jaggard fully recognized when he republished *The Passionate Pilgrim* with a new subtitle, *Or, Certaine Amorous Sonnets, betweene Venus and Adonis.*

Yet, Shakespeare continued to leave the sonnets in manuscript—both those "sugred Sonnets [found] among his private friends" and others, perhaps including these "certain other sonnetes." Not that there was anything peculiar, or even original, about such a decision. Sir Philip Sidney's 108-sonnet sequence, *Astrophil & Stella,* had been circulated among friends since some time before his death in 1586, but it was not until "a publishing adventurer," Thomas Newman, published the sequence, along with "sundry other rare sonnets by divers noblemen and gentlemen," in 1591, that the form enveloped the Elizabethan literati and would not let go till every able-bodied poet(aster) had demonstrated dexterity with what the French preferred to call a *quatorzain.*

Whatever Shakespeare's intentions regarding such sonnets, there can be little doubt that any publication of the main sonnet-sequence

(Q18–126) at this stage in his career would have opened him to possible charges of pederasty—still an offence technically punishable by death, as per Leviticus, and a charge Marlowe narrowly avoided by getting himself killed. Likewise, the numerous references to a noble patron that litter these letters-versified would surely have required a visit by Shakespeare to the Privy Council, at the very least, to explain himself. There was a specific offence—*scandalum magnatum*—when it came to the libeling of peers.

That the censors of books took their duties seriously is evidenced by the events of June 1, 1599, when the Bishop of London notified the masters and wardens "that all books by [Thomas] Nashe . . . be taken and never printed hereafter" for "containing matter unfit to be published." And if the J.D. of the 1600 *Amours* was Sir John Davies, then he now knew just how draconian and arbitrary the church's powers could be. As did the "W.S." who featured in a long poem called *Willobie His Avisa*, registered in September 1594, and involving a virtuous lady, Avisa; the tortured lover, H.W.; and his "familiar friend W.S." Both Davies' *Epigrammes and Elegies* and the anonymous *Willobie His Avisa* were among the "scurrilous and libellous works" ordered to be burned by the bishop, along with "all books by Nashe."

Presumed by many to be an allegorical version of some minor literary scandal—and subsequently seized on by optimistic Southamptonites as a depiction of the Dark Lady's duplicitous affairs with a playwright and Fair Youth—the belated condemnation of *Willobie His Avisa* does rather suggest there was "some element of scandal in the poem" [EKC]. Yet no contemporary ever connected the two W.S.'s, even though the poem continued to enjoy a healthy reputation and print-life throughout the first half of the seventeenth century—unlike the *Sonnets*.

Sir John Davies, one of those sonneteers who liked to have a little fun at other sonneteers' expense, wrote his infamous Gulling Sonnets around 1594 and, like Shakespeare, chose to circulate them in manuscript only (in Davies' case, it would be 1873 before they made it to the printing press!). The satirical vein struck by Davies and—on occasion—Shakespeare in their respective sonnets could suggest a joint plan to rain scorn down on their more sentimental fellow sonneteers.

Given the general literary context in which such sequences might have been composed, and the elusive personal circumstances of the Stratford poet, one productive path has been opened up by recognizing a satirical streak running through parts of Q. The object of such satire seems to be the sonnet-craze itself, suggesting said sonnets were written either just before or shortly after the fad burnt itself out. To satirize a discredited form would be a pretty redundant exercise; and to satirize a form that had as yet a handful of proponents and very little press—as was the case before publication of Sidney's *Astrophil & Stella* and Daniel's *Delia*, in 1591 and 1592, respectively—equally pointless.

But surely if Shakespeare was tempted to find mirth at the sonnet-form's expense, would it not be reflected in the plays of the period? It is. In *Love's Labours Lost*—which probably premiered circa 1595–96, and appears in a "bad" quarto edition in 1598—the characters fall in love at the drop of a hat, and when they do, they write sonnets. Even the title seems to be a play on something one of Shakespeare's near-contemporaries, John Florio, wrote in *First Fruits* (1578): "We need not speak so much of love, all books are full of love; with so many authors, that it were labour lost to speak of love."

Lee correctly recognizes "another conceit which Shakespeare develops persistently, in almost identical language, in both the sonnets and *Love's Labours Lost* . . . that the eye is the sole source of love, the exclusive home of beauty." And, like the sonnets themselves, *Love's Labours Lost* incorporates what Katharine M. Wilson calls "gradually deepening layers of meaning. It begins with parodying sonnet attitudes; [then]

widens to include all sorts of ridiculous fashions in language study and usage."

Love's Labours Lost contains four "sonnets" of its own, three of which subsequently appeared in The Passionate Pilgrim, albeit with enough verbal differences to suggest that Jaggard "printed stray copies which were circulating 'privately,' and did not find the lines in the printed quartos of the play" [SL]. In the context of the play, these sonnets are clearly satirical—less so in Jaggardian isolation. But the possibility, voiced by Lee, that they circulated independently, alongside other sonnets from Q, suggests a willingness on the author's part to lampoon his own conceit(s) to a more rarefied audience than the one which frequented the theaters.

After all, few contemporaries would have failed to notice the resemblance between the opening of the so-called fourth Dark Lady sonnet, Q130, and expressions like "thine eye's bright sun," a Petrarchian image Samuel Daniel used in Delia; or "Her sparkling eies in heav'n a place deserve," from the seventh "Passion" of Thomas Watson's Passionate Centurie of Love. Such a subtext a side-by-side comparison with Watson's own sonnet amply demonstrates (the original line numbers appear in brackets for the Watson poem; see note for full text):[2]

CXXX (Shakespeare)	VII (Watson)
My mistress' eyes are nothing like the sun;	Her sparkling eies in heav'n a place deserve; [3]
Coral is far more red than her lips' red;	Her lips more red than any Corall stone; [11]
If snow be white, why then her breasts are dun;	Her necke more white, than any swans yat mone; [12–13]
	Her brest transparent is, like any chrystall rocke; [12–13]
If hairs be wires, black wires grown on her head.	Her yellow lockes exceede the beaten goulde; [2]
I have seen roses damasked, red and white,	On either cheeke a Rose and Lillie lies; [9]
But no such roses see I in her cheeks,	
And in some perfumes is there more delight	Her breath is sweete perfume, or hollie flame; [10]
Than in the breath that from my mistress reeks.	
I love to hear her speak, yet well I know	
That music hath a far more pleasing sound.	Her wordes are musicke all of silver sounde; [5]
I grant I never saw a goddess go;	
My mistress when she walks treads on the ground . . .	

And yet, as Paul Kerrigan suggests in the 1986 Penguin edition of Q, "Some of the metaphors satirized in Sonnet 130 were used of the young man in earlier [sic] poems" in Q—the populist poet again demonstrating a rare capacity for mocking his own folly. Or, to fleetingly impose the *auteur* on lines delivered by one particular character in *Love's Labours Lost,* "By heaven, I do love, and it hath taught me to rhyme / And to be melancholy." Some have, not unreasonably, adduced that the Dark Lady's spirit infuses the entire play, citing Biron's verbal portrait of Rosalind:

> *O, if in black my lady's brows be decked,*
> *It mourns that painting and usurping hair*
> *Should ravish doters with a false aspect,*
> *And therefore is she born to make black fair.*

(It would be equally hard to overlook the parallel between "from thine eyes my knowledge I derive" (Q14.9) and a line in Act IV, Scene 3, of *Love's Labours Lost:* "From women's eyes this doctrine I derive.")

Shakespeare, bound as he was by popular tastes, artistically and financially, found himself obliged to reconcile opposite impulses—playing to them, while simultaneously sending them up. He certainly never modified his mordant view on popular expressions of lovelorn melancholia. Hence, Ophelia's snatches of song signifying her slide toward suicide, or, more whimsically, the scene in *The Winter's Tale* where Autolycus offers to sing "another ballad, of a fish that appeared . . . forty thousand fathoms above water, and sung this ballad against the hard hearts of maids. . . . The ballad is very pitiful, and as true."

But the element of satire in both *Love's Labours Lost* and the sonnets is simply that, and though I suspect Shakespeare began writing sonnets with a view to satirizing his contemporaries and providing comedic value, in plays and/or to amuse friends, there is no way he wrote *all* 154 sonnets in Q with such a lightweight purpose. The geneses of this particular play and these poems may be contemporaneous, but the poems do not operate as a single narrative; while any satirical intent in Q strikes me as essentially confined to the Dark Lady material.

Even if the positioning of the first 126 sonnets, the so-called "Fair Youth" sequence, reflects some kind of authorial intent—i.e., they appeared in (much) this order in the manuscript, and Thorpe decided not to second-guess his material—how they relate to the Dark Lady sonnets is not clear. A possible link with one of the plays, though, might provide a chronological end-bracket to these other poems. Q126—widely regarded as the "envoi" to the Fair Youth poems—uses the word "Quietus," meaning final settlement, an expression appearing just once in a Shakespeare play: "When he himself might his quietus make / With a bare bodkin?" (*Hamlet*, Act III, Scene 1, line 77). The final couplet of 126 reads: "Her [i.e., Time's] audit, though delayed, answered must be / And her quietus is to render thee." It is such a startling word to utilize at the end of a sonnet that one is tempted to view these usages as sharing a common conception. But even accepting such a premise would not provide us with a precise chronology—the play could have been composed at any point between 1599 and its July 1602 registration.

Hence, one of the problems of using such a "key word" approach. Not that this stopped A. Kent Hieatt, Charles W. Hieatt, and Anne Lake Prescott from conducting an experiment, running a study of rare word occurrences in the *Sonnets*. They designated certain rare words as either early (ERW), 1590s, or late (LRW), i.e., post-1600, and published their conclusions in the *PMLA* in 1991. Those conclusions, summarized by James Schiffer, were "that Shakespeare composed sonnets 1–60 in the first five years of the 1590s and then revised many of them after the turn of the century; sonnets 61–103 . . . were also composed early, but received 'little or no revision'; [whereas] sonnets 104–26 were probably composed around 1600." They also assigned sonnets 127–54 to "the first half of the 1590s"... but judged that they "were probably not revised."

However, the trio's choice of "early plays" from which they drew sample ERW words was almost immediately questioned, while the slightly arbitrary divisions in the Fair Youth sequence (at 60 and 103) rendered their conclusions regarding the sequence as a whole hard to embrace. At least their conclusions about the Dark Lady sonnets made some kind of sense within the context of Q.

A perceived lack of revision among the so-called Dark Lady sonnets (127–54) seems mirrored by a similar lack of any discernible pattern of organization. J. W. Mackail found a marked contrast with what comes earlier in Q, such that, "while in [his] opinion Sonnets 1 to 126 are a continuous, ordered and authentic collection, 127–54 are a miscellaneous and disordered appendix." Arthur Marotti goes further, supposing that, "if some of the 154 sonnets of the 1609 Quarto circulated in manuscript in the 1590s... they were more likely to have been those from the 'dark lady' section of the collection... as [these] verse [are] lacking the social exclusiveness of the more private encomiastic sonnets to the young man."

In other words, Thorpe could well have "unwittingly" added this "miscellaneous and disordered appendix," which came to him in its original, untreated form, to a consistent, coherent sequence. This might also explain why so many of the ideas imperfectly expressed in said appendix are reworked, with greater diligence, in the "core" sequence (the relationship between Q40–42 and the Dark Lady sonnets has been a starting point for many a sonnet "reorderer"). Like a modern bootlegger, who has stumbled upon assorted studio tapes of some well-known rock band, the Jacobean publisher perhaps failed to distinguish between the finished and the fatally flawed, between work intended for a public, and an abandoned notion never fully realized.

The notion that the bulk of the Fair Youth sonnets were revised shortly "after the turn of the century" (contemporaneous with a series of freshly composed sonnets?) accords with an authorial intention repeatedly expressed in the sonnets themselves—specifically Q18, 19, 55, 60, 63, 74, 81, 101, 107—to ensure that these poems were passed on to posterity. Of the half a dozen sonnets devoted wholly to this theme, perhaps the most revealing in terms of authorial intent is Q55, in which Shakespeare tells the reader he is reserving all the fame attendant to "this powerful rhyme" to the "Fair Youth" who has "cast the glamour over him," leaving none for himself:

> *Not marble nor the gilded monuments*
> *Of princes shall outlive this pow'rful rhyme;*
> *But you shall shine more bright in these contents*
> *Than unswept stone, besmear'd with sluttish time.*

Here Shakespeare has composed an entire sonnet emulating the Ovid of *Metamorphoses*. Specifically, he is alluding to the fifteenth book's epilogue, where the Roman, at the end of his arduous endeavors, finally bangs his own drum. Ovid is convinced that his own name shall live on as a result of his own powerful, not to say protracted, rhyme. And live on it did, albeit to Elizabethans in the 1567 Arthur Golding translation to which Shakespeare generally referred:

> *Let comme that fatall howre*
> *Which (saving of this brittle flesh) hath over mee no powre,*
> *And at his pleasure make an end of myne uncerteyne tyme.*
> *Yit shall the better part of mee assured bee too clyme*
> *Aloft above the starry skye. And all the world shall never*
> *Be able to quench my name . . .*
> *My lyfe shall everlastingly bee lengthened still by fame.*

Shakespeare conceives of a different kind of immortality, a self-effacing kind that memorializes the subject of his verses, not their creator. In Q81, he actually states that the verses will endure as long as Ovid's, "such vertue hath my Pen"—though not the name of the writer responsible: "I (once gone) to all the world must dye / . . . [But] your monument shall be my gentle verse." Meanwhile, in Sonnet 18, it is his "love" that "shall in my verse ever live young"; in Q60, this "verse" that "shall stand / Praising thy worth"; "His beautie," in Q63, that "shall in these blacke lines be seene"; and, most Ovidian of all, "thou in this shalt finde thy monument" (Q107).

All of these internal boasts, a repeating feature of the Fair Youth sequence, contain that extraordinary combination of poetic bravado and self-effacement which could come only from a man who wrote plays for the ages, and then left not a single play behind in what might be termed an "authorial text." Not that his attitude would have seemed so strange to a Jacobethan, for whom "the very concept of individual authorship in the Renaissance was a relative one . . . a large part of education [being] devoted to the practise of imitation, both of manner and of matter" [HRW].

What the poet is alluding to in the "immortality" sonnets, and perhaps envisaging by his actions, is a sequence that would, in the fullness of time, replicate the fate of Sir Philip Sidney's *Astrophil & Stella,* published posthumously when the personalities were "food for worms"; for, not only did Sidney's muse, Penelope Rich, a courtier's wife, duly end up immortalized in verse, but the knight's work served as a model for Shakespeare's own sequence in so many ways, not least structurally.

Should Shakespeare have intended such a passage from presentation to print there could be an allusion to the scuppering of this desire in Heminge and Condell's famous dedication of the First Folio to two noble kinsmen (one of whom has proven to be the most tenacious candidate for "Fair Youth" status). The King's Men lament the fact that their late friend did "not hav[e] the fate, common with some, to be exequutor to his owne writings." Are the pair making a subtle dig at those—like Thorpe and Jaggard (the printer of the folio)—who had taken it upon themselves to act as executors before the man had even passed on?

In the case of the sonnets, the internal references imply only that Shakespeare envisaged circulating the poems anonymously—hence, perhaps, "certain other sonnetes by W.S." This was not an uncommon conceit in a period when notions of authorship were held to be of far less importance than in our post-Romantic world. George Puttenham's treatise, *The Arte of English Poesie* (1589), was one important work that came into the printer Richard Field's hands, "with his bare title without any Authours name or any other ordinarie addresse." The work was all.

Of course, in order to even release these poems anonymously, Shakespeare would still have had to entrust his original to a copyist. It seems unlikely he would have done this if all he wanted to do was forward it to its "onlie begetter." But it could have been transcribed for the purpose of presentation. H. R. Woudhuysen describes how such "presentation manuscripts can [generally] be identified by prefaces and dedications . . . [and also] by the care and elaboration of their writing and decoration. . . . Examples of presentation inscriptions, in prose or verse, are common—Chapman, Daniel and Jonson made much use of them." It seems highly unlikely that such a presentation copy would have made its way to Thorpe during the author's lifetime, so other copies must have been made, either knowingly or surreptitiously.

Assuming that there was a period of sustained rewriting—and the internal clues are by no means as obtuse as some would like to imagine— such a revision process, directed at Q18–126 specifically, was almost certainly independent of the sonnets' 1609 appearance. It came about because the poet was preparing the work for dissemination in some suitably anonymous guise—perhaps as W.S.; most likely, initially at least, in manuscript. As I have indicated earlier, there were a number of reasons why he would have considered this course preferable to publication.

What Shakespeare is unlikely to have foreseen was the publication of his carefully structured sonnet-sequence bound up with discarded exercises he had previously passed around, perhaps concerning an earlier affair, as well as a handful of satirical sonnets, and even a couple of questionable rhetorical exercises concerning Cupid, based on an Ovidian text (Q153–54). Nor that a long, tedious narrative poem—by an entirely different poet—would be attributed by Thorpe to him whose pen "hath . . . such vertue."

Even if the manuscript itself identified only its initialized author and/or recipient, in the time it took for the manuscript to reach Thorpe, the identity of the poet, if not the "onlie begetter," was made known to the publisher. In the interim, it had probably already passed through the hands of one or more rival poets, as well as a certain Fair Youth.

CHAPTER THREE

1593–1603

"MY LOVE SHALL . . . EVER LIVE YOUNG"

One can only conclude that something in [our] liter-
ary response . . . ensures that in every century some
group of people will try to reidentify the Sonnets'
dramatis personae.

—JAMES SCHIFFER, 1999

There is a contradiction at the very heart of the sonnets that no amount of sophistry can shake. For all the protestations of immortality their author seeks to confer on his "lovely boy," the identity of said youth is a mystery wrapped in a conundrum, sealed up with an enigma. And to imagine that this is an accident is to credit Shakespeare with a great deal less artistry and intellect than he displayed elsewhere. Whether he feared a scandal, or was simply aghast at his own conduct, is a matter of conjecture and interpretation—there is evidence a-plenty for both positions in Q—but the proffered Eternity in Verse proved to be a rather anonymous one. At least, it did for 200 years or so.

Only in the nineteenth century, after William Wordsworth turned the key in this rusty lock, did it become an issue of importance to discern the identity of the Fair Youth, and therefore—it was hoped—the intent of the poet in writing such a sonnet-sequence—even though that intent undoubtedly shifted as the sequence itself took shape. What might have begun as a kind of cathartic, versified diary of an infatuation—directed at its object, yet selectively kept from him—changed into something else the moment it became a "sonnet-sequence," curtailed by a definite set of rhetorical rules.

As the poet dabbled in the form for fun and favor, a seriousness of purpose ultimately began to underlie and transform the process, which explains why themes explored in that core sequence also feature in the "disordered appendix." Shakespeare, methinks, was obliged to discard those themes that could only have been reworked into the primary sequence at the expense of structure and sense, or that simply lacked said seriousness.

Yet, giving a sense of purpose to what had previously been a private obsession was bound to turn the poet's innermost thoughts and fears into something less autobiographical, and more artistic. As Northrop Frye puts it in his important essay "Never the Twain," "Our ignorance is too complete to be accidental. . . . The world's greatest master of characterization will not give [his friend] the individualizing touch that he [gave] to the humblest of his dramatic creations."

And yet, Shakespeare throughout his life worked at perfecting the art of self-effacement, a state of affairs which prompted W. H. Auden to observe, "Shakespeare is in the singularly fortunate position of being, to all intents and purposes, anonymous. Hence the existence of persons who spend their lives trying to prove that his plays were written by someone else." As such, it would be surprising if any rewriting process didn't involve a certain amount of covering one's tracks. For, as Frye notes, "The

establishing of a recognized convention is of enormous benefits to po-
ets, as it enables them to split off personal sincerity from literary sincer-
ity, and personal emotion from communicable emotion." Or, to put it
more prosaically, it allows the poet to make the personal, universal.

This might serve to explain why the sonnets sometimes seem di-
vorced from their actual milieu. The poems have been stripped of their
context, so much so that not a single definite date for any sonnet's com-
position can be nailed down by contemporary circumstance—though
many have tried to do so. As C. S. Lewis once observed, á propos these
poems, "External evidence thus failing us, we look for internal, and
[still] find ourselves in a world of doubts."

The sonnets and the plays have virtually no direct references or allu-
sions in common. In fact, there is only one line in the sonnets that also
appears in a contemporary play—"Lillies that fester, smell far worst
then weeds" (94.14) also appears in *Edward III,* a script attributed to
Shakespeare as early as 1656, and possibly one of those for which he was
part of the scriptwriters' committee. But if so, his was not the main hand,
and the line in question cannot with any certainty be ascribed to him.
Indeed, the line, self-evidently a proverb, could well have existed in the
rich Elizabethan oral tradition, just waiting to be appropriated by print,
making it just another piece of historical driftwood. After all, as Rev-
erend Beeching put it a century ago, "A line that embalms a proverb may
be expected to occur in more than one context."

The only literary allusions in Q that have a measure of verisimilitude,
but have not been summoned up from the classical past, reflect back on
the sonnet-craze and its instigators. Thus, Q21 ("So is it not with me as
with that Muse") appears to contain clear allusions to Edmund
Spenser's *Amoretti,* published in November 1594; Q99 ("The forward
violet thus did I chide") can be shown to borrow imagery from Henry
Constable's *Diana,* also published in 1594; and Q38 ("How can my

Muse want subject to invent") seems to have adopted, if not purloined, the whole notion of the poet's own "muse, worthy and angel," as the tenth of nine, from Michael Drayton's "Amour VIII," first found in the 1594 edition of *Ideas Mirrour*.[3] But even if one were to consider these debts as definite, they would push the sonnets' possible composition only as far back as 1594—the year Shakespeare dedicated his epic poem *Lucrece* to the Earl of Southampton in terms that suggest he had finally found a patron who loved what he did with a rhyme-royal.

And if literary allusions do little to expel this Jacobethan fog, the lack of political allusions in Q—at a time when the world picture was in a constant state of flux, and portents of political upheaval were on everyone's lips—is palpable. The one definite reference to a historical personage, and event, "The mortall Moone hath her eclipse endured" (107.5), has defeated definitive dating at every turn, though no one now disputes that the "mortal Moone" is a reference to Elizabeth I.[4]

Yet here is where any general consensus ends, prompting Rollins to reckon, "This so-called 'dated sonnet' has been made to fit whatever theory each writer on the subject is addicted to." Those who would like to imagine that Shakespeare was still sonneteering when the old queen finally stopped imprisoning every potential patron, dying single and sad, have preferred to see "her eclipse endur'd" as a reference to James I's accession. According to the ever-sure Lee, the reference simply "cannot be mistaken: [it is] to three events that took place in 1603—to Queen Elizabeth's death, to the accession of James I, and to the release [from prison] of the Earl of Southampton." Unfortunately, what also cannot be mistaken is the meaning of "endured," which never means "expired." In fact, it always means the reverse.

The early birds have preferred to see the line as an equally unmistakable reference to the defeat of the Spanish Armada, on the grounds that everyone knows this was the queen's gravest threat and her finest hour.

Unfortunately, that would provide a date of 1588 for one of the last son-
nets in the Fair Youth sequence, a fantastical solution that would make
the sonnets Shakespeare's first poetic outpourings, anticipating the en-
tire Elizabethan sonnet fad.

Even those starting from likelier premises have found it impossible to
agree on the specific crisis in the reign of Good Queen Bess to which the
line alludes. Those who favor an "early" date have generally sided with
the passing of her Grand Climacteric, i.e., her sixty-third year ("The
most daungerous of all these passages or steps are the forty nine, com-
pounded upon seven times seauen: and sixty three standing uppon nine
times seauen"—Thomas Wright, *A Succinct Philosophicall Declaration of
the Nature of Clymactericall Yeeres,* 1604). Considered by astrologers as
the most significant year in a person's life because the mystic numbers
seven and nine are united, this year ended for Liz One on September 6,
1596. The astrological imagery, and the fact that "endured" fully fits its
poetic sense, make this date highly attractive, especially to the
Southamptonites, for whom—as we shall see—the earlier the better.

Advocates of Pembroke have tended to favor either 1599 or 1600, on
the grounds that Elizabeth was once again rumored to be ill in 1599, and
people feared for her life and the future (thanks to a still unresolved suc-
cession). There were also negotiations afoot for a lasting Anglo-Spanish
peace. This situation continued through the first half of 1600 (though a
lasting peace was not reached until 1604), and it is thought to be re-
flected in line 8 of Q107—"And peace proclaims Olives of endlesse
age."

The phlegmatic Chambers dates the sonnet even more specifically,
to August 1599, arguing that for most of that month the whole country
was in turmoil at the thought of a Spanish fleet sailing up the Channel.
A letter from John Chamberlain to a friend on the 23rd does capture
some of the feel of Q107, while suggesting how superstitious and

jumpy the natives had become: "The vulgar sort cannot be perswaded but that there was some great misterie in the assembling of these forces, and because they cannot finde the reason of it make many wilde conjectures, and cast beyond the moone; as sometimes that the Quene was daungerously sicke."

In these uncertain times, though, there were crises each and every year during the last decade of the old lady's reign. Still, there is something rather appealing about the astrological explanation—or, anyway, an astrological explanation. After all, Shakespeare could be referring to the peace of Vervins, signed in April 1598 between France and Spain, signaling an end to the Wars of Religion, which came just a month after the whole of Ireland, Scotland, and the north of England was bathed in a total eclipse (even if said treaty was a violation of France's solemn obligation not to conclude a peace separately, making it hardly a cause for general celebration).

Not that Q107 provides the one and only potential reference to that portentous astral event, the eclipse, in the *Sonnets*. Q35 has been seen as referring to the self-same eclipse—or to a less spectacular one in May 1594 ("Cloudes and eclipses staine both Moone and Sunne"). This should not surprise us. Shakespeare, as a man of his time, set great store in astrological computations derived from portents, a feature we find in poems and plays alike (over a hundred references reside in the plays, including one voiced by Edmund in *King Lear:* "I am thinking, brother, of a prediction I read the other day what should follow these eclipses.").

Meanwhile, in Q98, we find that Saturn is seemingly sitting in the April night sky: "When proud pide Aprill . . . Hath put a spirit of youth in every thing: / That heavie Saturne laught and leapt with him." If we are dealing here with an astrological occurrence, it can be computed easily enough. From the two decades that concern us, only 1600, 1601, or 1602 would fit, which would favor a Pembrokian association—especially if the lines relate to 1600, when he had yet to make earl. Shakespeare, more importantly, is equating Saturn with Melancholy, and Melancholy with himself. "Proud pide Aprill" could therefore be Pembroke personified. He was born on that most auspicious of days, April 8.

Whatever the case, in our search for internal clues we still find ourselves in Lewis's "world of doubts"; scrabbling for "evidence" within this most private of texts. The Shakespeare of the sonnets doesn't want us to know where we are, or even with whom we are dealing. If there is a profound shortage of calendar-based clues, there is almost too much information about the kind of man this Fair Youth was. Yet none about who he was. This is because, in an artistic sense, identifying the Fair Youth is unimportant; that we identify with the poet's predicament, vital. And so, the poet chooses to scatter enough clues about his Love's character and social background to engender the requisite empathy from the reader. But only in generalities. And he is too good a craftsman for this to be accidental—especially if we assume that a revision process afforded him the opportunity to further blur aspects of a once personal portrait.

The one place where he seems content to let generalities mutate into specifics is in his delineation of the poet-patron relationship. As we are informed by Lee, it is the one "distinctive fact" in the sonnets that he was Shakespeare's literary patron. This "fact" turns up in Q26, 38, 69, 79, 80, and 82–86. Beeching, likewise, felt that "there are indications in not a few . . . sonnets that the social interval between the poet and his friend was considerable. Sonnet 72 imagines the world remonstrating with the friend for his misplaced affection . . . while Sonnets 80 and 87 . . . give the [distinct] impression that he has worth in the world's estimation as well as in the poet's."

Even if we accept Seymour-Smith's qualification of his predecessors' assertions—making the Friend "either a literary patron of some distinction, *or* [my italics] . . . his beauty and influence inspired many poets to write about him"—he was evidently someone of rank and influence. Dover-Wilson argued, in his 1963 monograph, that "the importance attached to the young man's perpetuating his stock by begetting an heir [in 1–17] is almost enough by itself to indicate high rank[,] . . . [while] Sonnet 101 . . . claims that the Poet's praise will 'much outlive a gilded tomb,' which I take to be an allusion to the painted monuments beneath which Elizabethans of distinguished families lay after death." For Shakespeare the social-climber, this would presumably have been an important part of his allure. Hence, the ubiquitous references to his "beauty, birth, wealth and wit" (37.5).

Unless, that is, one subscribes to Stephen Booth's highly original suggestion that, in "addressing a man of high rank," Shakespeare was adopting a convention "that could just as well derive from the courtly love tradition of addressing beloved ladies as if they were feudal lords." Except that the point of such a convention is that it needs to be shared and understood by one's audience, whether of one or many. And though this convention was a feature of the popular ballads that Shakespeare would have heard in the taverns—derived no doubt from the metrical romances on which such ballads were often based—it was not one any Jacobethan sonneteer would have adopted, especially not directed at a man. Social niceties might permit a poet to call the most unladylike tramp a lady—then as now—but to attribute birth and wealth to a boy-actor, say, would offend certain contemporary sensibilities to which Shakespeare, of all people, subscribed wholesale.

It is hard to naysay William Archer's observation in 1897, that "beauty and wit, indeed, are matters of opinion . . . but [Shakespeare] would scarcely attribute birth and wealth to a youth who possessed neither." And Archer goes further, suggesting that, "the Young Man . . . being possessed of 'beauty, birth, wealth, and wit' can scarcely be unknown to fame." At least he recognizes the likelihood that we are dealing with an identifiable individual, a figure separated from the poet by a social gulf impossible for us to conceive, yet one that was all too real to the anguished versifier.

As James Boaden, the original Pembrokian, observed in an 1837 treatise, "There are many passages in these Sonnets, which, as they infer the superior condition of his young friend, express also the fear that reasons of rank and state might separate them: that an intimacy with the Player might sully the future Peer, and that it would be incumbent on the latter to 'hold his honour at a wary distance.'"

The sonnets, so the argument goes, can only be understood in the context of a relationship bound by established conventions of patronage and poetry. In the light of said context—"poems written in the context of patronage . . . [and therefore] distinct from that of the miscellaneous poems found in the 'dark lady' section of the collection"—the Rival Poet poems (Q78–86) represent "the major crisis of the young-man sonnets . . . the favouring of a rival poet [being] an act the speaker of the sonnets treats as a serious betrayal" [AM].

Assuming the main sonnet-sequence does reflect a "patron-client relationship," and were we to accept Archer's assertion that such a patron could only be found among the nobility, this would leave exactly three credible candidates, one of whom—through age—can be dismissed out of hand. These "three men of birth and wealth . . . positively known to have been acquainted with Shakespeare [are] Henry Wriothesley . . . and the brothers William and Philip Herbert. . . . No other man of birth and wealth is known to have known Shakespeare. . . . Therefore there is every probability that the Young Man was one of these three" [WA]. Once we dismiss Philip—who was not born until 1584—we are left with the two others.

Before considering the differences between Henry Wriothesley, Earl of Southampton; and William Herbert, Earl of Pembroke, perhaps it would be a good idea to acknowledge their similarities, which have been strong enough to keep both hats in the ring for nearly two centuries. As Chambers summarizes them, "Both are known to have shown favour to Shakespeare. Both were good-looking and had beautiful mothers. Both were much in the public eye. Both were the subjects of early negotiations for marriages which came to nothing. Both had amorous relations with ladies of Elizabeth's court and suffered disgrace and imprisonment as a result."

And, in a very real sense, both were what we would term patrons of the arts—one might go as far as to say the leading literary patrons of their day. As such, both presumably became aware of the playwright when his passage through Elizabethan literary London began to pique a number of potential patrons' curiosity. In Southampton's case, we know when this was. And how. Sometime in 1593 or early 1594, the earl responded positively to a brazen pitch for his patronage by the usually diffident dedicator, in his first piece of published poetry, *Venus & Adonis,* which the Stratfordian prefaced thus:

> To the Right Honourable Henrie Wriothesley, Earl of Southampton, and Baron of Titchfield, I know not how I shall offend in dedicating my unpolished lines to your Lordship, nor how the world will censure me for choosing so strong a prop to support so weak a burden . . .

Between that poem's well-received publication, circa April 1593, and the registering of its successor, *The Ravishment of Lucrece,* in May 1594, Shakespeare had learned that his previous poem, far from offending his Lordship, had delighted him. As such, the 1594 poem's dedication, again to the earl, is effusive and obsequious in almost equal measures, "The love I dedicate to your Lordship is without end. . . . What I have done is yours; what I have to do is yours; being part in all I have, devoted yours." Quite a contrast to the importuning tone a year earlier.

According to Tucker Brooke, "There is no other Elizabethan dedication like this." Other scholars have disputed this. A. L. Rowse asserted that, "Many people misjudge the relations between the poet and his patron by thinking of the high-flown language in modern terms: they are not sufficiently deep in the age to know that this was the proper decorum for a gentlemanly poet to use to a handsome young nobleman." Half a century earlier, Hermann Conrad noted that Elizabethan "dedications, no matter how effusive, are no evidence whatever of intimate friendship. Instead poets expected a cash acknowledgment; and when they were on terms of intimacy with noblemen, they did not address dedications and sonnet cycles to them."

One thing is sure. An Elizabethan dedication of whatever hue is an unreliable barometer of the poet's real feelings. Thomas Nashe, in *Pierce Penniless* (1592), put the convention in a manner blunt enough to explain the difficulties he had finding patronage and the insincerity underlying many a fellow poet's protestation, "What reason have I to bestow any of my wit upon him that will bestow none of his wealth upon me."

And yet, on such an issue hangs the very case for (and against) Southampton as our Fair Youth. Reduced down to its essence, sifted, refined, and clarified, the case for the twenty-one-year-old Henry Wriothesley is as follows: "Simply and solely the resemblance between the dedication of *Lucrece* and Sonnet 26." Or so William Archer thought, when mounting his "Case against Southampton" in the December 1, 1897, edition of *Fortnightly Review*. And he had a point. On the one hand, one would be hard-pressed not to notice a certain similarity of tone and diction between the *Lucrece* dedication and the following four lines (26.1–4):

> *Lord of my love, to whome in vassalage*
> *Thy merrit hath my dutie strongly knit;*

To thee I send this written ambassage
To witnesse duty, not to shew my wit.

On the other hand, it does not seem like an awful lot on which to build a case for the centuries. A certain similarity of tone and diction comes with the territory. To invoke Rowse again, might this not simply be "the proper decorum for a gentlemanly poet to use to a handsome young nobleman"? When coming from the same pen, why would he not swear a similar bond to his "new" patron, even alluding to a former fealty in kind? As that eminent Victorian antiquarian and founder of the New Shakspere Society, Frederick Furnivall, put it, "There is no evidence that Southampton kept up his alliance with Shakspere after 1594. He had plenty of other folk and work to look after; and we can't tie an enthusiastic poet down to his dedications for his whole life."

Fellow Shaksperean William Archer was not quite so coy. He portrayed the advocacy of Southampton as the literary equivalent of trying to put square pegs into round holes, by simply addressing the respective ages of the parties, "At the dates which the Southampton theory is bound to assume for the Sonnets (between 1594 and 1598) we should have at first a man of 30 addressing a youth of 21, and at last, a man of 34 describing himself as a thing of 'tanned antiquity' in writing to 'a sweet and lovely boy' of 25. . . . [Save for] the resemblance between the dedication of *Lucrece* and Sonnet 26, everything else . . . is not demonstrative but apologetic, . . . attempt[ing] to explain away an improbability."

Needless to say, the Southamptonites—led for many years by that late apostate from the Pembroke cult, Sidney Lee—saw things differently. Taking his lead from Nathan Drake, whose 1817 two-volume biography, *Shakespeare & His Times,* first posited Southampton as a candidate for Fair Youthdom, Lee advocated that the unambiguous language of patronage evident in sonnets like 26 and 78 could apply to just one literary figure, Southampton, adding for good measure, "No young man of like condition was the object of a greater number of dedicatory compliments," as if numbers served to prove the argument.

Southamptonites' greatest challenge, though, was demonstrating the likelihood of the sonnets being composed in the immediate aftermath of *Venus & Adonis,* i.e., after Southampton reciprocated Shakespeare's affection, when, at a stretch, the earl could still be deemed a fair young man. Again, Archer failed to spare his scorn, "Nothing really makes for an earlier date, *except* [my italics] the theory that the Young Man was Lord Southampton."

Chronologically, the sheer fact that the sonnets contain no hint of the earl's plans to travel for a year, for which he received leave from the queen in March 1597, argues against a date later than 1596. Equally problematic are the stylistic issues. As astute a critic as C. S. Lewis found he could "hardly conceive [of] a poet moving from the style of the best sonnets (which means in effect nearly all the sonnets) to that of *Venus & Adonis,* but can easily conceive one who had achieved Shakespeare's mature dramatic technique still writing some of the sonnets we have."

Even in making a great deal of the fact that the earl, after his intended marriage to Elizabeth Vernon was vetoed by the queen in 1598, vowed that "if he could not marry the object of his choice, he would die single," the Southamptonites were electing to play a dangerous game. Though they could (and, indeed, do) argue that this provides a credible context for the seventeen marriage sonnets that open Thorpe's quarto, unfortunately for their case, they clothe their theory in the loosest of garbs, while the counterargument—for the younger, wilder Pembroke—fits like a glove. As early as 1821, before Pembroke's name had even entered the frame, James Boswell turned the argument—first put by Nathan Drake in his 1817 biography—on its head:

> Dr Drake . . . contends that . . . the first seventeen in the collection
> were written with a view of remonstrating against a premature vow
> of celibacy . . . in consequence of his union with Elizabeth Vernon
> being forbidden by a mandate from the Queen. . . . We have no ev-
> idence, nor, I think, any probable ground, for supposing that the
> Earl had ever formed such a resolution as is here ascribed to
> him. . . . If we look to the poems themselves, they will afford no
> colour for such an interpretation. They have no reference to such
> a supposed case, nor allude in the slightest manner to wounded
> feelings or disappointed hopes; but contain only general exhorta-
> tions in favour of marriage.

Unlike the case for Southampton, the evidence for Pembroke's reluc-
tance to marry, period, was in no way confined to a specific object of af-
fection. Even when he got Elizabeth's own maid of honor, Mary Fitton,
pregnant, in June 1600, he refused to "do the decent thing," and was im-
prisoned for his impudence. Again Archer hits the target when he states
"that the sonnets are addressed, not to a man who is bent on marrying
one woman and no other, but to a beautiful boy who, 'contracted to his
own bright eyes,' has shown himself averse from the very idea of mar-
riage." The case for Pembroke as someone in need of the kind of guid-
ance offered in those early sonnets is demonstrably stronger.

This convinced Dover-Wilson, for one, who felt that the young pup
"badly needed the advice given in 1–17. After he had refused to wed
Elizabeth Carey in 1595, his parents tried in 1597 to make a match for
him with Bridget Vere, daughter of the Earl of Oxford; but it, too, came
to nothing. Once again, this time in September 1598, there was 'speech
of a match between . . . Lord Herbert, and Lady Hatton,' a woman much
older than he. . . . [And in] September 1599, the niece of the Earl of Not-
tingham, so Rowland Whyte tells [us], was proposed as a wife for Her-

bert, and her uncle approved the match." So, in the space of four years, the beautiful boy had "successfully evaded the bonds of matrimony" four times.

Of these repeated demonstrations of youthful willfulness, the second instance, the proposed marriage to Bridget Vere, tallies best with the variety of admonishments delivered across the seventeen sonnets that serve as a prelude to the main fare in Q. Those prefatory sonnets are self-evidently of a piece, and they have a conventionality of theme and rhetorical purpose that is entirely at odds with the remaining sonnets. They also "differ from the rest of the sequence in that they are less complex; the author is less involved in his theme, which is, quite obviously, a rhetorical instigation to a young man to marry and procreate his kind. . . . Nothing much happens in the[se] poems, except that the poet becomes intellectually . . . interested in the theme of narcissism" [MSS].

Further evidence of an independent existence has been afforded by the manuscript versions of Q2 and Q8 (discussed previously), which may have been circulated because they were indicative of these sonnets' central theme—persuading a recalcitrant youth to marry and preserve the family line. On a number of the others, Shakespeare untypically belabors the point—twisting the language this way and that to find a new way of saying what Erasmus had managed in a couple of sentences.

Even allowing for the craftsmanship by which he gives each *quatorzain* its own centripetal spin, the fact that Shakespeare should produce seventeen sonnets that stick doggedly to one idea suggests it was done in response to a very specific commission. For a specific reason. Rarely one to overgild his lyrical lilies, Shakespeare must have had a compelling reason to discourse so. At no other juncture does he belabor a subject like he does here. Even the so-called Rival Poet "mini-sequence" (Q78–86) stops well short of such repetitiveness.

And yet, according to Duncan-Jones, "The number of sonnets in the first section, 17, is not of obvious significance unless we accept Dover Wilson's attractive but quite unsupported hypothesis that these sonnets were commissioned by the Countess of Pembroke to mark her son's seventeenth birthday." For "quite unsupported hypothesis," read most plausible explanation. Given that the lady academic had spent part of her 1983 article on Q's "authorized" status, extrapolating a highly debatable import from the number of sonnets (28) in the Dark Lady sequence—as somehow "reflect[ing] a male disgust with the lunar, menstrual cycle"—it seems a tad perverse that she should fail to acknowledge the possibility of a concomitant significance in a sequence based on a prime number.

Would any self-respecting Elizabethan have written a sonnet-sequence around a prime number, save for a very good reason (and I think we can probably discount Alastair Fowler's explanation that seventeen is the union of 10—the Decalogue—with 7—Gifts of the Holy Ghost)? The number of sonnets in an Elizabethan sequence always had a mathematical significance. Yet the marriage sonnets are indivisible in number. Not only do none of the notable Elizabethan sonnet-sequences that precede Shakespeare's total seventeen, no other important sequence deals in units of seventeen.

The first seventeen sonnets have always stood apart. Even the many would-be reorganizers of Q have rarely messed with these sonnets. Even Lee noticed the "contradiction in terms between the poet's handling of [marriage in 1–17] and his emphatic boast in the two following sonnets that his verse alone is fully equal to the task of immortalising his friend's youth and accomplishments." By Q18 he is no longer concerned with marriage as a remedy for one's mortality, having decided that the adored one shall live in the collective memory thanks solely to his verse.

So we are left hunting for an explanation that actually fits these facts. The one credible explanation—seventeen sonnets represents seventeen years—took its time appearing. The suggestion of a specific commission originated with William Archer, in his battle with Sidney Lee. Yet Archer stops short of drawing a direct comparison with events of 1597. Instead, he tentatively posited a scenario where "the friends of a handsome and 'self-willed' youth were anxious to see him settled in life, and thought that literary exhortation might further that end, [and so] they would naturally apply to the poet who had become famous in virtue of the honeyed eloquence he had lent to the Goddess of Desire."

E. K. Chambers, taking up Archer's suggestion, preferred to date the marriage sonnets to 1595, when the willful future earl rejected an arranged marriage with Elizabeth, daughter of Sir George Carey. Chambers' argument relies on the fact that Elizabeth was the granddaughter of the Lord Chamberlain, who was the patron of Shakespeare's acting company. Hence the commission. Chambers therefore suggested that the playwright, having "made a reputation for himself, as something more than a mere player, by his *Venus & Adonis* and his *Rape of Lucrece,*" and being "a persona grata to Sir George Carey, the son of Lord Hunsdon, in whose company he was then a leading member," seemed like "a plausible man to stimulate the imagination of the young Herbert." But in 1595, the earl and the countess had no real sense of how intractable their son and heir would prove to be.

Twenty years on, it was Dover-Wilson's turn to reexamine the history of the Herberts in the light of this "commission" idea; and putting two and two (and thirteen) together, came up with seventeen. His suggestion that the Countess of Pembroke asked Shakespeare to meet the young lord at Wilton, on or around his seventeenth birthday, having commissioned him to compose an appropriate number of pro-marriage sonnets, had already been made by a German academic, Wülker, in 1896, but had drawn few moths to its flame. Dover-Wilson combined Wülker's thesis with an even earlier one, of William Minto's. Minto thought that the lines in Q3—"Thou art thy mother's glass, and she in

thee / Calls back the lovely April of her prime"—was a "clear" refer-
ence to Herbert's famously attractive mother (who was only in her
mid-thirties). The countess was widely known as a patroness of poets,
including Breton, Daniel, and Spenser, while certain lesser-known
writers—Fraunce, Howell, and Moffett—were also members of the
Pembroke household.

An invite to Wilton on Herbert's birthday may well be one of Dover-
Wilson's more fanciful ideas. But his suggestion "that sonnets 1–17 were
written as a last resort to work upon the boy's imagination when all else
had failed, and probably at the suggestion of his mother who [w]as sis-
ter of the Sir Philip Sidney who wrote *The Defense of Poesie*," ticks all the
right boxes. Equating April with young Herbert, Dover-Wilson took the
literal view, making the sonnets a sequence commissioned for the birth-
day boy. Yet it was only later in the same year that Herbert really
demonstrated that he had a mind of his own when it came to marriage.
By September 1597, the second earl had a new candidate for his elder
son's wife. An ill man, he wanted the matter resolved before he passed
on. Bridget Vere was Lord Burghley's granddaughter, and daughter of
the Earl of Oxford. But once again, after protracted negotiations, and
perhaps even after getting input from the most persuasive pen in the
land, young William rejected the proffered bride out of hand.

A date of 1597 for the first series of Fair Youth sonnets tallies well
with the more credible chronologies constructed for their composition
and his infatuation, which, if Q104 can be taken at face value, survived
long enough to see at least "three April perfumes in three hot Junes
burned." And, as Archer persuasively argues, "The youth of the Young
Man is emphasized in almost every sonnet. . . . [So,] the greater the dif-
ference in age between Shakespeare and his friend, the more compre-
hensible do such allusions become. . . . The Pembroke theory, placing
the Sonnets between 1598 and 1601, represents, at first, a man of 34 ad-

dressing a boy of 18; at last, a man of 37 addressing a youth of 21." A year earlier, better still, for if the glove doth fit, Pembroke is it.

By 1597, Southampton would have been out of the frame. Off on his military adventures, he is unlikely to have retained any special bond he might once have established with the young(ish) playwright-poet. But Pembroke, as the son of the widely admired countess, the nephew of Sir Philip Sidney, and the future Earl of Pembroke, was a patron-in-waiting for just about every erstwhile aspirant to Southampton's largesse.

Confirmation that William—and his brother Phillip—*were* "patrons" to the Stratford artist is duly provided by the Heminge and Condell dedication to the 1623 First Folio. There, the noble brothers are thanked for having "prosequuted both [the plays], and their Authour living, with so much favour: we hope that (they outliving him, and he not having the fate, common with some, to be exequutor to his owne writings) you will use the like indulgence toward them you have done unto their parent." Clear enough. Shakespeare once enjoyed the brothers' "favour" and "indulgence."

Unlike Southampton, though, we lack specifics as to how and when the two brothers "prosequuted . . . their Authour . . . with so much favour." Just that such "favour" appears to have been ongoing, hence this joint dedication seven years after the playwright's death—despite Southampton still being alive in 1623, and fully restored to court favor. Lee argues that the players couldn't help but dedicate the folio to the two earls, to whom nearly every work of any literary pretension was dedicated in this period, choosing to ignore the language of the dedication, which is quite specific. The King's Men are thanking Pembroke (and his brother, Montgomery) for favors *already* rendered.

There is one other internal clue thought to tie William Shakespeare to William Herbert (or at least a namesake). It lies in three sonnets from the "disordered appendix," principally the infamous Q135 ("Whoever hath her wish, thou hast thy Will"), which demonstrates that the playwright's love of a pun was not mere grandstanding to the playhouse pit. This sonnet, one of those probably passed amongst "private friends" for their mutual mirth, tries to utilize every possible meaning of "Will." Here, in sonnet form, is a wit contest between "Will" and some other "Will" as to who shall have their will(y). Archer probably got it right when he argued that said sonnet "was not intended for critical analysis, but simply to be smiled at by two at least of the persons concerned."

Out of joint with the serious tone of the first 126 sonnets, Q135 is a slightly smutty satire on sonneteering. It was omitted from the primary sequence, just as Sidney initially omitted the one sonnet (37) from *Astrophil & Stella* that twice punned on the name of his own paramour (Lady Rich). And it does rather suggest that Shakespeare's rival for the Dark Lady's affection (if he was indeed the Fair Youth) shared the same Christian name—and perhaps a love of punning. As does its sequel, Q136, which asks of the dusky lass, "Swear to thy blind soul that I was thy Will." Nor are these the only plays on the battle of Wills found among the Dark Lady sonnets. There is Q143, for instance, of which Beeching wrote, a century ago:

> If the pun be allowed at all, it cannot refer to the poet's own name, but must refer to the name of his friend. In this sonnet the "dark lady", pursuing the poet's friend while the poet pursues her, is compared to a housewife chasing a chicken and followed by her own crying child. It concludes . . . "So will I pray that thou mayst have thy Will, / If thou turn back, and my loud crying still." The word "Will" is printed here in the original text in italics, and the pun is in Shakespeare's manner. . . . That there are more Wills than one concerned in the matter is made more evident still by other passages, where the poet jocosely limits his claim on the lady's

favour to the fact that his Christian name is Will, acknowledging that not a few other people have as good a claim as he.

That Pembroke could take a joke at his name's expense, even after he became a lord, is amply demonstrated by a dedication to him from that other contributor to Q, John Davies of Hereford. At the outset to his *Select Second Husband for Sir Thomas Overbury's Wife* (1616), Davies wrote thus: "Wit and my Will (deere Lord) were late at strife, / To whom this Bridegroome I for grace might send. . . . / Wit, with it selfe, and with my Will, did warre: / For Will (good-Will) desir'd it might be YOU. . . . "

It would be appealing to think that Shakespeare and the young Herbert might have shared a relationship akin to Prince Hal and Falstaff in *Henry IV Part I.* Unfortunately, that play had been written by 1597. But the similarities between the (fictionalized) future king and the future earl are not entirely fanciful. Pembroke, after coming to London in 1598, hoping to escape his parents' constant marriage-arranging, showed a propensity for sowing his wild oats that caused concern, just as Hal's activities had worried Henry IV. Indeed, Clarendon's generally glowing portrait of the boy-noble suggested he had just one marked character flaw:

> He was immoderately given up to women. But therein he likewise retained such power and jurisdiction over his very appetite, that he was not so much transported with beauty and outward allurements, as with those advantages of the mind as manifested an extraordinary wit and spirit and knowledge, and administered great pleasure in the conversation. To these he sacrificed himself, his precious time, and much of his fortune. And some who were nearest his trust and friendship were not without apprehension that his

natural vivacity and vigour of mind began to lessen and decline by
those excessive indulgences.

Among those "nearest his trust and friendship" for a while—who
were understandably concerned "that his natural vivacity and vigour of
mind" might begin "to lessen and decline by [such] excessive indul-
gences"—could well have been a poet who had given seventeen warn-
ings to the unmarried young man in the days when the writing of love
poetry remained merely a theoretical exercise.

That the two Wills shared a love of poetry is not in doubt. Another
early biographer of Pembroke, John Aubrey, specifically states that he
"delighted in Poetrie: and did sometimes (for his Diversion) write
some Sonnets and Epigrammes, [the quality of] which deserve Com-
mendation." (Duncan-Jones goes as far as suggesting that Pembroke
actively "responded to Shakespeare's Sonnets. One of his own poems . . .
opens with a verbal and thematic elaboration of Sh.'s sonnet 116, 'Let
me not to the marriage of true minds,' and incorporates the phrase
'love is not love.'")

Ultimately, nothing definitively disposes of Southampton. Nor nails
down the claim made on behalf of Pembroke. But as William Minto
concluded, after conducting his own, typically methodical Victorian in-
vestigation into the matter, "The more one looks into this vexed ques-
tion, the more does one find little particulars emerging, singly
inconclusive, but all increasing the weight of the probability that Pem-
broke was the man."

Yet, even if we settle on this fortunate son as the Fair Youth, it does
not resolve other, altogether more contentious issues—how deep was
their friendship, and how much or little did it reflect the internal story
of the sonnets, one of jealousy, betrayal, and self-abnegation? Those
who have argued, as Marotti has, "that the poems were initially written

to an aristocratic patron and [so] their language and imagery of courtly love should be read as conventional rather than as genuinely amorous," will have a hard job convincing anyone who has actually read the likes of 26, 33, or 57 that there is anything conventional about either the relationship, or its poetic expression. As C. S. Lewis observed, "The self-abnegation, the 'naughting' . . . this transference of the whole self into another self without the demand for a return, have hardly a precedent in profane literature."

What is just as remarkable about these poems is the degree of self-awareness displayed by the poet throughout the tortured relationship. A sense of futility infuses the entire infatuation. The gulf in age, status, and feelings is stated almost ad nauseum. But the cycle does come to a conclusion, as presumably the infatuation did. How many of the sonnets that conclude the Fair Youth sequence—those coming after Q104's despairing final line, "Ere you were born was beauty's summer dead"—he composed after the fateful falling-out, I doubt we shall ever know.

Pembroke certainly did not heed the warnings in Shakespeare's sonnets—if they were directed at him—or those of his family, for in February 1601, a couple of months from his majority, having been earl for less than a month, he was accused of seducing Mary Fitton, one of the queen's maids of honor, who, upon finding herself with child, named Pembroke as the father, perhaps in the hope that he would accede to what would have been a rather advantageous marriage.

According to Dover-Wilson, it was actually he who had been seduced, and she who targeted her beau. She had made "herself conspicuous as the leading lady in a masked dance before the queen at the wedding festivities on 16 June 1600 of a cousin of Herbert's," and later, "found her way late at night and disguised as a man to Herbert's private quarters." His reputation as someone "immoderately given up to women" evidently preceded him. However, even though Pembroke, upon "being examined, confesseth" he did the deed—as Robert Cecil reported in a letter the following February—he still "utterly renounceth all marriage." Fitton's gambit, if it was one, had failed. And even the threat of imprisonment—along with the Earl of Southampton, who had been imprisoned for "life" for his part in Essex's rebellion, the previous year—failed to intimidate the unrepentant youth.

A short spell in Fleet prison, followed by exile to the country, may, however, have had the effect of forcing the boy-noble to rethink his lifestyle. More likely, the death of his father, Henry, in January 1601, and assumption of the earldom forced him to succumb to his responsibilities, and finally, in 1604, to the inevitable arranged marriage, with Mary Talbot, daughter of the Earl of Shrewsbury. The marriage was a disaster, for, in Clarendon's piercing phrase, "he paid much too dear for his wife's fortune by taking her person into the bargain." Thankfully, it does not seem to have entirely quelled his questing spirit.

But his assumption of the title, and perhaps fear of any further scandal, may have finally convinced a wavering sonneteer that he should return the sequential sheaf of sonnets to a locked drawer till "Ruin hath taught me thus to ruminate" (64.11). Attendant upon such concerns is the suspicion that Shakespeare had tired of the form, and perhaps of lyric poetry itself. The almost impenetrable *Phoenix & the Turtle*, published in 1601, widely regarded as his "farewell" poem, seemed—or so C. S. Lewis believed—to be another attempt "to expound a philosophy of love; the last word, presumably, that he has given us in his own person on that subject. Its doctrine consummates that of the Sonnets. In them the 'naughting' had been one sided. He had lost himself in another but that other had not lost himself in Shakespeare. Now Shakespeare celebrates the exchanged death, and life, of a fully mutual love."

A convenient explanation for an inconvenient truth: Shakespeare had had enough of versifying "the perplexities of Love."

As for Pembroke, he simply bided his time, and after Elizabeth's reign was finally eclipsed in March 1603, he found himself almost immediately restored to royal favor on the accession of James I, from whom he received the royal garter that summer. Before that, James had already ventured to wrap Shakespeare's troupe—again facing hard times, as the plague closed the playhouses through a long, hot summer—in his ermine-lined protection, making the former Chamberlain's Men into King's Men.

Though I cannot share Boaden's belief that it was Pembroke's "friendship for our Poet [that] procured the above license from King James," for which there is not a shred of evidence, the days when Shakespeare aspired to be a patronized poet had passed and gone. Happily, he soon had the opportunity to (further) impress both earl and king with his playwriting skills when the King's Men were commanded to perform for king and court, then staying at Pembroke's ancestral home, Wilton House, on December 2, 1603. The play in question was almost certainly *As You Like It*. At last, both Wills had gotten what they wanted, thanks to "the highest Stuart o' all."

CHAPTER FOUR

1609–1639

"NOTHING IN MY CONSCIENCE . . . DID NEED A CYPHER"

There is no good reason for believing that Shake-
speare himself voluntarily gave to the world those
beautiful records of the errors of a great man.
—*The Edinburgh Review, 1840*

When, in 1983, Katherine Duncan-Jones first put her case for an authorized publication in 1609 of a set of poems almost no one dated later than the accession of James I (and many dated a decade earlier), she was challenging what she viewed as a cozy consensus that had gone on too long. In asking, "Was the 1609 *Shake-speares Sonnets* Really Unauthorized?" she sought to extend their composition and/or revision beyond 1603 to a time when one might have expected the playwright to rest on his poetic laurels. Instead, she preferred to have him jeopardizing his literary and social standing, and possibly alienating a former patron, with a set of poems that even on a single reading demonstrate a worrying propensity for masochistic infatuation—with woman and man.

Having transformed the sonnets themselves into a lifelong obsession, not a fleeting fancy, for their author, Duncan-Jones was obliged to recast the publisher, Thomas Thorpe, into a man of taste known for fastidious editions of the great and the very great, not a man of piratical disposition, minimal capital, and literary pretensions that fifteen years in the trade had failed to disabuse. In this act of transforming Thorpe from a "well-wishing adventurer" into a well-respected publisher of literature, she necessarily took certain liberties with the facts.

Even more improbably, she hoped to explain away the seeming deficiencies in the 1609 edition by bringing in the one solid factual snippet that tied Shakespeare down to a place and a time that year—his June 7 court case in Stratford. Seeking legal redress for an unpaid debt apparently resulted in him leaving London in a hurry. Rather than insisting on a delay to Q while he took care of a minor legal squabble in his hometown, we are required to believe that he left Thorpe (and printer George Eld) to it. Yet this was the exact opposite of everything he had done when he sought the epithet "Poet," in 1593–94. Back then, he had used a fellow Stratfordian, with a respectable name and capital to spare, to print his two long poems, *Venus* and *Lucrece,* both of which he dedicated to a named patron, and a renowned one at that.

By overlooking the weight of evidence to the contrary, accumulated by two and a half centuries' worth of Shakespearean scholarship, the lady was seeking to suggest that the order of Q was Shakespeare's; that the dedication was his in spirit, if not actual wording; and that the identity of "Mr W.H." was known not only to author and publisher, but to various other members of the London literati. Oh, and that Shakespeare had reworked some of the sonnets long after he had ceased to display any interest in composing further poetry.

The lady scholar thus reopened a debate that had once raged without respite (and now rages again): Were the sonnets—"those beautiful records of the errors of a great man"—ever intended for publication, and if so, why had it taken Shakespeare so long to get around to publishing them; so long, in fact, that it was a full decade after the Elizabethan sonnet fad had dissipated? If Q was Shakespeare's idea, he assuredly broke a number of patterns established two decades earlier, when he was still scrabbling to make his way in the literary world.

A certain amount of groundwork, undertaken by Shakespearean scholars in the quarter of a century before Duncan-Jones's article appeared, anticipated her thesis. The most necessary reinterpretation for anyone who longed to take Q at "face-value" was provided in 1964/1965 by a professorial pincer movement. An anthologized article and an academic monograph almost simultaneously decided that "A Lover's Complaint"—the forty-seven-verse narrative poem in rhyme royal that comes at the end of Thorpe's edition of the *Sonnets* (uncredited on the title page, but credited to Shakespeare within)—was indeed by Shakespeare.

First to break ranks with the past was a twenty-five-year-old New Zealand scholar, MacDonald P. Jackson, who brought out a thirty-nine-page pamphlet entitled *Shakespeare's 'A Lover's Complaint': Its Date and Authenticity*. He was rapidly followed by the English scholar Kenneth Muir, who published his own essay, "'A Lover's Complaint': A Reconsideration."

The effect of this "double whammy" on contemporary literary scholars was remarkable. "A Lover's Complaint" had, for most of its largely secret history, been subordinate to the sonnets. Omitted from almost every non-facsimile edition of the sonnets since Malone, few believed it belonged with these poetic gems. Rejected by Lee, who thought it "a literary exercise on a very common theme by some second-rate poet," its last rites were seemingly given by J. W. Mackail, in a 1912 article in *Essays and Studies*. After thoroughly examining its vocabulary, syntax and phrasing, Mackail concluded that "careful study leaves its authorship doubtful."

The die seemed cast. In 1927, the highly respected John Dover-Wilson called the poem "an elaborate jest." Professor Hyder Rollins, when commissioned to compile his monumental, two-volume, variorum edition of *The Sonnets* (1944), chose to leave "A Lover's Complaint" elsewhere, among the disputed items at the end of his edition of Shakespeare's other poems. And, in his 1954 volume for *The Oxford History of English Literature*, C. S. Lewis called it "a still-born *chanson d'aventure*, in rhyme royal, corrupt in text, poetically inconsiderable, and dialectically unlike Shakespeare."

Yet its importance in determining the "validity" of Q could not have been greater. As Mackail noted, in his highly influential article, "It obviously cannot be ignored in considering the problem of the Sonnets, and more particularly, that part of the problem which deals with the way in which they reached Thorpe's hands, the Mss. from which they were printed, and the circumstances of their publication."

Rather than addressing those issues, most scholars took Muir and Jackson at their word, and decided it was Shakespeare's work, after all. The restoration of the poem to the canon had begun with Martin Seymour-Smith's own edition of *The Sonnets*, the previous year, in which he took Lewis to task. Seymour-Smith suggested Lewis's curt dismissal of the poem had meant "that general readers have been led to ignore it. This is a pity, because . . . the poem seems certainly to be by Shakespeare." He still didn't incorporate the poem into his own edition, though he otherwise adhered to Q with a tenacity rare among modern editors.

He need not have worried. Paul Kerrigan put "A Lover's Complaint" in the Penguin edition of *The Sonnets* in 1986 and, not surprisingly, Duncan-Jones did the same for her 1997 Arden edition. More significantly, it was included alongside the sonnets in the 1988 Oxford edition of *The Complete Works,* edited by Stanley Wells and Gary Taylor, who merely observed that it is "clearly ascribed to Shakespeare" and that "stylistic evidence suggests [it] was written in the early seventeenth century and . . . may have been intended as a companion piece." Not even a mention of its disputed status. Thus one troublesome issue was not so much resolved, as dissolved. (And, clearly, should anyone successfully prove "A Lover's Complaint" to be the work of another poet, then the whole issue of Q's "authorized" status becomes instantly null and void.)

Another awkward encumbrance to any conception of an authorized Q lay with its rather belated appearance. Why would Shakespeare wait until 1609 to publish what are generally regarded as much earlier compositions? A. L. Rowse, writing in 1973, thought he knew why: "The story that is revealed . . . is highly dramatic and that of a poet who was already beginning to be well known as a dramatist. That is why they were not published at the time. . . . They were too near the bone."

Even before any general consensus treated Q as an authorized edition, there remained no shortage of apologists for this "delayed for fear of scandal" thesis. Indeed, the 1960s saw a new variation on an old theory as to the exact nature of the scandal—first advanced by Arthur Acheson in the early part of the century—gaining favor in certain quarters: that the publication itself was an act of spite from Southampton's old tutor, John Florio, who helped himself to the manuscript and gave it to Thorpe to embarrass and humiliate Shakespeare.

But Duncan-Jones felt she had found an alternative explanation for the belated publication, and it was all because the plague had returned to London. This "prolonged plague outbreak . . . deprived Shakespeare of income from the theatre. He may [therefore] have finished work on [the] Sonnets during this period, before selling the manuscript to Thorpe." As for the man who "brokered" this deal with Thorpe, why not fellow playwright Ben Jonson? According to Duncan-Jones, "If Shakespeare in 1608–9 wanted to raise some money by selling an unpublished literary manuscript, Jonson . . . would have been an obvious friend to consult on the matter. . . . It seems more than possible[!] that Shakespeare himself sold the copy to Jonson's friend Thorpe entire, though without troubling himself to correct the normal crop of errors which appeared in Eld's text."

So, in one swell foop, Duncan-Jones aimed to account for the transmission of the manuscript from author to publisher, and at the same time dispense with a previously insurmountable logistical obstacle: Why is Thorpe's edition riddled with errors if the author was party to its publication? What she failed to address was the sheer unlikelihood of Thorpe and Shakespeare being parties to a mutually beneficial financial transaction. As Charles Nicholl notes, in his engaging literary investigation, *The Lodger* (2007), "If Shakespeare was a man of substance, it was the substance of money and property. Shakespeare's earnings were high—estimates vary wildly, but something around £250 a year is plausible."

That kind of income would have made William a very wealthy man in Jacobean England. Thorpe, by contrast, couldn't even afford his own printing press. He was, by his own admission, an "adventurer," a common enough euphemism for "pirate." The idea that Shakespeare— even if he had decided to publish these poems, irrespective of the wishes of a (former) patron—would have sold them to Thorpe verges on the fantastical.

All the evidence, i' truth, when examined in an undistorted light, lines up against Duncan-Jones. Arthur Marotti, one of those who has challenged Duncan-Jones's thesis, points out that Jacobethan "authors might sell texts for modest sums and/or for complimentary copies of their books, but they were more likely to benefit economically from dedicating their works to patrons and patronesses than from any direct payments from publishers for their texts." As a matter of fact, when John Stow delivered his life's work, *The Survey of London,* to the publisher John Wolfe, in 1598, he was paid the princely sum of £3, plus forty copies of the work (and for his *Brief Chronicle,* he was paid a third of that). An examination of Elizabethan translator Richard Robinson's accounts shows that twelve of his books only produced about £40—a desultory sum when spread over some fifteen years. In addition, he was given twenty-five copies of some of his publications.

The notion that these sonnets had long ago been consigned to the author's private locker has a great deal more to recommend it. The 1609 edition Thorpe published certainly shows precious few signs of a carefully marked-up manuscript, and there is plenty of (admittedly circumstantial) evidence to suggest that the book was either suppressed, or quietly sidelined. In fact, Thorpe's career never recovered from the disaster that was Q, leaving him obliged to continue his piratical ways.

Admittedly, the text itself begets a clear contradiction between the avowedly private nature of the discourse and the repeated, unambiguous professions of the immortality the verses will confer on their subject. But it is a discrepancy we have already addressed. Assuming the poems will be published anonymously and/or posthumously, after a period of discreet circulation, is quite a different mindset from the one that would be required to publish them under one's own name, during one's own lifetime.

The Victorians certainly had no problem holding both ideas simultaneously. As Charles Armitage Brown states, in an 1838 essay, "That the poems were eventually intended for publication is certain, since they were to immortalize the 'only begetter of them.'" And yet, he was still inclined to conclude, "The confused manner in which they were printed, rendering them wholly enigmatical for so long a period, exculpates the author from any share in the transaction." A year earlier, Boaden doubted whether "the collection of Sonnets addressed to W.H. . . . were ever seen by any eye but his, to whom 126 of them were addressed," further pointing out that "they are entirely personal, and never intended for the public view. . . . Nay, when at length they are 'set forth,' the person addressed by the writer is obscured, rather than revealed," an interpretation seemingly at odds with Shakespeare's internally expressed intent.

In modern times another "W.H.," Auden, a preeminent poet himself, simply could not conceive of the sonnets having been written from the artistic remove generally required to create art. He used this to defend Shakespeare against the charge of allowing such wildly varying work to appear in his name, "For the inferior ones we have no right to condemn Shakespeare unless we are prepared to believe—a belief for which there is no evidence—that he prepared or intended them all to be published. . . . Wordsworth defined poetry as emotion recollected in tranquility. It seems highly unlikely that Shakespeare wrote many of these sonnets out of recollected emotion."

Whereas Martin Seymour-Smith sees their private nature as an intrinsic aspect of their worth: "The Sonnets seem to have . . . been written from day to day and from week to week, without much thought, at any rate at the time they were written, of publication, [which perhaps explains why] the Sonnets are of a higher poetic value than Shakespeare's two ambitious narrative poems; . . . *because* they were not written with the public in mind." And yet, "there are few readings of the Sonnets that do not [at least] tacitly assume that Shakespeare's prime intention was to create art."

This distinction is not mere Whatifism. If Shakespeare had elected to publish poems of such a private nature, it would have been a monumental decision. As Duncan-Jones herself points out, "Where Jonson, through such a figure as Horace in *The Poetaster,* makes a clear definition of his artistic personality and ideals, Shakespeare nowhere asserts his presence in the plays, either as a writer or as a personality." What I, for one, extrapolate from such an observation, and a close reading of the sonnets, is that a key characteristic of the great wordsmith was self-effacement. This was something William Hazlitt noticed as far back as 1826, when he observed how, in "some of Shakespear's Sonnets . . . he appears to have stood more alone and to have thought less about himself than any living being."

And one thing seems sure. The author of the sonnets cannot have ever imagined they would fit easily into the genre that inspired them. Simply put, "Autobiographical confessions were not the stuff of which the Elizabethan sonnet was made. The typical collection of Elizabethan sonnets was a mosaic of plagiarisms, a medley of imitative or assimilative studies" [SL]. Which perhaps explains why modern tastes find it so hard to equate Shakespeare's sonnets with those of technically superior contemporaries.

Shakespeare himself was consciously adopting the "inferior," quintessentially English, Surrey-inspired sonnet-mode—"the first twelve rhym[e] in staves of four lines by cross metre, and the last two rhyming together," as defined by Sir Philip Sidney—rather than the more convoluted Petrarchan model, with which he would have been equally conversant. As one critic opined, "The only explanation seems to be that he considered the form evolved by Surrey and other English poets to have, on the whole, for English practise, the advantage."[5] But then, he was not trying to impress an audience with his literary dexterity. He was hoping to communicate with a directness and immediacy altogether lacking in those contemporaries.

All of this argues against a wealthy, semi-retired playwright opening his drawer for a second time, and letting Thorpe do what he wilt. As, indeed, doubtful Thomas did—however he came by the manuscript(s). Hence, E. K. Chambers' uncharacteristically categorical statement, "The volume cannot have been 'overseen,' as *Venus and Adonis* and *Lucrece* may have been, by Shakespeare."

It is an uncomfortable fact for advocates of an authorized Q, noted as early as Malone's 1780 edition, that there are some fourteen instances in sonnets 26–70 where the printer has mistaken "their" for "thy" (said confusion doubtless arose from the common use of certain abbreviations at that time: "yʳ" for "their" and "yⁱ" for "thy"). This does rather suggest a printer who reprinted what he saw in his "copy," even when it made poor sense, and thus that there was no author on hand to consult, and that the printer-publisher had only the original scribal copy with which to work.

Three obvious and embarrassing errors—even for a Jacobean printer—also argue against an overseer with a vested interest in textual consistency. The last couplet of Q96 repeats that of Q36; while Q99 ("The forward violet thus did I chide") has an additional line (probably line 5), perhaps transposed from another page in the printing process; and the phrase "my sinful earth" closes line 1 and opens line 2 of Q146 ("Poor soul, the center of my sinful earth"). Even though George Wyndham in 1898 went to great pains to demonstrate that the "use of italics, capitals, and punctuation [shows] evidence of design," any such design was mangled by an uncomprehending compositor.

Actually, one suspects that the italics did originally serve an important purpose, and this purpose is occasionally apparent in Q (as in the italicizing of *Will* in sonnets 135, 136, and 143). But the printer either failed to consistently discern the meaning of markings in manuscript, or there were intrinsic textual inconsistencies he simply could not reconcile. Tucker Brooke's supposition that words like "mighst" (57), "unstayined"

(70), and "preuenst" (100) were the poet's attempt to avoid "harsh clusters of consonants" likewise retains its appeal. As does Wyndham's idea that "Rose," when italicized, "stands . . . for the Idea or Eternal Type of Beauty." But at every turn, Q obliges us to guess the author's intent. Oh, the irony, that a minor publisher's carelessness should culminate in more books on Q than the entire output of all his contemporaries.

Thorpe certainly failed to adopt the *modus operandi* of Bartholomew Yong, who in his address "to divers learned Gentlemen, and other . . . friendes" that precedes his translation of Jorge de Montemayor's *Diana* (1598), asked the reader's pardon for "the faults [that] escaped in the Printing, the copie being verie darke and enterlined, and I loth to write it out againe . . . [and] could not intende the correction." This "wellwishing adventurer" saw little wrong with what he wrought. And, anyway, he had no one to whom he need answer.

The corollary of this is distasteful only if one's primary intention is to do away with the textual difficulties that a "bookleg" edition of the English language's most revered love-poems generates. And that has been the direction most academics have been moving in for the past half-century, more in love with the idea of an "authorial" text than in the historical reality. Thankfully, the occasional voice in the academic wilderness has cried wolf. Heather Dubrow, for example, asserts in her necessarily revisionist 1999 essay, "Incertainties Now Crown Themselves Assur'd": "The 1609 edition represents not that dream of traditional textual editors, the author's final intention, but rather a set of poems in various stages of composition. If this is so, the division between poems to one addressee and those to another is not likely to be perfect."

To further compound the improbability of a middle-aged Shakespeare letting Thorpe publish "a set of poems in various stages of composition," we are required to believe that this was because he had to hurry back to Stratford on pressing personal business. In fact, Shakespeare's documented financial prudence makes Duncan-Jones's explanation for his departure from London rather unlikely. The matter that required his personal attendance was the recovery of a debt totalling six pounds, with twenty-four shillings interest attached, from one John Addenbrooke, the hearing for which was convened at the Stratford Court of Record on June 7, 1609.

Not only was the sum a trivial one for a man whose annual income was forty or fifty times that, but the judgment in the playwright's favor in no way resolved the matter, or resulted in the recovery of the debt (the case had already been dragging on since the previous August). Addenbrooke simply failed to appear, and the court finally instructed his surety, a local blacksmith, to show cause why *he* should not pay. Samuel Schoenbaum ruefully notes, in his *William Shakespeare: A Documentary Life,* "Whether Shakespeare ever collected is not recorded."

So Shakespeare had traveled 100 miles to his country home, at a time when this was a two-day journey, to recoup a debt he would have had some expectation would end up unpaid whatever the judgment of the Court of Record. And, as a result, he "knowingly" allowed his first published collection of poetry in fifteen years to appear riddled with typos, and with a dedication more obtuse than any part of *The Phoenix & the Turtle*?

And yet, precious few have dared vouchsafe the suggestion of W. L. Phelps, in a 1939 article in the *Proceedings of the American Philosophical Society,* that the appearance of Q was the real reason why the dramatist left town, it having "caused Shakespeare to leave London and to retire to the seclusion of Stratford," at least temporarily, while the hubbub died down, à la James VI leaving Edinburgh after the murder of the Earl of Moray. Though permanent retirement was still a couple of years away, the timeline fits such a premise rather well.

Registered on May 20, the *Sonnets* probably appeared in early June (though the so-called receipt for a copy purchased by Edward Alleyn on

June 19 is almost certainly another Payne-Collier forgery). If Shakespeare's reaction has gone wholly undocumented, that unabashed homosexual poet, W. H. Auden, expressed very little doubt as to what it would have been:

> It is impossible to believe either that Shakespeare wished them to be published or that he can have shown most of them to the young man and woman, whoever they were, to whom they are addressed. Suppose you had written Sonnet 57, "Being your slave, what should I do but tend / Upon the hours and times of your desire?" Can you imagine showing it to the person you were thinking of! . . . Of one thing I am certain: Shakespeare must have been horrified when they were published. . . . The poets of the period, like Marlowe and Barnfield, whom we know to have been homosexual, were very careful not to express their feelings in the first person, but in terms of classical mythology.

Though the above statement probably says more about Auden than it does about Shakespeare. Yet there is no getting away from the fact that no Jacobethan—even Barnfield—wrote sonnets of such ardent desire to a man. And, as Seymour-Smith points out in his edition, "It is unlikely that Shakespeare would have failed to remember that one of the charges outstanding against Marlowe at the time of his murder had been that he was alleged to have said, 'All thei that love not tobacco and boyes are fooles.'"

That the state took such matters seriously is indicated by the fact that, in 1533, "buggery," which to date had only been an ecclesiastical crime, was made a felony punishable by death, and though that statute was repealed by Edward VI, it was reenacted in 1562. Nor would the king's own infatuations have saved Shakespeare from a visit to the Privy Council.

There was one rule for king and court, another for commoners—as would be the case even after the Restoration, when the Earl of Rochester could boast in rhyme, "There's a sweet, soft page of mine / Does the trick worth forty wenches."

Assuming that the emotions pouring off the pages of Q were now as embers to the older, wiser man, any reminder the appearance of these poems provided must have been painful; as must the shabby way they had been collected and printed, a sick shadow of what the poet probably once intended. But that self-effacing streak still probably propelled the playwright to run and hide, not challenge and confront. After all, he had a long-established pattern of "uncomplainingly submitt[ing] to the wholesale piracies of his plays and the ascription to him of books by other hands" [SL].

And it must have been especially galling to find he was obliged to share this edition of the *Sonnets* with a wordy narrative poem by one of those "alien pen[s]" of which he complained in Q78. And yet he made no documented public complaint—unlike three years later, when he found himself in a similar situation, having the work of a.n.other attributed to him. In that case, a quiet word with the publisher, our friend William Jaggard, probably through a third party, sufficed to have the title page of a revised edition of *The Passionate Pilgrim* canceled and a new one, no longer bearing the dramatist's name, substituted in its place (further demonstrating that self-effacing streak).

We are obliged to a caustic aside from the fellow dramatist whose work had been attributed to Shakespeare for evidence of the playwright's annoyance. That peeved polemicist was Shakespeare's acquaintance Thomas Heywood. And it was in his *Apologie for Actors* (1613) that he reported, "The Author [i.e., Shakespeare] I know [was] much offended with M. Jaggard (that altogether unknowne to him) presumed to make so bold with his name." What inspired William's ire was the inclusion of poems from Heywood's own *Troia Britanica,* originally published in 1608, in a third edition of *The Passionate Pilgrim.* As Rollins relates, "A reader who did not know the exact details of the situation might conclude that [Heywood] had plagiarized these poems from Shakespeare and that Shakespeare to expose his dishonesty was printing them under his own name."

The annoyance of the "much offended" Shakespeare may have stemmed in part from the fact that this dubious collection, from another century, had returned to vex him. Or it could be that he felt the charge of plagiarism, whether directed at him or Heywood, was not one he could let stand unchallenged. It was, after all, an accusation that had stained him before.[6] Of course, there could be other explanations—none quite as original as Duncan-Jones's: "Jaggard's 1612 piracy was all the more brazen in its audacity because, as Heywood said, 'he [Shakespeare] since, to do himself right, hath published them in his own name.' That is, in 1609 Shakespeare had assumed control of his own text of his Sonnets, by selling the collection to Thorpe."

Yet again, the audacity of the lady takes my breath away. By carefully excising a choice phrase from its context, Duncan-Jones has transformed a hypothetical statement from Heywood—i.e., that the appearance of his own poems under Shakespeare's name in the 1612 work "may put the world in opinion I might steale them from him; and hee to doe himselfe right, hath since published them in his owne name"—into an altogether different complaint. The poems that "hath [been] published . . . in his own name" no longer apply to Heywood. They have been transmuted into a reference to the 152 Shakespearean sonnets that do not appear in *The Passionate Pilgrim.* Such an interpretation would qualify as arch-revisionism even if Duncan-Jones had also provided readers of her influential Arden edition with the generally accepted interpretation of Heywood's barb.

Heywood responded to this act in the only way he knew how. He had no comeback legally, because Jaggard owned the *Troia Britanica* poems outright, having published them back in 1608 (with Heywood's blessing). Likewise, the original edition of *The Passionate Pilgrim* had been published twice thirteen years earlier, explicitly attributed to Shakespeare.

The chances of getting the Stationers' Company to suppress a book of poetry (even one that was never registered, like *The Passionate Pilgrim*) on any grounds save prurience or the ruffling of religious or political sensitivities was small. Shakespeare, the hapless author on the receiving end of more bookleg quartos than any other Jacobethan, undoubtedly knew this. Which makes the suggestion proposed by John Kerrigan, "that Thorpe diverted copies [of Q through two booksellers] to avoid the suppression of his volume by Shakespeare," a most uncharacteristic misunderstanding of the nature of Jacobethan publishing.

Yet, at the time of Q's appearance, there were still a couple of options available to Shakespeare, if he wanted to put pressure on Thorpe. Unfortunately, they would have required him to draw attention to the *Sonnets* at a time in his life when he probably no longer held them, or the feelings that originally kindled them, in high regard. There were two recent precedents for the recalling of unauthorized works, both of which, in all likelihood, he personally knew about. The first of these concerned Spenser's *Complaints*, registered by William Ponsonby on December 29, 1590. It contained a classically Elizabethan publisher's preface:

Gentle Reader, SINCE my late setting foorth of the Faerie Queene, finding that it hath found a fauourable passage amongst you; I haue sithence endeuoured by all good meanes (for the better encrease and accomplishment of your delights,) to get into my handes such smale Poemes of the same Authors; as I heard were disperst abroad in sundrie hands, and not easie to bee come by, by himselfe; some of them hauing bene diuerslie imbeziled and purloyned from him, since his departure ouer Sea. Of the which I haue by good meanes gathered togethaer these fewe parcels present.

All protestations to the contrary, Ponsonby is here brazenly proclaiming his act of piracy—and not expecting any comeback. And yet, according to Woudhuysen, "By the next year there is evidence that [all] the unsold copies [of *Complaints*] were called in by the authorities." However, unlike Thorpe's act of piracy, Ponsonby's had its own reward. Even with the attempted suppression, a large number of copies of his edition survived.

Altogether more pertinent to the history of Q is the successful suppression of the first quarto of Sir Philip Sidney's *Astrophil & Stella*. Like Ponsonby, who had himself registered Sidney's *New Arcadia* a couple of years earlier, the publisher of Sidney's sonnet-sequence, Thomas Newman, claimed due diligence for his edition, asserting that he had "beene very carefull in the Printing" of the poems from manuscript, "and whereas being spred abroad in written Coppies, it had gathered much corruption by ill Writers: I have used their helpe and advice in correcting & restoring it to his first dignitie, that I knowe were of skill and experience in those matters." (He then added assorted sonnets from other authors after Sidney's sequence, which is hardly the act of a concerned publisher.)

Nonetheless, sometime in September 1591 the Stationers' Company took action against Newman, demanding that he bring his books to Stationers' Hall, and consulting Lord Burghley about the matter, even though he was "on progress" with the queen. Something about Newman's publication had led to its "takinge in," and though the Stationers' Register gives no indication of why such action was undertaken or who initiated it, it was surely at the instigation of Sidney's sister, the Countess of Pembroke. The nature of Newman's crime is unclear, but "may have involved compromising the honour of the Sidneys by publishing Sir Philip's adulterous poems, or by associating him with dubious characters; [or] it may simply have been to steal the thunder from the Countess of Pembroke's plans" [HRW] to publish her own edition.

Whatever the case, when a new edition, prepared from a more accurate text, appeared, albeit still under the auspices of Newman, the incursions of "alien pen[s]" had been removed. At the same time, one of those "alien pen[s]," Samuel Daniel, set about publishing heavily revised versions of twenty-four sonnets that Newman had incorporated into the original edition of *Astrophil & Stella* as part of his own sonnet-sequence, the delightful *Delia*. Dedicating the edition to the Countess of Pembroke, he insisted that he had previously been "betraide by the indiscretion of a greedie Printer."

Given his undoubted knowledge of (and debt to) Sidney's *Astrophil & Stella* sonnet-sequence, it seems unlikely that the Stratford dramatist would not have known something of its publishing history. And one of two options would probably have been available to the King's Man: to ask for any unsold copies to be impounded, pursuant to an approved edition appearing; or, to take the more contentious route, to simply publish the sonnet-sequence as he had originally intended, in a rival edition, just as "good" quartos of *Hamlet* and *Romeo & Juliet* had succeeded "bad" ones. The fact that Shakespeare adopted neither course rather suggests that the last thing he wanted was for his own sonnet-sequence(s) to become another cause célèbre, à la *Astrophil & Stella*.

Thorpe had probably already calculated that he had little to fear from the author of the *Sonnets*. But there remains the contentious issue of what feelings the unexpected publication of these once-private poems might have induced in the Fair Youth with "beauty, birth, wealth and wit," now that he was no longer so "fresh" or "green." If the Fair Youth was in fact Southampton, there was very little—save scuttlebutt—to connect the earl, now released from prison and restored to favor, with these sonnets. He may therefore have been content to let the matter lie.

However, if Pembroke was the "W.H." to whom these poems were directed—and dedicated—then Thorpe would never have knowingly "dared the hazard of offending the most powerful nobleman at court" [CAB]. Even if William Archer's investigation into Pembroke's character left him convinced that the earl, "never a man of scrupulous morals, may have been privately far from ashamed of the episode, and [was] willing enough to permit a dedication to which only the initiated had the key," the powerful peer would have surely responded to a request from the poet to put the screws on the upstart publisher. As we know, he "prosequuted ... their Authour living with so much favour."

The scraps of evidence that exist favor the thesis that Thorpe knew nothing of his dedicatory *faux pas*. For one, there is quite a contrast between the Q dedication and one published the following year, where Thorpe sought Pembroke's favor as the "poore delegate" of John Healey, now in Virginia. Healey's translation of *Civitas Dei* was dedicated on his behalf by Thorpe to "the Honorablest Patron of Muses and Good Mindes, Lord William Earle of Pembroke" (this dedication could predate Q, given that the book was registered as far back as 1608).

Neither dedication brought Thorpe any favor, and when he published a new English edition of the *Manuall* of the Stoic philosopher Epictetus, translated into English by the same John Healey, later in 1610, he dedicated it to the more susceptible John Florio, despite Healey's expressed wish that his "translations ... might only bee addressed" to William, Earl of Pembroke. This rather suggests that Thorpe felt he had nothing to gain from (further) courting the earl.

Possible further "evidence" that Thorpe was not "in on the joke" has been deduced from two subsequent dedications by bit-players in our little drama. In 1613, the poet George Wither seemingly parodied Thorpe's Q dedication—with, "To himself, G.W. wisheth all happiness"—in his preface to *Abuses Stript and Whipt.* Though it is likely he was simply sending up a general convention, not Thorpe specifically, it is possible that the satirist—a friend of John Davies of Hereford— was responding to that earlier, cryptic dedication in a knowing way. Wither somehow managed to annoy somebody grand with the book in question, being incarcerated in the Marshalsea in Southwark for his pains.

No direct connection, however, ties George Wither to either Shakespeare or Thorpe. But if anyone in London, save the personalities themselves, would have known of a hidden history behind those initials, it would have been Ben Jonson, the one known friend of Shakespeare already published by Thorpe. And in the 1616 edition to *Epigrammes*— published as part of his own first folio—Jonson apparently decided to share a private joke with the playwrights' patron, dedicating the work to "William, Earle of Pembroke" in almost Thorpean terms:

> MY LORD. While you cannot change your merit, I dare not change your title: It was that made it, and not I. Under which name, I here offer to your Lo[rd]: the ripest of my studies, my Epigrammes; which though they carry danger in the sound, doe not therefore seeke your shelter: For, when I made them, I had nothing in my conscience of which I did need a cypher.

The Jacobethans certainly did love their in-jokes, though I wouldn't necessarily agree with Gerald Massey's claim in 1872 that Jonson's epigram "tells us plainly enough that the Earl's title had been changed in some previous dedication." But his reference to "nothing in my conscience of which I did need a cypher" appears designed to counterpoint some previous work which had need of a cypher.

In the same year, coinciding with Shakespeare's passing, Thorpe finally decided to give Healey his wish, dedicating the second edition of his translation of Epictetus' *Manuall* to Pembroke, using the most obsequious language at his command. But by then his career as a publisher was nearing its end, and it is unlikely that Pembroke, who was now Lord Chamberlain, took the slightest notice of Thorpe's belated pleading. Or that he greatly cared to know that Thorpe's troubles had begun when he had published the sonnets of a former favorite.

My supposition that the publication of the *Sonnets* predicated the collapse of Thorpe's publishing dreams seems borne out by everything we know concerning his business before and after its fateful registration. Lee's account of the publisher, in his 1905 facsimile edition of Q, records that Thorpe finally managed to occupy a shop of his own in 1608, a fact given due prominence on the title pages of all three publications he issued in that year, "but his other undertakings were described on their title-pages as printed for him by one stationer and sold for him by another; and when any address found mention at all, it was the shopkeeper's address, and not his own." Well, by the time the *Sonnets* appeared, he had already been obliged to give up the shop in St. Paul's Churchyard.

Thorpe also seems to have chosen to give up at least one publication he'd previously planned in order to devote himself to the popular playwright's "lost" poems, assuming, as seems likely, that he acquired the manuscript(s) around January 1609. It was on the 18th of that month that he had entered at Stationers' Hall *A Discovery of a New Worlde,* a translation by "an English Mercurye" of Joseph Hall's satirical treatise *Mundus alter et idem.* However, before the book could appear, the copyright was transferred to his old friend Edward Blount, who issued it later that year in collaboration with William Barrett.

Nor was this the only copyright Thorpe was obliged to surrender—for what one must assume were financial reasons—in those pivotal years 1609–10. If, as Duncan-Jones would like us to believe, it was Jonson's association with Thorpe that gave Shakespeare the impetus to enter into a transaction for his own "sugred sonnets," then it was almost the last time Jonson did anything to help Thorpe's business. Less than a year after the publication of the *Sonnets*, Thorpe transferred his rights in Jonson's *Sejanus* and *Volpone* to a former fellow-apprentice, Walter Burre; and as Leona Rostenberg has observed, "With this transfer of copyright, Thorpe's association with Jonson was concluded."

Such a transference hardly comes across as the transaction of a shrewd businessman. Rather, it suggests pecuniary pressures had begun to bite. The two plays in question were just about the only potentially valuable copyrights Thorpe now held. Perhaps he simply had no option—he needed money. Or maybe Jonson, unhappy at the unwarranted publication of his friend's private poems, wanted nothing more to do with the piratical publisher. A leap, I know. But it seems clear that Thorpe fell on hard times on or around the time he published Q. To start with, it was the only publication he registered that year (excepting the Healey translation that he "gave" to Blount to publish)—and however much he had paid for the manuscript(s), this kind of thin quarto was hardly a costly production.

Matters had not greatly improved by the following year, when he dedicated the *Manuall of Epictetus* to John Florio in terms that suggested he was hoping for a handout. He calls himself "your poor friend," and compares himself to "distressed Sostratus," while alluding to Florio as "more fortunate Areius." Having recently become a groom of Queen Anne's privy chamber, Florio now enjoyed an annual salary of a hundred pounds, whereas Thorpe was struggling to raise enough money to publish Healey's monumental translation of *Civitas Dei* (registered in May 1608—to Eld, not Thorpe—it did not appear until 1610).

Meanwhile, the *Sonnets* proved to be neither the kind of "bestseller" Thorpe had been hoping for, nor a copyright that would come in handy in his old age. Which brings us back, neatly I trust, to the highly charged issue of whether the *Sonnets* were in fact suppressed. Many have thought so—though, according to Duncan-Jones, "There is no evidence whatsoever of suppression."

By which, she presumably means there is no direct evidence. There is more than enough circumstantial evidence to mount a solid case, the salient features of which J. M. Robertson summarized back in 1926, "[Q] is now a very rare book; yet the natural presumption would be that in 1609, at the height of Shakespeare's contemporary fame, it would have found a considerable sale if it were not interfered with; and that a second edition would have followed in a few years. . . . There is fair ground for a presumption that . . . [Q] was stopped, whether through the intervention of Shakespeare or another."

Duncan-Jones has suggested that thirteen is actually quite a large number of copies to survive the centuries, given the relatively flimsy nature of seventeenth-century quartos. But I would counter that thirteen is statistically too small a number to draw any inference with confidence. If the number of copies in any way equated with the number of contemporary references to Q, or manuscript transcriptions of poems therein, she'd have a stronger case. It does not. And is it really so hard to imagine that there were a dozen or so Jacobeans who recognized the genius of this uniquely English sonneteer and, knowing of the book's scarcity, treasured their precious quarto enough to bind it well and preserve it?

No reasonable person could fail to be struck by the contrast between the continuing popularity of Shakespeare's two narrative poems and the disappearing act that is the 1609 *Sonnets*. Just three decades on, the second publisher of the sonnets couldn't even find a copy of Q to cross-reference with his text (see next chapter). And that invisibility manifests itself most pertinently in the total lack of contemporary references to the collection, compounded by an equal absence of its contents in Caroline commonplace books or manuscripts—even though, as was shown in Chapter 2, at least one sonnet in the collection had begun to circulate widely from a manuscript source.

The manuscript culture lent itself to this kind of indirect fame. John Donne's "poems circulated extraordinarily widely in manuscript during his lifetime, principally in the 1620s" [HRW]. In fact, some seventy-three contemporary manuscript-miscellanies containing Donne's poems have survived, a marked contrast to the dearth of Shakespearean sonnets so anthologized.

But the most salient point Robertson made back in 1926 was that the sonnets secured "no second edition." From this Seymour-Smith drew the obvious conclusion: "It is significant that Thorpe, who did not entirely cease publishing activities until 1624, never reissued [the *Sonnets*]. Why not, unless the edition had been bought up, withdrawn or otherwise suppressed?" Certainly, by the time Thorpe got around to republishing the one other book he issued in the same twelve-month period, the *Manuall*, in 1616, he had all but stopped publishing new books, though he remained a member of the Stationers' Company a while longer.

Unfortunately for Thorpe, whatever the status of the original edition of Q, the days when Shakespeare's foul papers were "fair game" apparently died with the playwright. When that old rogue Jaggard, in cahoots with fellow stationer Thomas Pavier, decided to issue quarto editions of at least four Shakespeare plays and one pseudo-Shakespearean offering

(*Sir John Oldcastle*), in or around 1619, he found that the King's Men had a powerful new ally whom they could call upon to stop the pair in their tracks. (Some time in 1618–19, Pavier issued new quartos of *The Merry Wives of Windsor, Pericles, The Yorkshire Tragedy,* and *Henry VI Part 2* and *Part 3,* and, in partnership with Jaggard, fresh editions of *A Midsummer Night's Dream, The Merchant of Venice, Henry V, Sir John Oldcastle, and King Lear.*)

The actors and/or their agents persuaded the Lord Chamberlain to send a letter to the Stationers' Company in May 1619 saying that none of the plays belonging to them could be printed without their express permission. Such a "request" was quite unprecedented. But the Lord Chamberlain's powers over what could and could not be published were as great as those he enjoyed when regulating the theater. And since 1615, the Lord Chamberlain's office had been occupied by William Herbert, Earl of Pembroke, whom Heminge and Condell would thank, four years later, for having "prosequuted both [the plays], and their Authour living, with so much favour."

Evidently, Heminge and Condell had already begun to assemble the First Folio of their late friend's plays when Jaggard and Pavier began to queer the pitch. This time the pirate-publisher was suppressed, though Jaggard did not go quietly. Canceling title pages was a favorite ruse of the man, and soon enough these piratical quartos had reappeared bearing a series of new "publication dates"—either 1600 or 1608. The only way to stop him from continuing to run interference with their ambitious project may have been to let him join the syndicate. Jaggard, that pirate extraordinaire, thus ended up being the chief (of two) printers who, along with two respected booksellers, William Aspley and John Smethwick, produced the most important volume in English literature. The other printer was Edward Blount. Small world.

Because the Chamberlain's office was scrupulous about their paperwork, we know all about the Lord Chamberlain's May 1619 letter. But if the same individual, or someone of equal stature, directly or indirectly made it clear to Thorpe privately back in 1609 that there would be no second edition of Q, and that he would be strongly advised to let *Shakespeare's Sonnets* disappear quietly, it is unlikely it would have crossed Thorpe's mind to argue, even if it meant financial ruin. There would, of course, be no public record of any such "agreement." The object of such a (wholly hypothetical) exercise could only have been to avoid a scandal. After all, several sonnets of Shakespeare's had been in print by then for more than a decade, without upsetting the cart; and piracy of his work had long been a fact of life.

The most compelling evidence for such a covert suppression of the *Sonnets* is the conspicuous "failure" of Thorpe to sell the copyright to a fellow publisher, even after the First Folio appeared in 1623, or after Pembroke's death in 1625. It was *his* property. And as late as November 1624, he assigned, in tandem with Edward Blount, "all their estat and interest in a booke called *Hero and Leander* begun by Christopher Marlowe and finished by George Chapman" to the London stationer, Samuel Vicars. And this wasn't even a book Thorpe had personally published.

In fact, there was a former business associate to whom, one would assume, the copyright to the *Sonnets* would have held instant appeal. Back in 1609, William Aspley had been one of two booksellers who received printed editions of Q. Since then, Aspley had become a junior partner in the publication of the First Folio (thanks to the copyright he held in two of its plays); had acquired the copyright on the still-lucrative *Venus & Adonis* (presumably at quite a cost); and had become an equal partner in the 1632 publication of the Second Folio. By the time of his death, in 1640, he was the master of the Stationers' Company.

Given his increasing involvement in the company's affairs, Aspley must have known all about Thorpe's increasingly dire straits (and probably of his death, sometime after 1635). So why would he not have made Thorpe an offer he couldn't refuse, unless he had already had his fingers burned, and/or there was an aura to this particular volume from which he was keen to dissociate himself?

Subsequent to Q's appearance, a chastened Thorpe learned to be more discreet, or at least less brazen, when attempting to publish any of his more dubious ventures—something he continued to do. When he published a translation of Lucan's *Pharsalia* by Sir Arthur Gorges in 1612, he was remarkably coy about how he had procured his "copy." This time, when he concocted a preface, he did so in the name of Gorges's son, Carew, who had apparently stumbled on the poem "in my father's study, amongst many other of his Manuscripts." Carew was ten at the time.

Likewise, when Thorpe attributed a third-rate poetic eulogy for a murdered Devon landowner to a certain "W.S." the very same year, he refrained from even putting his initials, T.T., to the production (as he had with the *Sonnets*, almost the only instance when drafting his own dedication that he did not put an abbreviated version of his full name—Tho. Thorpe). The title page of "A funerall Elegye in memory of the late virtuous master WILLIAM PEETER of Whipton neere Exetour" merely named the printer, his old partner-in-piracy George Eld. There seems little doubt that he and/or Eld hoped to convince some potential purchasers that "W.S." was a rather well-known dramatist.[7]

One doubts, though, that in even his most fevered dreams, Thorpe imagined that this formulaic tripe would, 380 years later, be added to the "official" Shakespeare canon on the say-so of a single Shakespearean scholar. And if that was not ironic enough for him, that his anonymous publication of this dirge would be used as evidence of his own publishing credentials, and of a connection between the dead man and the London-based playwright that never existed.

Just as one assumes that when Thorpe was lying in his bed in the room he had been provided with in the hospital of Ewelme, Oxfordshire, in the last few years of his long life, he finally accepted that he had never been cut out to be a publisher. By the time he arrived at Ewelme in December 1635, a broke(n) man, it had been twelve years since he had last paid his Stationers' dues. In that time, he may well have noticed how Shakespeare's standing had only continued to grow. In 1632 there had even been the Second Folio, which added more than its fair share of errors to the slowly formalizing official canon. In the next three years, two more plays attributed to the late bard (this time with justification), *Pericles* and *The Noble Kinsman,* appeared in quarto form. But the *Sonnets* seemed destined to remain Shakespeare's greatest secret, a fact that probably brought a rueful smile to the old man, in his comfortable almsroom. If only he had known.

CHAPTER FIVE

1639–1640

"SCORN NOT THE SONNET"

[These] excellent and sweetely composed Poems . . .
had not the fortune by Reason of their Infancie in his
death, to have the due accomodatio[n] of proportion-
able glory, with the rest of his everliving Workes.
—JOHN BENSON, PREFACE TO 1640
EDITION OF SHAKESPEARE'S *Poems*

I f the first booklegger of the *Sonnets,* Thorpe, has recently been re-
deemed from the "stain" of piracy, at least temporarily, the second
so-called booklegger of these poems, John Benson, has continued
to be damned for daring to republish them. His 1640 edition of *Poems*
Written by Wil. Shakespeare. Gent, has been called a lot of names, none
nice. As temperate a scholar as Hyder Rollins accused Benson of taking
"great pains to conceal his piracy," called his edition "completely devoid
of textual authority," and even sarcastically rebuked Benson for being
"so thoughtful and independent" an editor that he somehow managed
to omit eight of the Q sonnets.

So perhaps now is a good time to restore some balance to the traditional account of Benson's book, while presenting the flipside of Stuart book-publishing. In order to understand not just the history of the *Sonnets*, but of all seventeenth-century editions of Shakespeare, it is important to recognize, as Gary Taylor does in *Reinventing Shakespeare*, that "copyright was held by . . . a trade cartel of printers and booksellers, who held those rights in perpetuity and could buy or sell them like any piece of real estate." Which is why the greatest mystery underlying Thorpe's edition is the lack of documentary evidence that he transferred its copyright at any time between that original 1609 publication and his death in the late 1630s.

Perhaps he did. If he transferred his rights after 1624, when he ceased being a contributor to the Stationers' Company coffers, it would not necessarily have been recorded in the company registry. It seems unlikely, but perhaps Thorpe did give his blessing to a later edition, for a consideration. One recent writer has suggested that, when the copyright reverted to the company itself on Thorpe's death, Benson turned to William Aspley, who was then master of the Stationers' Company, for a copy of the scarce book. Which merely begs the question, Why would Aspley not have just reissued it himself?

It is tempting to see some significance in the publication date of Benson's redaction of the *Poems*—as if he, or his copublisher, knew that the only potential counter-claimant had now passed away without issue. We have no record of Thorpe after he entered the Oxfordshire hospital, but it is unlikely that he was still alive in November 1639, when part of *Poems* was registered with the Stationers' Company.

By said date, any other party that might have known the "true story of the sonnets"—if, indeed, there was one—had also already passed on. Shakespeare himself had died in April 1616. The Earl of Southampton lived long enough to see the First Folio's publication, but died the following year, and the Earl of Pembroke lived until his fiftieth birthday (just), in April 1630. Ben Jonson, who made it to sixty-five, passed away in August 1637, not in an alms-house, but in dire straits financially.

One must assume that any scandal concerning Q died with these men—unless, as some have argued, there is a significance to the reorganization and mingling of the sonnets by Benson above and beyond an attempt to—in Rollins's words—"hoodwink the wardens of the Stationers' Company." Massey thought he saw something self-aggrandizing in the preface that Benson wrote (quoted above), which was a way of attesting "to the purity of [the] Sonnets." "This vindication," Massey said, "would not have been made unless some contrary charge had been brought against them."

And perhaps there was still some general stench of scandal attached to Shakespeare's sonnets per se. But it seems more likely that, knowing only of Q's existence, Benson set out to make it part of his own collection. The editorial work he apparently undertook would certainly have sufficed to obscure any connection. Yet I have to agree with Dover-Wilson that, however much it may be "commonly assumed . . . it was fear of infringing Thorpe's copyright that led [Benson] to disguise his wholesale borrowing from that collection, . . . the work Benson put into the preparation of the volume seems in excess of anything such fears demanded."

Many have assumed that Benson's avoidance of the word "sonnet" at all times, as well as his attempt to violate the form itself by ganging together several sonnets at a time, reflected a general critical opprobrium that was now attached to the form. At some point, someone certainly turned the 146 [sic] sonnets into somewhere between 72 and 80 poems, putting sonnets together in groupings of between two and six quatorzain stanzas. Said person then gave these newfound poems titles, and apparently made a handful of changes to gender in three of the poems (Q101, 104, and 108).

The groupings and the emasculated titles that Benson gave many of the sonnets—if he was the textual editor of *Poems*—seems on the face of it to suggest an attempt to sanitize the sonnets' thematic concerns. And so, in *Poems,* the "master-mistresse" sonnet (Q26) becomes, hilariously, "A Dutifull Message," and the sonnet that so offended a correspondent to *Fraser's Magazine* (Q42) becomes "Losse and Gaine." The infamous pairing where the poet offers his obeisance, Q57 and 58, have been combined into a single poem, entitled "The Force of Love." Which is one way of putting it.

However, the practice of putting names to untitled sonnets was hardly uncommon in this time period. We already know that someone gave Q2 the title "Spes Altera," and that the title stuck. Likewise, a contemporary copy of Q8 found in a manuscript commonplace book in the British Museum has a Latin heading found nowhere else, "In laudem musice et opprobrium contemptorii eiusdem." The facile titles found in Benson's book share common ground with other collections from the period.

This could be because Benson sought consistency, even as he laid the poems published by Thorpe and Jaggard side by side, in an order that has defied any subsequent attempt to discover his logic. And, aside from the use of titles often tenuously related, and generic to the point of inconsequence, Benson also adopted one of Jaggard's little tricks: He pads out his collection with a smattering of non-Shakespearean offerings that he had registered to himself on November 4, 1639.

In fact, if one didn't know better, one might suppose that both the *Poems* and *The Passionate Pilgrim* were drawn from the same kind of source-document—the single-poet manuscript miscellany—and that the publishers simply took unreliable attributions, titles, and orders at face value when they had no means of restoring the "right" ones. Arthur Marotti asserts that "Benson did what other English publisher-editors did back to the time of Richard Tottel's famous miscellany: he took the verse that originally had specific social coordinates and handled it as conventional lyrical utterances within the context of the usual literary depiction of amorous experience." And he could well have done so in ignorance of its "specific social coordinates," not in contempt thereof.

Jaggard's original 1599 edition of *The Passionate Pilgrim* was almost certainly compiled from one or two such miscellanies—which, I suspect, is why he failed to acquire more than just a handful of the privately circulated "sugred sonnets," and gave it the title he did. Benson's collection also resembles a miscellany, albeit a more ambitious one, centered around the poems of William Shakespeare, and one that has been heavily edited and organized by someone, whether for purely private or ostensibly commercial reasons.

We should remember that "in a system of manuscript circulation of literature, those into whose hands texts came could, in a real sense, 'own' them: they could collect, alter and transmit them" [AM]. The "reorganization" of Q given in *Poems* makes no real sense in terms of any commercial imperative—Benson had little to fear and no one to fool by such an act—but as a private document that someone has collected, altered, and then transmitted, it is hardly at odds with other "single-author" miscellanies of the period.

If a compiler of a manuscript miscellany had already done the work for Benson—combining the *Sonnets, The Passionate Pilgrim,* "A Lover's Complaint," *The Phoenix & the Turtle* &c. into a handy "private" compendium of works otherwise unavailable to devotees of the dramatist— it suggests that such material was already scarce. Yet Benson seems to have known that the material had been previously published, which explains why he registered only the "additional" poems in November 1639.

He also doubtless knew something of the history of *The Passionate Pilgrim.* His chosen printer certainly knew not only that William Jaggard had died (in 1623, with the First Folio barely off the press), but also that his son and heir, Issac, had died just four years later, leaving his wife Dorothy to sell all the copyrights the Jaggards owned in the works of William to another stationer. That stationer was none other than Thomas Cotes, the man responsible for printing Benson's *Poems*. And Cotes was, as Lee points out, "the printer who was . . . the most experienced of any in the trade in the production of Shakespearean literature." J. W. Bennett goes further: "The fact that Cotes did the printing makes it highly improbable that there was anything surreptitious about the 1640 *Poems*."

Any rights attendant upon *The Passionate Pilgrim* now belonged to Cotes. Even though the book is not specifically named in the transfer of rights from Jaggard's widow on June 19, 1627, the last two lines of the assignment, "her parte in SHACKSPHEERE playes. / Seven godly sermons upon 'the temptacon' &c." covers a multitude of sins. Jaggard's copyrights had become Cotes's, even when—as was the case with *The Passionate Pilgrim*—the book had never actually been entered in the Stationers' Register. This, in turn, provides the most likely explanation for why Benson sought out Cotes as a printer, rather than using his usual printer, J. Okes. Buying off a claimant to a copyright by giving him the printing contract was not that apparently uncommon.[8]

So Benson did not register *The Passionate Pilgrim* because he had Cotes's word that he had already acquired those rights (and, who knows, maybe the rights for the sonnets, too). A blank page in the register (and there is one for 1610) could suggest a gap in registering, and Cotes had been steadfastly acquiring copyrights to the works of Shakespeare for the past twelve years. Three years after he bought Jaggard's rights, he purchased those of Thomas Pavier, Jaggard's old partner in the 1618 "Quartos scam."

And yet, Cotes did not necessarily display a great deal of discrimination about what he published under that esteemed name. After he printed the so-called Second Folio in 1632, he followed it up with a 1635 reprint of the mangled 1618 quarto of *Pericles,* published by Pavier; and then put two more plays, *The Yorkshire Tragedy* and *Sir John Oldcastle,* back into the world. These were again attributed to Shakespeare, demonstrating that there were already questions-marks about some of the material which even Cotes chose to publish under such a saleable name (both plays were purchased from Master Bird in November 1630, and would reappear again as part of the 1664 Third Folio).

The issue of authenticity was rearing its head barely three years after the dramatist's death. That situation, confused enough prior to the appearance of the First Folio, was not entirely settled by its appearance. Partly, this was because Heminge and Condell, apparently deliberately, omitted some of the plays Shakespeare coauthored, as well as all of Shakespeare's poetry, thus leaving this aspect of their friend's art wholly uncataloged. Their example led "many later editors to treat the Poems as if they were not an integral part of the Works of Shakespeare" [SB].

In an era when the works of William Shakespeare remained caught betwixt Apocrypha and Authentick, one should be wary of assuming that any publisher, let alone a relative novice like Benson, knew precisely the parameters of his poetic canon. As Benson told his readers in the Preface to *Poems,* he was not so much concerned with copyright as with getting his readers to recognize these poems as "seren[e], cleere and eligantly plaine" enough to "raise your admiration to his praise." In this, he might have been unduly optimistic, but was probably, nonetheless, sincere.

The Preface Benson appended to his collection, rather than implying he was skating on thin ice with the Stationers, as has been suggested, seems to strike the tone of someone hoping that the work will be accepted as genuinely Shakespearean: "[These] sweetely composed Poems of Master William Shakespeare, Which in themselves appeare of the same purity, the Authour himselfe then living avouched . . . yet the

lines of themselves will afford you a more authentick approbation than
my assurance any way can." In the highly confused climate that suc-
ceeded Shakespeare's fatal shuffle, Benson—"in good faith"—at-
tempted to collect together the "non-narrative" poems, thus producing
a compendium of the genuine and the misattributed that would become
the standard Shakespeare poetic miscellany for 150 years.

But why did Benson undertake such a venture? It was hardly his forte.
It is curious that it should even be Benson, and not Cotes, who was the
main force behind the project (and we have to assume this was so, since
it is his name on the Preface). Given the freedom to publish by the Sta-
tioners' Company in 1631, Benson had only published half a dozen
books before *Poems,* displaying precious few credentials as a publisher of
poetry or literature (though he had "desired leave to print" Sir William
Davenant's *The Tragedy of Albovine* back in July 1639, then changed his
mind). In Henry R. Plomer's *Dictionary of Printers and Booksellers,* he is
described as "chiefly a publisher of ballads and broadsides," and his
most famous legacy, *Poems* excepted, would be as the printer of John
Playford's *The English Dancing Master* in 1650–51. (Playford had, in
fact, been apprenticed to Benson back in 1640.)

Actually, Benson is not identified as the publisher on the title page of
Poems. It simply says, "Printed at London by Tho. Cotes, and are to be
sold by John Benson," suggesting more of a joint project. And the only
registration in the Stationers' records is for the additional poems that
come at the end of the volume. The registration itself, entered on No-
vember 4, 1639, is positively cryptic: "An addicion of some excellent Po-
ems to *Shakespeares Poems* by other gentlemen." Were one to endorse
Rollins's premise, that Benson was looking to "hoodwink the wardens of
the Stationers' Company," why draw attention to the book, and pay a
registration fee, when the bulk of its contents infringed extant copy-
rights anyway?

The registration rather suggests that Benson was reasonably sure they did not. Indeed, his use of the phrase "the Authour himselfe then living avouched" leads me to believe that he knew more of the history of Q than he was telling. Of course, it could just be simple sales-speak, but he did have a connection to another playwright of the period that has gone largely unexplored. This "contact" probably provided the "copy" of "Q" that he utilized, and an examination of their association raises the intriguing possibility that it was a manuscript version.

So what, if any, are the arguments for the text of the *Poems* deriving not from Q, but from a manuscript copy thereof? That Benson knew of the book's existence seems indisputable. One, he made no attempt to copyright the sonnets as part of his November 1639 registration. Two, in the Preface he carefully avoids saying that the sonnets had never been published. Rather, he says they lacked the "due accomodatio[n] of proportionable glory, with the rest of his everliving Workes," strongly implying that copies of Q had already become bloody rare. The total absence of contemporary references to—or manuscript transcriptions from—a collection of sonnets by someone as notable as Shakespeare suggests they had a collectibility of which Benson was only too aware.

Even if the dozen or so copies that have survived the centuries had already acquired the status of secret texts, one would have expected the sonnets to have cropped up in some of the seventeenth-century commonplace books known to exist. As H. R. Woudhuysen observed, in his work on the circulation of literary manuscripts 1558–1640, "The emergence of an apparently print-dominated culture did not result in a movement one way only. As movable type transformed manuscript into print, so print . . . could be transformed back into manuscript. Whole books which were rare or had been suppressed were transcribed, and favourite poems, speeches, or letters would be extracted for private use."

In manuscript, more likely, omissions would go unobserved. And the most compelling evidence that Benson utilized a manuscript version is the omission of eight Q sonnets (18, 19, 43, 56, 75, 76, 96, 126) from *Poems*. This alone convinced Sidney Lee, who in his 1905 facsimile edition, "doubted whether Benson depended on Thorpe's printed volume in his confused impression of the sonnets. . . . He avows no knowledge of *Shakespeares Sonnets* . . . [and his] text seems based on some amateur collection of pieces of manuscript poetry, which had been in private circulation. . . . It is difficult to [otherwise] account for the exclusion of these [eight sonnets]."

These omissions have been troubling commentators ever since Edmund Malone's edition in 1780. Many have looked for an explanation in the sonnets themselves. Unfortunately, there is nothing that obviously connects the six groups—taking 18–19 and 75–76 together—either conceptually or thematically. The octet even includes one of the more beautiful, and perhaps the most famous, sonnet of them all, Q18, "Shall I compare thee to a Summers day?"

One can immediately discount the possibility that the absence of the sonnets stems from an incomplete copy of Q, given Benson's inclusion of other sonnets found on the same pages. And the eight sonnets absent from Benson's edition are hardly among the more damning, should one be looking for evidence of a poetic pederast. Only one of them can be said to represent that small number of sonnets which are unambiguously directed to a male (Q126, "O thou my lovely Boy who in thy power"). Likewise, if the editor's changes to three closely grouped sonnets—which seem designed to modify the message, turning "him" and "he" into "her" and "she" in Q101, and "friend" and "boy" to "love" in Q104 and 108—were part of a plan to mislead readers as to the nature of this infatuation, these would not have been the sonnets with which I, or any modern bowdlerizer, would have started.

And, as Margreta de Grazia points out in her 1997 essay, "The Scandal of Shakespeare's Sonnets," "Of the seventy-five titles Benson assigned to Shakespeare's Sonnets, only three of them direct sonnets from the first group . . . (Q1–126) to a woman . . . [while] the very first fourteen lines printed in the 1640 *Poems* contain eleven male pronouns, more than any other sonnet." Hardly the act of a scandalized scribe. So, all in all, these omissions cannot be easily explained away as demonstrating evidence of deliberate design.

Nor did the reorganization and entitling of the volume, whatever their purpose, suffice to fool the one careful contemporary reader who left his thoughts behind. A seventeenth-century copy of Benson's book, which now resides in the Folger Library, has someone starting to mark up his copy, changing the poem titles to more appropriate ones and correcting obvious typos. Among his emendations is a new title for Q20, "The Mistress Masculine" (from "The Exchange"); while for the first three sonnets, bundled together by Benson, he has written "Motives to procreation as the way to outlive Time"—a title of which even Shakespeare might have approved.

As to whether such amendments would have fooled the wardens of the company—which Rollins claims to have been Benson's main intention—one is obliged to point out that the wardens did not go out of their way to challenge their members' copyrights. They relied on other members, if their copyrights had been infringed, to raise such matters. And, as we've already noted, there was no one around who was likely to do so (or would even know the history of Q).

What is also clear, from the other contents in the collection, is that Benson intended for his edition to be the "complete" poems—save for the two well-known narrative poems, *Venus* and *Lucrece*, whose copyright he could not obtain, and dare not infringe. Not only does he include "A Lover's Complaint," but he also incorporates *The Phoenix &*

the Turtle, taken from either the 1601 or 1611 edition of Robert Chester's *Love's Martyr, or Rosalin's Complaint* (where it is explicitly attributed to Shakespeare), plus the entire 1612 edition of *The Passionate Pilgrim* (Heywood's incursions included). There are even two songs from the plays, the first of which, "Take, O take these lippes away," has two stanzas, when only one appears in *Measure for Measure.* The second, from *As You Like It,* also looks like it came from a manuscript copy.[9] Evidently, "the compiler used everything . . . which he found attributed to Shakespeare in print" [JWB].

In this light, Benson's protestation that he had been "somewhat solicit[o]us to bring this [book] forth to the perfect view of all men" has as much claim to our credulity as Heminge and Condell's assertion that they rescued play texts that had been "maimed and deformed by the frauds and stealthes [of] injurious imposters." Marotti is surely right to suggest that Benson was offering "his volume as the completion of The Complete Works of William Shakespeare, as it were."

And yet, the publisher managed to omit eight sonnets from Q. The only tenable explanations are that either the printer was incompetent—an accusation not generally leveled at Cotes—or that the papers from which *Poems* was compiled and/or printed were incomplete, and that no one directly responsible for its publication knew any better.

Even if the printer had accidentally omitted these sonnets at the outset, Benson would have been able to restore them in any subsequent reprint. And, as Lee points out in the 1905 facsimile edition, there was a catalog of books for sale at a shop "at the Prince's Armes" in 1654 that included an edition of *Poems* "printed for Humphrey Moseley."

All of which suggests that the full edition was unavailable personally to Benson, though he remained aware of Q's existence. At what stage these sonnets became detached is pure guesswork, of course, but there are a couple of clues that it was after the material was reorganized. The fact that these eight sonnets should include two sets of consecutive sonnets—which, as a random happenstance, would be around a one in 5,000 shot—is unlikely to be accidental. We know that many of the sonnets were paired together in the "reorganizing" process.

Given the sheer cost of paper in Caroline England, the likelihood of four other, disconnected sonnets being on single sheets that had become individually detached also seems remote (the scene in *Shakespeare in Love* where the young William scrunches up sheets in dissatisfaction at what he has written would never have happened). The eight missing sonnets probably made up a single unit that became detached after they were grouped together. If they were in a single sheaf, without the numbering system found in Q, it would have been all too easy for them to go astray in their passage from private hands to publisher to printer.

Let me be clear. I am not suggesting that Benson's text provides an alternate source for Q, just that it was a copy—and a good one at that—probably directly derived from Thorpe's edition. We can be fairly sure that the organizer was working from an actual copy of Q because, as Rollins notes, "In the case of italicized words—the item least likely to be dependent on ms. copy—there is not a single instance of divergence." But if that collator was Benson—or the printer Cotes—one would expect them to have referred back to Q before going to press, and not just some scribal copy—let us get all synoptic and call it Q/2. Likewise, one would have expected Cotes and/or Benson to have compared the versions of Q138 and 144 with the versions included in *The Passionate Pilgrim*. But they simply used the *P.P.* variants verbatim—as did the transcriber of Q/2.

Maybe Benson just didn't give a damn. Except, we know he did care about the textual quality and appearance of what he published. The supplement to *Poems* contains a frontispiece facing the title page, presenting a carefully elaborated cut of the Droeshout engraving of the First Folio by the highly regarded William Marshall, hardly a demonstration of cost- or corner-cutting. We also know that Benson dramatically reworked another book when it was already at the press, a mere three months after he registered *Poems,* and that the book in question could well have come from the same source as Q/2. That work was a previously unpublished masque by Shakespeare's contemporary Ben Jonson, and it was registered to Benson, under the title *The Masque of the Gypsies,* on February 20, 1640.

What Benson had here acquired, as W. W. Greg notes in his introduction to the 1952 variorum edition, was already "a good manuscript, possibly one prepared for presentation on the occasion of the first performance." "But before the book was issued," Greg writes, "Benson . . . somehow acquired a manuscript of the fuller composite version, and though this was in fact a rather inferior copy, he decided to amplify the already printed text in accordance with it. To do this he cancelled the leaves D6–10 and E5–11 and replaced them by two newly printed quires."

This does not sound like someone who, upon realizing he had omitted eight sonnets from the collected poetic works of William Shakespeare, would have simply shrugged his shoulders. The work involved in resetting the Jonson masque was considerable, and furthermore, had no obvious bearing on its salability. In all likelihood, no one would ever have known. We only know what happened because a single printed copy survived in which three of the canceled leaves were "scored through," but not removed by the binder.[10]

These two versions of a single Jonson masque also tell us that Benson had recently chanced upon a supply(er) of literary manuscripts, ostensibly from the pen of Ben Jonson. And the timeline of these Jonsonian acquisitions aligns exactly with his registration of *Poems.* In a period of just over three months from November 1639 through February 1640, Benson registered the "additional poems" for his Shakespearean anthology (November 4), and then, in rapid succession, three works by Jonson: *Execration against Vulcan with Other His Smaller Epigrams* (December 16); *The Art of Poetry*, a translation by Jonson of Quintus Horatius Flaccus (February 8); and *The Masque of the Gypsies* (February 20).

The clincher? Among the "additional poems" registered on November 4, 1639, were two of Jonson's own, "His Mistress Drawne" and "Her Minde," both of which appeared in the 1640 *Poems*, as does an eight-line testament to Shakespeare from Jonson. The first six lines of this testament may be "drawn at haphazard from Ben Jonson's eulogy in the First Folio" [SL], but the concluding couplet—"For ever live thy fame, the world to tell / Thy like no age shall ever parallel."—appears to have been original. Did it appear this way in one of Jonson's papers—some of which Benson, and a fellow stationer, had recently acquired? If so, among them was also probably a three-page riposte by Leonard Digges to Jonson's tribute in the First Folio, in which Digges is "taunting Johnson with the lack of popularity of his plays and the great drawing power of Shakespeare's" [JWB]. This, too, Benson published in *Poems*. Where did this material come from?

One tantalizing suggestion, made first by Keith Whitlock in a 1999 *Folk Music Journal* article, is that the papers were obtained from Richard Brome, who for many years had been "an Ingenious Servant, and Imitator of his Master, that famously Renowned Poet, Ben Jonson." Brome had worked for Jonson since at least 1614, and possibly since 1609,[11] his duties apparently including transcribing parts for dramatic entertainments. By the time Charles I dissolved Parliament in 1629, Brome had developed into something of a playwright himself. In that year he wrote two highly successful productions for Shakespeare's old troupe, the King's Men: *The Lovesick Maid* and *The Northern Lasse*, the latter of which appeared in print in 1632 with commendatory verses by Jonson himself.

But Brome was dogged by the same problem as his mentor, Jonson. Without a direct financial stake in one of the acting companies, he was a scribe for hire, surviving from play to play on the advances doled out by the companies. Even after a huge success at the Salisbury Court Theatre in 1635, with *The Sparagus Garden,* which Brome estimated earned the company concerned over a thousand pounds, he was still essentially "on retainer." On a salary of fifteen shillings a week (plus one day's profit per delivered play), he was signed to a three-year contract by the manager of the Salisbury Court, Richard Heton. Required to write some three plays per annum, a daunting regime even for a prolific playwright, he almost immediately buckled under the strain.

When, as a result, his stipend dried up, he turned to Christopher Beeston, actor, self-styled impresario, and owner of the Cockpit Theatre and the Red Bull. In August 1636, Beeston "loaned" Brome £6, in return for a commitment to write a play for him. But another outbreak of the plague closed the theaters. They stayed shut until October 1637, by which time Brome was living from hand to mouth and Jonson was already dead.

Despite these difficulties, Brome remained in demand, and in August 1638 he was offered a new contract by Heton. This one was for seven years at a pound a week, but also required him to supply the plays he still owed from their previous agreement. It was a recipe for disaster, and Brome and Heton were soon at loggerheads. In April 1639, Brome finally walked out on the Salisbury Court players for good and went to the Cockpit. His former employer immediately commenced a legal action for breach of contract, leaving Brome fearing for his financial future. While working on a new play, *The Court Beggar,* Brome—short of funds again—revived *The Northern Lass.* He also arranged for his two most no-

table Salisbury Court plays—*The Sparagus Garden* and *The Antipodes*—
to be published.

Whether he even had the rights to do so is unclear. It seems unlikely.
The company usually owned its plays outright. But the gesture would
have served two purposes—it gave Brome a little money, as he contin-
ued trying to make ends meet, and it served to annoy his former em-
ployer, whose suit continued to be pressed. It also introduced him to
new contacts in the world of publishing. Any initial contact between
Brome and Benson may have been provided by Benson's regular
printer, and fellow stationer, John Okes, who was simultaneously
charged with printing the two plays from Brome's Salisbury Court days.

Brome, we can assume, would probably have been in a position to ac-
cess a copy of Q from Jonson, and he would have had the literary inter-
est to do so. He also may have had the inclination, and certainly the
aptitude, to reorganize the material in a manner he preferred, transcrib-
ing it into a volume of Shakespeare's poems. If he did indeed take that
task upon himself, Brome could have reorganized and transcribed Q at
the same time. Or he could have had a scribal transcript made, or ac-
quired one already in existence. (As Woudhuysen observes, such copies
were frequently made, with good reason: "A scribal copy . . . provided an
insurance against loss or destruction in or outside the printing-house.")
As it happens, we have evidence that the going rate for such work was a
penny a sheet. Sir Edward Dering paid 4 shillings, i.e., 48 pence, to "mr
Carington for writing oute ye play of K: Henry ye fourth" in February
1623. At this time, the First Folio had not yet appeared, and any old
quartos of *Henry IV* had largely disintegrated.

Benson may even have specifically asked Brome to produce a text of
Shakespeare's poems, and if so, Brome may have taken it upon himself
to edit them in the manner of the day. In which case, he may well have
provided the publisher with anecdotal information concerning the

scarcity of the material, to which Benson appears to be alluding in his preface. After all, Brome had known others who had moved in Shakespeare's circles, notably Thomas Heywood, with whom Brome had coauthored three plays. To the end, though, he struggled to make ends meet—leaving his posthumous editor, Alexander Brome, to observe, "Poor he came into th' world and poor went out." Benson expressed a personal sense of debt toward the man shortly before Brome's death in 1653, providing a commendatory verse—under the initials J.B.—to the quarto edition of *A Joviall Crew,* beginning, "Nor [i.e., What] need the Stationer, when all th' Wits are past."

Accepting the existence of Q/2 does not, unfortunately, bring us any closer to Q's source text, fair or otherwise. *Poems* replicates all of the most problematic errors found in Q. But it does return us to a world where manuscript and print were in a state of constant flux. It also suggests that Q had disappeared real fast, whether through interference, carelessness, or just a general distaste for its style and content (though one might expect some contemporary reference if this final scenario applied). Therefore, when Benson claimed it lacked "due accomodatio[n] of proportionable glory, with the rest of his everliving Workes," it was probably said with a straight face, and with a keen awareness of the difficulties he had experienced obtaining *any* text.

However, in the immediate aftermath of its publication, *Poems* was the least of Benson's problems. Having obtained miscellaneous "Jonson papers" (in tandem with the unfortunately named Andrew Crooke), presumably from the hapless Brome, both Benson and Crooke found themselves accused by another stationer-publisher, Thomas Walkley, of "having obtayned by some casuall or other indirect meanes false and imperfect Copies of the said workes." (In fact, Benson's edition of the *Masque of the Gypsies* is markedly superior to Walkley's, which Jonson editors C. H. Herford and Percy Simpson branded as "execrable.")

Walkley's financial concerns lay not with Shakespeare's poems, but with Jonson's masques, fifteen of which he had obtained from Jonson's "executor," Sir Kenelm Digby, who, according to Walkley, "in pursuance of the said truste reposed in him delivered [them to Walkley] to have them published and printed according to the intenc[i]on of the said Benjamin Jonson." Actually, Digby sold the papers to Walkley for the relatively high sum of £40—a sum that would have far exceeded whatever Benson and Crooke paid Brome for their own set of papers.

Rather than registering the masques with the Stationers' Company, Walkley simply set about printing his edition, oblivious to the fact that Benson and Crooke had already registered five of these masques (in February-March 1640). When they discovered Walkley's intentions, Benson and Crooke referred the matter to the Stationers' Company, and proceedings were obtained against Walkley. This led to the forfeiture of his own stock, along with "goodes and wares . . . of the value of three hundred pounds," a considerable sum of money back then. (A new decree, passed in July 1637, required "every printer . . . to enter into a bond [of] £300 to print no books but such as are lawfully allowed to him." Walkley was deemed in breach of this decree.)

So much is documented. And as Greg makes clear, Walkley was the one who "formally infringed the rights of Benson and Crooke, rights based upon regular entries in the Stationers' Register." Nevertheless, by directly appealing to one of the secretaries of state, Walkley was able to get the forfeiture overturned and a warrant issued "prohibiting the sayd Benson and Crooke from further printing or publishing the same workes or any of them." By now Benson and Crooke were caught up in a far larger spat. Walkley, who had a history of failing to register his publications, as well as out-and-out piracy, "was using the royal authority to defeat the Stationers' right to grant copyright. . . . This was no bit of private chicanery, but the might of the City guilds against the royal authority on the eve of the Civil War" [JWB].

Not surprisingly, despite an appeal to the Chancery court, Walkley, like his fellow Royalists, was fighting a losing battle. As late as 1648 he was still trying to get a license to publish the "peece[s] of Poetry of Mr Ben Johnsons which cost him £40." The following year, he had greater concerns. A warrant for his arrest was issued "for dispersing scandalous declarations sent from the King's son in Jersey."

Benson, who probably had very little interest in reprinting Jonson's *Masque of the Gypsies,* comes across as the injured party throughout. Having acquired the masque in good faith, he registered it properly and had even gone to the trouble of resetting his edition to make his text as complete as possible. And yet, damned as just another booklegger by Malone and the many other editors of Shakespeare's sonnets who came along in the scholar's wake, he was summarily judged the guilty party in the Benson-Crooke-Walkley dispute by twentieth-century Jonsonian scholars C. H. Herford and Percy and Evelyn Simpson.

In their authoritative eleven-volume set of Jonson's collected works (1925–52), Herford accused Benson of obtaining *"certainly by dishonest means* [my italics], a copy of the fully revised and enlarged text" of the gypsy masque. But Herford had no grounds for making such a claim. In fact, like Walkley, he had no idea what means—legal or illegal—the publisher had used (he certainly should have realized that Walkley emotively claiming Benson had "obtayned [them] by some casuall or other indirect meanes" demonstrated ignorance of the actual circumstance).

If the Jonson masque did come from Richard Brome, any charge of underhandedness holds no water. Even if Digby's rights to Jonson's literary papers were marginally stronger than Brome's, Walkley was the one who acted like a pirate. Herford was convinced that Walkley was "the true owner of the copyright," though Benson had the *a priori* claim. Which is why it took Walkley eighteen years to get the Stationers' Company to "recognize" his copyright, by which time he had been obliged to sell these ill-defined rights to another stationer, Humphrey Moseley.

At least Benson had better luck with *Poems,* which sold better than Thorpe's edition—some sixty-plus copies are known to have survived to the present day, and around a dozen examples of the poems therein were transferred to extant Caroline commonplace books (one of which uses twenty-three quotes from the 1640 edition). There is also evidence that the book was still available in 1654, when the same Humphrey Moseley included it in an advertisement for his prodigious wares. And perhaps such an edition did appear, just without the Moseley imprimatur.

Moseley, a one-man publishing industry, may have reached an agreement with Benson, who had all but retired from publishing—he has a single entry after 1654 in the register—to put the book back in print (or to sell unsold stock). There is no evidence that Benson ever surrendered his own copyright to Moseley. But it may be that no "Moseley" edition ever appeared. After all, Moseley was the same publisher who just a few months earlier had registered a play called *The History of Cardenio,* "by Mr Fletcher and Shakespeare," for publication. There is solid contemporary evidence that such a play once existed, but it singularly failed to appear in print, either from Moseley or any other seventeenth-century publisher. It remains one of the more enticing entries in that remarkable document, the Stationers' Register.

Either way, by the time of the Restoration, Benson had left his ballads and books behind. The lack of any entry for a transfer of rights in *Poems,* and the nonappearance of further editions throughout the remainder of the seventeenth century, suggests that Benson, like Thorpe, had learned the hard way that these private poems, even when anthologized, struggled to strike a chord with Caroline sensibilities. His one "crime" against their composer—"arranging" the material in such a way as to render any sense of an underlying story moot—probably did the poet a favor. Sparing the sonnets further scandal would allow the first shoots of bardolatry to take root before anyone dared to reconstruct their original sequence.

THIS KEY...
UNLOCKED
HIS
HEART

CHAPTER SIX

1709–1821

"I, ONCE GONE, TO ALL THE WORLD MUST DIE"

> *For a long time . . . the Sonnets were not read. . . . [But Shakespeare] was always in the hearts of the people. There, in that deep, rich soil, have the Sonnets rested during two centuries . . . [until] all young imaginative minds now rejoice in their hues and their fragrance.*
> —CHARLES KNIGHT, 1841

Whatever Benson's source, it seems clear that his intention in 1640 was to bring together the flotsam and jetsam of Shakespeareana into a single, affordable edition. But his timing was off. By the time he registered the additional material, Charles I was already at loggerheads with Parliament, and the country was on the brink of civil war. On September 2, 1642, a parliamentary edict forbade the performance of plays. Shakespeare's name suffered as much as those of his Jacobethan contemporaries. During the Interregnum, just three of his plays appeared in quarto form (*Merchant of Venice, Othello,* and *King Lear*). In the climate of the times, the dramatist's name was becoming increasingly aligned with his latter-day tragedies. By the time Charles II reclaimed the throne in 1660, Shakespeare had become the Great Tragedian, who wrote occasional comedies and histories—oh, and the odd narrative poem.

By the Restoration, editions of his poetry had all but fallen into abeyance, save for a sacrilegious edition of *Lucrece* in 1655, which was forced to share its pages with John Quarles's *The Banishment of Tarquin*. The "Moseley" edition of *Poems*, if it ever existed, disappeared altogether, and though the occasional sonnet copied from *Poems* made it into commonplace books, Benson had stopped publishing, and the status of his edition soon became shrouded in almost as much mystery as Thorpe's original.

For the rest of the century, the dramatist's devotees were obliged to rely on new folio editions of the plays, of which there were three (1663, 1664—both called the Third Folio—and 1685—the Fourth Folio, and the last), plus regular quarto editions of the more popular tragedies—the pulp fiction of their day—which continued to be reworked weekly at the revived London theaters. The two great histories of English poetry compiled at the end of the century—Gerard Langbaine's *Account of the English Dramatick Poets* (1691) and Charles Gildon's *Lives and Characters of the English Dramatick Poets* (1699)—failed to devote a single line to Shakespeare's sonnets. It seemed like Shakespeare's several uncharacteristic claims to immortality in the poems themselves had become the idle boasts of a false prophet.

And when, in 1709, an impressive six-volume edition of Shakespeare's *Dramatic Works* appeared, edited by tragic dramatist Nicholas Rowe, its esteemed editor openly admitted, in his introduction, "There is a book of Poems, publish'd in 1640, under the Name of Mr. William Shakespear, but as I have but very lately seen it, without an Opportunity of making any Judgment upon it, I won't pretend to determine, whether it be his or no." Thus did Shakespeare's first biographer cast doubt on the authenticity of *Poems'* contents, let alone its right to inclusion in an authoritative collected works.

The fact that the man who began one of the most enduring mini-industries in publishing—biographies of the chimerical dramatist from Stratford—should be wholly unaware of even the existence of Q, a mere hundred years after its publication, and after all his research into the life and works of the man, suggests just how sidelined these poems had become.

And yet, there were those who knew about the existence of these poetic pearls, and in the new dawn that succeeded the 1709 Copyright Act, sought to restore them to the canon. For, as had been the case throughout the seventeenth century, it was largely the vagaries of English copyright law that decided what did and did not get published and/or widely disseminated during the first quarter of the eighteenth century, as new copyright-holders waited for the dust to settle after "The Statute of Anne," a.k.a., "An Act for the Encouragement of Learning, by vesting the Copies of Printed Books in the Author."

In this period, there remained one publisher who was determined to retain his iron grip on the Works of William. His name was Jacob Tonson. Tonson had been publishing poets and playwrights since 1678, most notably the works of Dryden and Milton. The latter continued to prove the most lucrative lyricist of the old school, with *The Poetical Works of Mr John Milton* (1695 & c.) being a mainstay of Tonson's business well into the eighteenth century. Tonson's strategy was simple enough: He would acquire a part share of a valuable copyright, and then gradually buy out the other copyright-holders until he owned the property outright. By 1709, he effectively owned the rights to all of Shakespeare's dramatic works, having purchased the rights to the Fourth Folio in his usual methodical way.

Unfortunately for Tonson, there was a cloud on the horizon—the new copyright act, which aimed to restrict new copyrights to just fourteen years' duration, renewable for a further fourteen years, but only if the author was still living. Tonson galvanized his fellow stationers into lobbying for a special exemption when it came to existing copyrights. Though he did not entirely succeed, he did play a key role in getting a one-off "extended" copyright for preexisting works, which afforded an extra twenty-one years protection on his personal publishing monopoly of seventeenth-century poets. As such, until 1730 he had much of English literature to himself. And therefore plenty of time in which to ensure that Tonson was the brand name associated with splendid editions of the works of Shakespeare, Dryden, Milton, and the still-popular Beaumont and Fletcher.

Rowe was just the first of several well-known editors commissioned by Tonson (and his family) to keep a steady flow of Shakespeare's dramatic works in the marketplace. As Gary Taylor states, "The Tonsons did not base those decisions on . . . who was best qualified to edit Shakespeare; they wanted editors who were already famous." Which explains why Rowe was succeeded in time by the likes of Alexander Pope (in 1725) and Samuel Johnson (in 1765). Each succeeding editor—and there would be six in as many decades—would be obliged to refute the scholarship of his predecessor, proclaiming his own edition as the final word, usually in that disdainful tone eighteenth-century scholars liked to reserve for their peers.

But not one of Tonson's retinue of revered literary editors felt the slightest urge to tackle the sonnets. In part, at least initially, this was because Tonson only retained rights to the Fourth Folio. Everything else in the canon remained fair game. As such, Rowe, for all his biographical endeavors, used as the basis for his celebrated 1709 *Works,* the Fourth—i.e., least best—Folio. He even printed the plays in the same order, ending with *Pericles* and the six spurious plays added to the canon with the 1664 reprint of the Third Folio.

In response to Rowe's work, Charles Gildon published his own, unauthorized supplement within a couple of months, dubbing it—a tad impertinently—volume VII of *Works*. He used the firm of Curll and Sanger, who were doubtless delighted to put Tonson's nose out of joint. Gildon, author of *Lives and Characters of the English Dramatick Poets*, was making a novel point: Editors of Shakespeare should take account of his work as a poet. Here, for the first time, were the two narrative poems of the 1590s and the entire contents of Benson's *Poems* (*Passionate Pilgrim, Sonnets*, et al.) in one place. Gildon, like Rowe, remained oblivious of the existence of Q, but published all of Benson's collection, save for the "Addition of Some Excellent Poems . . . by Other Gentlemen."

There was clearly an element of two raised fingers aimed in the general direction of Tonson and his tenant-editor(s), blended with sound commercial sense, in the publishing of these poems as a "supplementary volume." If the Tonsons were not yet sure they were the target, all was made self-evident when a revised edition of Rowe's *Dramatic Works*, released in 1714, immediately prompted another revised supplement, again by Gildon (now volume IX, Rowe having reduced his efforts to eight duodecimo volumes).

And when Rowe was superseded by that self-congratulatory Shakespearean scholar Alexander Pope—who published his own six-volume *Works* under the Tonson umbrella in the years 1723–25—the hackwriter George Sewell was entrusted with revising Gildon's efforts, thus providing his own "supplement" to Pope's edition (Gildon had died the previous year). In his Preface, Sewell traded on Gildon's name and credentials to aver the authenticity—and conventionality—of the sonnets and their subject-matter:

> [Gildon] uses many Arguments to prove [these poems] genuine,
> but the best is the Style, Spirit and Fancy of SHAKESPEAR, which
> are not to be mistaken by any tolerable Judge in these Matters. . . .
> If we allow the rest of these Poems to be genuine (as I think Mr
> Gildon has prov'd them) the occasional ones . . . will appear to be
> the first of his Works. A young Muse must have a Mistress to play
> off the beginnings of Fancy, nothing being so apt to raise and ele-
> vate the Soul to a pitch of Poetry as the Passion of Love.

Thus was the status quo maintained for almost sixty years—editions of *Poems* being issued in counterpoint to the ever-burgeoning library of new Tonson editions of the plays. There was just a single sniff at a genuine edition of *Shake-speare's Sonnets*. In February 1711, in the wake of Gildon and Rowe, Bernard Lintott, a little known London publisher, came out with his own edition of the sonnets. It was part of an expanded two-volume version of an earlier *Collection of Poems*. (The first version, issued in July 1709, had been a single-volume edition of *Venus, Lucrece,* and *The Passionate Pilgrim.*)

Evidently, in the eighteen months that separated the two editions, Lintott, who produced both editions himself, had come across a copy of Q, which he now published as volume II with commendable fidelity. What he did not apparently find time to do was read the poems, since he published them under the marvelously misleading title "One Hundred and Fifty Four Sonnets, all of them in Praise of his Mistress."

Lintott advertised both editions in the *Post-Boy* periodical, even preparing a third issue which changed the individual title-pages for the sections. But he lacked the distribution to take on Tonson, and his collection failed to alert the likes of Rowe, Pope, or Lewis Theobald (Pope's equally curmudgeonly successor) to the existence of an edition that was genuinely Shakespearean, at least as far as the sonnets were concerned.

The Tonson dynasty would maintain its grip on publishing the nation's favorite former playwright until 1772, when the grandson of Tonson's nephew died and the family copyrights were duly auctioned off. Finally, the shackles were removed from Shakespeare's works. Indeed, for a while, it seemed like every able-bodied literary editor from this golden era for English antiquarians was preparing his own take on Shakespeare—the irascible, the incorrigible, and the plain industrious.

Edward Capell was all of these. While preparing his own edition of Shakespeare's dramatic works (published in 1768)—which abandoned the amendments of all the previous Tonson-commissioned predecessors, returning to the original folio and quartos for "elucidation"—he began to turn his attention to the sonnets, too. That he intended to return to Q, via Lintott, is clear from the Preface he prepared, in which he dishes out disdain not just to Benson, but to all those who had followed in the maligned bookseller's literary footsteps:

> In 1640, his Sonnets were set out by one Benson; not as in their only true copy, and as they lye in this volume, but in groups of his own invention and with titles prefix'd to them; and the rubbish of both those pamphlets of which account has been just give[n], is either thrown at the end, or intermix'd along with them. And this is the identical volume, that . . . has been follow'd, from that time to this, in impressions of all sizes, and now passes upon the world for the genuine poems of Shakespeare.

But Georgian London, having virtually invented the literary clique, had long ago decided that Capell was "an outsider, an arrogant loner who did not belong to that privileged inner circle of literary London, the circle of Johnson, Boswell, Garrick, Burke, Reynolds, Steevens, Reed, Malone" [GT]. The act of publishing his own edition of Shakespeare's

Works just three years after Johnson's own, unscholarly edition was considered bad form. Capell's edition of the plays, which was actually published by Tonson, was never reprinted, and his edition of the sonnets never completed, though he anticipated Malone's methodology in so many ways.

If Tonson no longer held the reins of copyright, it was not necessarily any easier to publish an edition of the bard-who-could-do-no-wrong if one's face didn't fit, or made no attempt to fit. Multivolume sets of the plays were expensive, labor-intensive productions. Aimed at England's burgeoning bourgeois, they were highly dependent—then as now—on positive press in the literary periodicals of the time, which, again, required entry to the "inner circle of literary London." The splenetic Joseph Ritson, the most meticulous antiquarian of his age, also found the ranks of London society closed against him. In return, in an open letter "To the Monthly and Critical Reviewers," he went as far as to lambast any potential reviewers before they reviewed his 1792 monograph on Edmund Malone's edition of the *Plays & Poems* (1790):

> I have desired my publishers to send each of you a copy [of my monograph]; for . . . the title of a book, read in a newspaper, or through a shop-window, may not be always a sufficient ground for unqualified condemnation and virulent abuse. On second thoughts, however, I believe I might as well have saved them the trouble; since you will, most probably, allow Mr Malone the grateful privilege of reviewing it himself.

By 1792, Ritson knew his voice would not be heard in the coffeehouses of London. When, in an earlier monograph highlighting many supposed flaws in George Steevens's (and Johnson's) 1778 edition of the dramatist's works, he had announced that he was currently preparing his own edition of "THE GENUINE TEXT OF SHAKESPEARE," he found himself headed off at the pass. Before Ritson could raise any interest for his edition, Malone, at this juncture a close friend of Steevens, issued a "family" edition along the lines Ritson had outlined, thus ensuring the eternal enmity of the most bilious man in London.

As it happens, Ritson never got to publish that "genuine text," though one doubts it would have included the sonnets, about which he noted, in passing, in his *Historical Essay on National Song* (1784), "How much ought we to regret the valuable time he sacrificed to the false taste of his age, in the composition of above 150 sonnets (the most difficult and insipid metrical structure ever invented), which, though from the pen of this immortal bard, we can scarcely endure to read."

Ritson's opinions were notoriously subjective, but in this instance he was in tune with many of his more sociable contemporaries. Johnson, in his *Dictionary* (1755), suggested that the sonnet form itself was "not very suitable to the English language." Whilst George Steevens rather famously offered as an explanation for their exclusion from his own revised edition of the plays in 1793,

> The strongest act of Parliament that could be framed, would fail to compel readers into [the sonnets'] service; notwithstanding these miscellaneous Poems have derived every possible advantage from the literature and judgement of their only intelligent editor, Mr Malone. . . . Had Shakespeare produced no other works than these, his name would have reached us with as little celebrity as time has conferred on that of Thomas Watson, . . . [a] much more elegant sonneteer.

Steevens's outburst is all the more curious given that he was directly responsible for restoring Q to its rightful place in the canon. He, after all, published it faithfully in 1766, as part of *Twenty of the Plays of Shake-speare* [*sic*]—effectively the collected Quartos—causing Capell to abandon his own edition. He thus provided the impetus, and initially the text, for Malone to publish his own edition in 1780, where the latter "drap[ed] the poems in the full dignity of an introduction and commentary" [GT]. (Malone did not obtain his own copy of Q until April 1779, when he paid an unprecedented twenty guineas for a bound edition of *Venus & Adonis* and the *Sonnets;* though he had access to Steevens' copy in the interim.)

Ironically, Malone's 1780 *Supplement*—the sonnets excepted—was almost entirely composed of apocryphal works: i.e., those plays attributed to the Stratford dramatist in the 1664 Third Folio, before they were removed from "the canon" at Pope's insistence in 1725. Malone's volume was another of those ubiquitous supplements to yet another "authorized" Tonson edition of the dramatic works. At least this particular *Supplement to the Edition of Shakespeare's Plays Published in 1778* by Samuel Johnson and George Steevens had the blessing of both Tonson editors.

Of the seven plays excluded from all subsequent editions of the work—but now placed alongside the sonnets by Malone—just *Pericles* had any claim to be the work of Shakespeare. Malone included these errant sons in order to reject them from the canon, not because they lacked "all distinguishing marks of his style, and his manner of thinking and writing," as Pope thought, but rather because their historical provenance was unproven and unreliable. It was a highly unusual way to further a growing reputation as a leading authority on Shakespeare, formed by his groundbreaking *Attempt to Ascertain the Order in which the Plays of Shakespeare Were Written* (1778).

Though it would be Malone's benchmark 1790 edition of Shakespeare's works—where he finally incorporated the sonnets "into his prestigious full-scale edition of the *Plays and Poems,* so that for the first time they became an integral element of the canon" [GT]—that marked their return to center-stage, the sonnets had initially returned through this supplemental back door. Now, after 171 years in the shade, Q was rediscovered; and Benson was consigned to a footnote in just about every future edition, with a wave of Malone's prefatory pen:

> It is somewhat extraordinary, that none of his various editors should have attempted to separate his genuine poetical composi- tions from the spurious performances with which they have been so long intermixed, or taken the trouble to compare them with the earliest editions. Shortly after his death, a very incorrect impres- sion of his poems was issued out, which in every subsequent edi- tion [sic] has been implicitly followed.

The sonnets would never again be separated from Shakespeare's work. Nor would any homoerotic subtext—which Malone revealed by the simple act of restoring the order in which Thorpe had published them (and by stating, on the first page of his introduction to the sonnets, "To this person, whoever *he* [my italics] was, one hundred and twenty- six of the following poems are addressed")—ever elude any editor again. Even though it clearly conflicted with Ben Jonson's eulogistic ide- alization of "my gentle Shakespeare . . . sweet swan of Avon," which eighteenth-century bardolatry had conspired to cultivate.

Not that George Steevens modified his own conflicted bardolatry in the interim, providing a caustic counter-commentary to Malone's notes in both the *Supplement* and the *Plays & Poems.* In one extraordi- nary exchange after another, Steevens and Malone carved out the terri- tory for two centuries of controversy about the worth and subject matter of the sonnets. When Steevens, describing his reaction to

Q20—the "master-mistress sonnet"—admitted that he found it "impossible to read this fulsome panegyrick, addressed to a male object, without an equal mixture of disgust and indignation," Malone leapt to Shakespeare's defense:

> Such addresses to men, however indelicate, were customary in our authour's time, and neither imported criminality, nor were esteemed indecorous. . . . To regulate our judgment of Shakespeare's poems by the modes of modern times, is surely as unreasonable as to try his plays by the rules of Aristotle.

Methinks Malone doth protest too much. His true opinion of the merits of what he restored to the popular consciousness was not so far from Steevens's. Thankfully, it was the historian in Malone that won out. He demanded that they be restored to their rightful position, alongside the plays, even as he damned them with faint praise. In the longest of his notes, to the first of the Dark Lady sonnets (Q127), he wrote:

> I do not feel any great propensity to stand forth as the champion of these compositions [even if] it appears to me that they have been somewhat under-rated. . . . When they are described as a mass of affectation, pedantry, circumlocution, and nonsense, the picture appears to me overcharged. Their great defects seem to be, a want of variety, and a majority of them not being directed to a female, to whom alone such ardent expressions of esteem could with propriety be addressed. . . . Though many of them are not so simple and clear as they ought to be, yet some of them are written with perspicuity and energy.

Malone was a methodical man, and with the sonnets, as with the plays, he ensured that there was a textual authority to his edition that had been previously lacking, even if his re-punctuation of the poems has been challenged in recent years, for "ignor[ing] both poetic subtlety and rhythmic function . . . result[ing] in impoverishment of the poetry" [MS-S].

What is also worth observing is how economical Malone's annotations usually are, and how influential they have proven to be. It was he who first drew attention to the likelihood that "Mr W.H." was the intended addressee for those first 126 sonnets. He also states that "as one of these Sonnets [Q135] is formed entirely on a play on our authour's Christian name, the first name of said person was also, in all probability, Will." (Unfortunately, he attaches undue importance to a pun in Q114.8, "in hew all Hews in his controlling," which convinced him that Hughes was W.H.'s surname—an idea Oscar Wilde would later adopt for his short-story, "A Portrait of Mr W.H.")

Malone also unequivocally established the division into 126 and 28 sonnets, addressed to a man and a woman, respectively; and even ridiculed William Oldys, who had been working on a biography for two decades, for believing that Q92 and 93 were "addressed to his beautiful wife" (Oldys never completed the biography). Malone responded, "He must have read our authour's poems with but little attention; otherwise he would have seen that these, as well as the preceding Sonnets, and many of those that follow, are not addressed to a female."

But Oldys was not alone in his error. As we have seen, Lintott had fancied every sonnet to be "in praise of his mistress," and Sewell, possibly disingenuously, wrote about the inspiration of "a Mistress to play off the beginnings of Fancy." In 1797, George Chalmers came up with the incredible notion that Shakespeare's sonnet-muse and mistress was

Elizabeth I, on the grounds "that Spenser addressed his *Amoretti* to Elizabeth; [and] Shakspeare was ambitious of emulating Spenser." In fact, in his determination to prove that "a husband, a father, a moral man," would never, under any circumstances, address "a hundred and twenty-six Amourous Sonnets to a male object," no absurdity was a bridge too far for Chalmers.

Malone was not fettered by such blinkers, even if he did his best to advocate that "such addresses to men were common in Shakespeare's time." By the simple act of restoring the sonnets to their "correct" order and stanza-pattern, and removing the misleading titles given them around 1640, he brought into the public domain the full sonnet-sequence(s), all the while recognizing that they told a story that, like the age itself, came across as "very indelicate and gross" to the eyes of a Georgian. He had also lit the fire of inquiry into this private man whose work preoccupied so many eighteenth-century literary luminaries. As he had written at the outset of his first published essay on the dramatist, back in 1778:

> Every circumstance that relates to those persons whose writings we admire, awakens and interests our curiosity. The time and the place of their birth, their education and gradual attainments, the dates of their productions and the reception they severally met with, their habits of life, their private friendships, and even their external form, are all points, which, how little soever they may have been adverted to by their contemporaries, strongly engage the attention of posterity.

Though Malone had rescued these poems from their first Bowdler, in Benson, he had also unwittingly bequeathed them to a new type of literati, the Romantics, for whom the sonnets and narrative poems provided—or so they believed—both a newly revealed insight into the man behind the plays, and "an opportunity to enjoy the novelty of their own critical perspective, while claiming Shakespeare as a precursor in their own favoured genres" [GT]. What the Romantics espoused was a new-found cult of personality for all true poets. The effect on Shakespearean studies has been long-lasting. As Arthur Marotti very recently wrote, "Malone's late-eighteenth-century edition and the romantic interpretation of Shakespeare's work [have long] set the terms by which the Sonnets were received, . . . as the heartfelt utterances of an eloquently self-expressive master-poet."

For these fledgling versifiers, the fact that this paradigmatic poet had been, to all intents and purposes, "invisible," biographically speaking, was a situation demanding immediate remedy. The principal Romantic revisionists who set about asserting the sonnets' importance as biography and art, removing them from the cloisters and coffeehouses, were William Wordsworth and Samuel Taylor Coleridge, those coauthors of the new Romanticism's defining text, *Lyrical Ballads* (1798).

Indulging in their own form of Post-it notes, the two poets initially took to scribbling in the margins of a copy of Robert Anderson's thirteen-volume set of *Poets of Great Britain* kept at Greta Hall, Keswick. Wordsworth started things off by suggesting that the Dark Lady sonnets—"to his mistress"—were "worse than a puzzle-peg," but that "the others are for the most part much better, have many fine lines . . . [and] are also in many places warm with passion," though hampered by a certain "sameness, tediousness, quaintness and elaborate obscurity." Coleridge responded, at length, on November 2, 1803, with a note ostensibly to his newborn son, Hartley, "These sonnets thou, I trust, if God preserve thy life, Hartley! thou wilt read with a deep interest, having learnt to love the plays of Shakespeare, co-ordinate with Milton, and subordinate only to thy Bible. To thee, I trust, they will help to explain the mind of Shakespeare."

It is doubtful Coleridge was aware of similar views expressed by the German poet-critic A. W. Schlegel, in an as-yet-untranslated 1796 article. He was certainly the first English literary figure to suggest that the sonnets might "help to explain the mind of Shakespeare." It would take Wordsworth a while longer to come around to the same point of view, arriving there only after John Black's 1815 translation of another Schlegel lecture, this one given in 1808 in Vienna. In this highly influential lecture, Schlegel pulled back the covers of Q₁ and said, Let there be light:

> It betrays more than ordinary deficiency of critical acumen in Shakespeare's commentators, that none of them, so far as we know, have ever thought of availing themselves of his sonnets for tracing the circumstances of his life. These sonnets paint most unequivocally the actual situation and sentiments of the poet; they make us acquainted with the passions of the man; they even contain remarkable confessions of his youthful errors.

Almost immediately, Wordsworth set about voicing similar sentiments in a supplementary essay he inserted alongside the Preface to a new edition of *Lyrical Ballads*. Here, he talked about "a small volume of miscellaneous poems, in which Shakespeare expresses his own feelings in his own person," before advancing the thesis that "in no [other] part of the writings of this Poet is found, in an equal compass, a greater number of exquisite feelings felicitously expressed." Having evidently located a copy of the sonnets independent of Anderson's cumbersome anthology, Wordsworth's doubts about the poetic worth of its contents had been largely dispelled. The sonnets were now ripe for rediscovery by every wanderer in search of a solitary cloud.

John Keats, too, felt the calling and, having brought along an edition of the sonnets as he traveled from Dorking to Devon in the autumn of 1817, wrote to his friend J. H. Reynolds, proclaiming, "I neer found so many beauties in the Sonnets—they seem to be full of fine things said unintentionally—in the intensity of working out conceits." And inspired he was, because on the same day he penned his famous letter to Benjamin Bailey, asserting "the truth of Imagination, [for] what the imagination seizes as Beauty must be truth." Truly, the sonnets had begun to work their magic on the Romantic imagination.

And though Keats did not live long enough to alchemize his passion for Shakespeare's sonnets into a like-minded sequence, he did put seventeen sonnets in his first published collection, *Poems*, the same year. He also evidently passed on this passion to his good friend Charles Armitage Brown, who, lacking the poetic gene, turned literary detective. By June 1830, Brown was excitedly writing about the sonnets to Keats's former editor and dedicatee, Leigh Hunt: "I have made a discovery, a key to the whole, which Landor declares incontrovertible—it is a discovery of which I am almost ashamed, as no one else discovered it before me."

It would take Brown another eight years to complete his studies and to publish the results in a book, which required a sixteen-word title to fully represent its outlandish thesis: *Shakespeare's Autobiographical Poems: Being His Sonnets Clearly Developed: with His Character Drawn Chiefly from His Works*. Exactly what took Brown so long is unclear, given that by his own admission, he had "no need of extracts from the writings of his contemporaries, or from any extraneous work whatever . . . relying on the Sonnets before me, and on them alone, for their natural interpretation."

Despite such a handicap, he was ready and willing to take up arms against a sea of sonnets, responding to the call from Schlegel, who, according to Brown, "directed our particular attention to [these poems], surprised at our neglect, and assured that, by competent diligence, something of Shakespeare's life might be revealed, or, at any rate, be illustrated by them." Brown also added, "[Yet] since that time few have attempted to unfold their meaning; none with success." His solution turned out to be disappointingly banal: He considered each of the sonnets as a fourteen-line stanza in a series of six long poems, which when examined afresh, would reveal "events which had occurred to [Shakespeare], and of his feelings attendant on them." It was a marvelously wrongheaded solution to a problem that few had expended energy on until Malone had come along, but now became the main preoccupation of an entire class of diligent detectives.

Malone himself did not live long enough to see what he had planted bear such mixed fruit. He died in 1812, while working on another edition of his 1790 *magnum opus*, which was to have included his own attempt at biography. For reasons that are not entirely clear, but were probably bound up more with a nagging dissatisfaction concerning the dearth of data available than with his failing eyesight, he never came close to finishing his life of Shakespeare. The man he assigned to assemble what he left behind—and who published a heavily revised edition of the *Plays & Poems* in 1821—held little truck with those who indulged in any sonnet-based biographical speculation:

> There are few topicks connected with Shakspeare upon which the ingenuity and research of his criticks have been more fruitlessly exercised, than upon the questions which have arisen with regard to the poems before us, the individual to whom they were principally addressed, and the circumstances under which they were written.... Whoever the person might be to whom the greater part of these Sonnets was addressed, it seems to have been generally admitted that the poet speaks in his own person; and some of his criticks

have attempted, by inferences drawn from them, to eke out the
scanty memorials, which have come down to us, of the incidents
of his life.

It is one of literature's more piquant ironies that the man here bewail-
ing any attempt to "eke out the scanty memorials which have come
down to us" concerning Shakespeare should be the younger son and
namesake of the man who single-handedly invented modern biogra-
phy, James Boswell. It is another that he was already too late. More po-
tent wordsmiths were ranged against him. Even the influential critic
William Hazlitt had taken time off from determining *The Characters of
Shakespeare's Plays* (1817) to observe that "the subject of [the sonnets]
seems to be somewhat equivocal; but many of them are highly beautiful
in themselves, and interesting as they relate to the state of the personal
feelings of the author."

Few, any longer, seemed prepared to vouchsafe Boswell's steadfast in-
sistence "that these compositions ha[ve] neither the poet himself nor
any individual in view; but [a]re merely the effusions of his fancy, writ-
ten . . . for the amusement of a private circle." Even those who once held
such a position began to rethink it. Nathan Drake, an indefatigable gen-
tleman-scholar, had dismissed the sonnets in an 1804 review in *The Lit-
erary Hour* for being "buried beneath a load of obscurity and quaintness;
nor does there issue a single ray of light to quicken, or to warm the heavy
mass."

Thirteen years on, the sonnets became the cornerstone of Drake's
800-page, two-volume biography, *Shakespeare & His Times* (1817). He
not only nominated the Earl of Southampton as the Fair Youth, but set
about laying the groundwork for a thousand fanciful theories by taking
the sonnets, no longer buried in obscurity, at face value. At least he did
not trouble to identify the Dark Lady, not because of any qualms about

his methodology, but rather from a distaste for the woman herself as she was portrayed by the great poet. Who she was, he felt, was hardly worth the effort of enquiry, "for, a more worthless character, or described as such in stronger terms, no poet ever drew."

Drake proved, once and for all, that no biographer of Shakespeare need be stymied by a singular lack of biographical information. All one had to do was assume a direct relationship between the poet's output and personal circumstance. For him, and for all who followed in his fanciful footsteps, the sonnets had become the key biographical document. And quite a battalion traipsed along behind him. As Edward Dowden was able to write, in the introduction to his 1881 edition of the sonnets, "With Wordsworth, Sir Henry Taylor and Mr Swinburne; with Francois-Victor Hugo, with Kreyssig, Ulrici, Gervinus and Hermann Issac; with Boaden, Armitage Brown, and Hallam; with Furnivall, Spalding, Rossetti and Palgrave, I [do] believe that *Shakespeare's Sonnets* express his own feelings in his own person." Quite a pantheon.

The romantically inclined had fully claimed the sonnets for their own, so much so that in 1827, Wordsworth was emboldened to write, without fear of ridicule, his own sonnet to the sonnets, beginning thus:

> *Scorn not the Sonnet; Critic, you have frowned,*
> *Mindless of its just honours; with this key*
> *Shakespeare unlocked his heart . . .*

The sonnets—and the sonnet—for all their wavering status across two centuries, were destined to endure "so long as men can breathe or eyes can see." Just as their author had predicted.

CHAPTER SEVEN

1821–1973

"CASTLES OF CONJECTURE"

If any should be curious to discover
Whether to you I am a friend or lover,
Let them read Shakespeare's sonnets, taking thence
A whetstone for their dull intelligence
That tears and will not cut.
　　　　—PERCY BYSSHE SHELLEY, *Epipsychidion,* 1821

Good heavens! What do I notice in rereading some of
the first sonnets? He instead of she? Nearly all are in
direct discourse: you and thee. Can I be mistaken?
Can these Sonnets be addressed to a man? Shake-
speare! Great Shakespeare! Did you feel authorized
by Virgil's example?
　　　　—LÉON DE WAILLY, *Revue des deux mondes,* 1834

The 1821 Boswell-Malone edition of the *Plays & Poems* not only provided an ur-text for most would-be editors of the sonnets, but also gave necessary impetus to a classically Victorian consensus concerning the validity of the experiences detailed in the sonnets.

If Boswell found few comers prepared to embrace his thesis "that these compositions had neither the poet himself nor any [other] individual in view," there was a greater willingness to endorse Boswell's Malonean inclination to view "this singular mode of writing" as stemming from "a fondness for classical imitation." In confirmation of such a notion, Malone had even co-opted Thomas Warton, who, in his *History of English Poetry,* suggested that "in the reign of Queen Elizabeth whole sets of Sonnets were written with this sort of attachment . . . particularly . . . *The Affectionate Shepherd,* of Richard Barnfield," a most unfortunate analogy. Barnfield was, of course, homosexual.

In other words, it was not merely "the anti-personalists"—as Schoenbaum duly dubbed the younger Boswell's disciples—who were anxious "to redeem the god of their idolatry from self-confessed impurities of the flesh." Those who felt they'd found the key to Shakespeare's heart also preferred to shy away from the logical outcome of their position: a bisexual bard. Charles Armitage Brown, like Malone, sought to depict the period as a time when "friendship, in poetical and prosaic addresses, adopt[ed] the language of love [and] to express its utmost sincerity . . . breathed of tenderness." Coleridge anticipated Keats's friend in his 1803 marginalia to Anderson's *Poets of Great Britain,* when he qualified at length his suggestion to his son that these poems would "explain the mind of Shakespeare":

> If thou wouldst understand these sonnets thou must read the chapter in Potter's Antiquities on the Greek lovers. . . . This pure love Shakespeare appears to have [also] felt—[and] to have been in no way ashamed of. . . . Yet at the same time he knew that so strong a love would have been made more completely a thing of permanence and reality . . . if this object of his love had been at the

same time a possible object of desire. . . . In this feeling he must have written the twentieth sonnet. . . . [Yet] it is noticeable that not even an allusion to that very worst of all possible vices . . . [occurs] in all his numerous plays—whereas Jonson, Beaumont and Fletcher, and Massinger are full of them. . . . I pray fervently that thou may'st know inwardly how impossible it was for a Shakespeare not to have been in his heart's heart chaste.

It took another century for someone with a less sentimental view of Elizabethan literature, H. C. Beeching, to point out that there are linguistic conventions, and there is the language of love. The Edwardian author awaited convincing "that there is nothing in Shakespeare's sonnets beyond the Elizabethan note of patron-worship, [and] it will at least require by way of parallel a poem with some passion in it . . . for example, [someone] speak[ing] of his love for his patron as keeping him awake at night." The closest "contemporaneous" comparison to the specific sonnet that upset Steevens and Coleridge so, Q20, perhaps lies with the king's description of "Willie o' Winsbury" in Child Ballad 100,[12] but unless Shakespeare took a trip to Scotland in his "lost years," he is unlikely to have heard sentiments such as these:

> But when he cam the king before,
> He was clad o the red silk;
> His hair was like to threeds o gold,
> And his skin was white as milk.
> "It is nae wonder," said the king,
> "That my daughter's love ye did win;
> Had I been a woman, as I am a man,
> My bedfellow ye should hae been."

For the anti-personalists, at least their position was straightforward, if intellectually circumlocutory: i.e., Shakespeare cannot have had any homosexual yearnings; therefore, since even they had to admit some oddball sentiments were expressed therein, Q1–126 must be a work of fiction. It took C. S. Lewis to raise an insurmountable objection, "Here . . . we have a sequence which really hints a story, and so odd a story that we find a difficulty in regarding it as fiction. It is the story of a man torn between passionate affection for another man and reluctant passion for a woman whom he neither trusts nor respects. No reading of the sonnets can obscure that amount of 'plot.'"

Yet even Lewis, from the vantage point of a more liberal time, could not bring himself to consider Shakespeare a sodomite, going on to insist that this was not "the poetry of full-blown pederasty. . . . If he had intended in these sonnets to be the poet of pederasty, I think he would have left us in no doubt." By which one must presume Lewis would like us to believe that Shakespeare's relationship with the Fair Youth was akin to the close bond he shared with J. R. R. Tolkein and Charles Williams. Methinks not.

Leaving his readers "in no doubt" would have been the very last thing Shakespeare would have done. Leaving aside the legal imperative, his own chameleon character would never have allowed such an unambiguous proclamation. Indeed, the entire sonnet-sequence goes out of its way to blur genders at times. Many of the Fair Youth sonnets—according to one twentieth-century sonnet-editor, as many as sixty-nine[13]—have a problematic addressee, and nine sonnets address a young man, but only in the third person (19, 63, 64, 65, 66, 67, 68, 100, and 101).

These are artistic decisions that make no sense unless the author is seeking to disguise an unconventional relationship. Even that "monstrous" sonnet, Q20 ("A woman's face, with Nature's own hand painted") can be given a more heterocentric spin (as Malone did when he argued that it "does not perhaps mean man-mistress, but sovereign mistress"). And yet it still failed to fool the one seventeenth-century near-contemporary who left his thoughts behind in the margin of his copy, where he wrote next to Q20, "The Mistress Masculine."

Even Victorians who allowed the sonnets to inform their own prejudices, like one mid-century correspondent to *Fraser's Magazine,* were unable to accept that anyone "guilty of the base pusillanimity of such sentiments [as Q42] could . . . have been so destitute of the sense of shame as to proclaim them to the world." Focused on the subject matter, not the poetry, of the sonnets, the Victorians one by one began to construct alternate scenarios, introducing a cast of characters that would give them the opportunity to solve the conundrum at their core, thus redeeming "the god of their idolatry."

If Drake had provided one candidate for the Fair Youth, it was a particular article in the *Gentleman's Magazine* in 1832 that put a large Cheshire cat among these paternalistic pigeons. James Boaden was hardly a scholar in the Malone-Boswell mode, rather enjoying a jack-of-all-trades career as an editor, biographer, novelist, and playwright. But his article, "To What Person the Sonnets of Shakespeare Were Actually Addressed," opened up whole new vistas of contention. Here he advocated entirely new, and quite plausible, candidates for the roles of both Fair Youth and Rival Poet.

For the Fair Youth, as we know, he offered up William Herbert, a.k.a. Pembroke, thus drawing the battlelines for 150 years of further debate. He also reinvigorated what had been to date a merely diversionary discussion as to the possible identity of the Rival Poet, thus amplifying the importance of a brief interlude at the midpoint of the Fair Youth sequence (Q78–86) dealing with a rival intent on stealing the poet's patron away.

Here we see gentle Shakespeare infused with several deadly sins—jealousy, resentment, self-loathing, even overweening pride—while he displays uncharacteristic venom for rival wordsmiths, bemoaning how "every alien pen hath got my use / And under thee their poesy disperse" (Q78). (Similar sentiments are voiced, somewhat more characteristically, by Bob Dylan in "Idiot Wind"—"Lady killers load dice on me / While imitators steal me blind.") Shakespeare also entertains doubts about his own worth as a poet: "O, how I faint when I of you do write / Knowing a better spirit doth use your name" (Q80), only to erase them in the blast of bravado that is Q81 ("Or I shall live your epitaph to make"). But in the end he finds himself wanting again, contrasting "the proud full sail of [the] great verse" of his rival with "that enfeebled [verse of] mine" (Q86).

This last among the so-called Rival Poet sonnets has stirred critics the greatest, taunting them to identify the figure he was writing about. Malone, back in 1780, started from the peculiar premise that "this better spirit . . . to whom even Shakespeare acknowledges himself inferior" must be someone whom posterity, too, would deem a worthy rival. He thus alights on Spenser, who was then "in the zenith of his reputation." Unable to envisage the possibility that our greatest poet may also have been one of our poorer critics, he selects someone from the previous generation whose influence on Shakespeare's own sonneteering was negligible, bordering on nonexistent. And there matters lay for a full half-century.

Until Boaden introduced his own candidate-sonneteer, Samuel Daniel—aiming to bolster his argument for Pembroke as the Fair Youth—it seems no one had thought of connecting the two. Boaden felt he'd solved the identities of both in a blizzard of supposition. And therein lies the rub. Almost everyone who followed in Boaden's wake had the same motive and adopted the same methodology: Start with preferred candidate; pour scorn on rival theories; attempt to prove connection by hook or by crock.

The results were often more entertaining than edifying, but Daniel was a good guess on Boaden's part. To start with, he was one of two sonneteers largely responsible for the fleeting sonnet craze that Shakespeare was reinventing/responding to. Having "contributed" twenty-four sonnets to the piratical edition of Sidney's *Astrophil & Stella* in 1591, Daniel belatedly ingratiated himself with Sidney's incensed sister, the Countess of Pembroke, by dedicating his own *Delia* to the lady the following year. And there is little doubt that Shakespeare was inspired by Daniel's example (not least in the brazen way he pitched his own poetry to a potential patron). Malone, though rejecting Daniel's candidacy for Rival Poet, willingly admitted that Daniel's sonnets "appear . . . to have been the model that Shakespeare followed."

Boaden, meanwhile, with a little requisite contextualization, took care of Malone's own candidate, Spenser: "The modern reader would be apt to think that Shakespeare could only regard Spenser as his superior— but this is to be unacquainted with the estimates of poetry in the age of Elizabeth. Acknowledged learning greatly predominated over genius. . . . I have no doubt that Shakespeare actually vailed his bonnet, not only to Spenser, but to Daniel and Chapman." He thus unwittingly offered up the main challenger to Daniel's own candidacy, George Chapman.

Because Chapman did not have the connection to Pembroke that Daniel assuredly did, Boaden remained focused on Daniel, who was a tutor to Herbert at Wilton, and dedicated more than one book to his mother, the countess. He also dedicated his *Defence of Rhyme* (1601) to Pembroke himself, now ascended to the earldom. This convinced Boaden that Shakespeare's allusion to "the dedicated words, which writers use / Of their fair subject" (Q82.3–4) was a direct reference to Daniel, who actually spent most of that dedication praising Herbert's parents—"your most worthy and honourable mother" and that "worthy Lord, the fosterer of me, and my muse"—rather than "spend[ing] all his might . . . speaking of your fame," as Shakespeare suggests the Rival Poet did. (Not surprisingly, Boaden omits any reference to Daniel subsequently devoting one of his 1603 epistles to the Earl of Southampton.)

Boaden even went to some pains to suggest "that affable familiar ghost / Which nightly gulls him with intelligence" (Q86.9–10) was a reference to mathematician and alchemist John Dee, who had been a tutor to Herbert's father and continued to enjoy the family's favor. Dee had claimed to communicate with angels "nightly"—apparently conversing with them in their own angelic tongue, Enochian—but one somehow doubts that the "proud full sail of his great verse" (Q86.1) was intended as a reference to the unintelligible drivel that Dee, and his sidekick Edward Kelley, published across two volumes of Enochian poetry in 1583–84.

It took another half century for a more worthy critic, William Minto, to highlight a more credible candidate for the Rival Poet to whom the Stratfordian might have deferred. In his important *Characteristics of English Poets* (1873), Minto devoted an entire chapter to some of the sonnets' thornier problems. After concluding that "the weight of probability" favored Pembroke as the Fair Youth, he turned to the issue of the Rival Poet, adopting that incredulous tone so many sonnet-detectives adopt when about to outline an explanation that has eluded everyone to date:

> I hope I shall not be held guilty of hunting after paradox if I say that every possible poet has been named but the right one, nor of presumption if I say that he is so obvious that his escape from notice is something little short of miraculous. . . . There was another to whom the allusions [in Q86] apply more pointedly than to Mar-

lowe [advocated by Robert Cartwright in 1859], and that was George Chapman, a man less honoured now, but numbered in his own generation among the greatest of its poets.... No-one who has read any of his poetry, and who knows his own lofty pretensions and the rank accorded him in his own generation, will think that his "proud sail" has been unduly honoured by the affected jealousy and good-humoured banter of the "saucy bark" of Shakespeare.

Chapman was always an obvious candidate—though by no means the only one—and Minto argued his case with great tenacity and intellectual vigor. A classical scholar who attended Oxford, and made most of his contemporary reputation from translations of the classics, Chapman also fancied himself a great poet and a worthy playwright. Unfortunately for Chapman, he had none of Shakespeare's success, either as a playwright or as a patron's favorite. Two of his erstwhile patrons, Robert Devereux, the second Earl of Essex, and the Prince of Wales, Prince Henry, both died prematurely—the former executed for treason, the latter smitten by typhoid when barely eighteen.

And that is the main problem with the Chapman thesis: Any claimant has a hard time alighting on any direct association connecting him to either Pembroke or Southampton. Indeed, Minto has to resort to a connection via Chapman's other main patron, Sir Francis Walsingham, "whose daughter Sir Philip Sidney had married." "Nothing," we are told, "could have been more natural than that the old man should introduce his favourite to the Countess of Pembroke or her son." Natural or not, there is no evidence he actually did.

Where Minto is better able to marshal his facts is among the minutiae of the poetry itself. Addressing the nightly visitations of the "familiar ghost" in Q86, he points out that Chapman alludes to such a figure in the dedication to his 1594 poem "Shadow of Night," in language that bursts with self-importance. Reserving muse-status for the mother of knowledge, who "will scarcely be looked upon by others but with invocation, fasting, watching; yea, not without having drops of their souls like a heavenly familiar," Chapman brags that his own poetic insights alone are equal to the task.

Another contemporary convert to Chapman's cause, Frederick Furnivall, convinced by Minto, then proceeded to examine a late Chapman poem ("The Teares of Peace"), in which he appears to suggest that Homer's *anima* came to him and said, "I am that spirit Elysian, That . . . did thy bosome fill, With such a flood of soule"—i.e., directly inspired his mammoth translation of the *Iliad*. If such a claim had indeed come to Shakespeare's attention—and Chapman's translation of Homer began to appear in 1598—then the use of the phrase "gulls him with intelligence" suggests that his earlier depiction of "the proud full sail of his great verse" may have been in some sense sarcastic. Such an interpretation in no way precludes Chapman's credentials as that "better spirit" who tormented Shakespeare so. Recognizing strengths and ridiculing weaknesses go hand in hand for the less gentle bard of the sonnets.

The Chapman Rival Poet thesis soon supplanted all others, though other claimants continued to cloud the literary landscape on occasion. The ever-contrary Sidney Lee dismissed Chapman on the grounds that he "had produced no conspicuously 'great verse' till he began his translation of Homer in 1598," i.e., in plenty of time for a Pembrokian chronology that dated the sonnets to 1597–1601, but not in time for the Southamptonite alternative to which he was predisposed. Instead, Lee came up with the extraordinary suggestion of Barnabe Barnes, on the grounds that he wrote sonnets influenced by the French rather than the more favored Italian model. Needless to say, Barnes also fit the strict timeline Lee had imposed.

Other candidates, such as Marlowe (too early) and Jonson (too late), drew few to their flickering flame. Nor did the two rival poets advocated by Henry Brown in 1870: Francis Davison, who dedicated sonnets to Pembroke in his *Poetical Rhapsody* (1602); and John Davies of Hereford, whose work is riddled with allusions and references to Shakespeare. Davies could certainly claim to be an "alien pen," though, as we shall see, it is hard to fit him to the right time period. He didn't begin publishing until 1602, though we can place him at Wilton in 1599, working on an edition of David's *Psalms* for Pembroke's mother, intended as a presentation copy for the queen. And though we can be pretty sure that Davies was not the author of "great verse" in Shakespeare's or any other contemporaries' minds, there is no reason to suppose Shakespeare was targeting a single rival. Indeed, he specifically tells us, in Q78, that every "alien pen" caused him concern.

Chapman could and did claim to write "great verse," and his advocates continued to hold the high ground well into the twentieth century. Indeed, in 1917, one scholar devoted an entire book to this (largely perceived) co-relationship between Chapman's work and Shakespeare's. John M. Robertson's *Shakespeare and Chapman* has been largely discredited, but he does point out that in the dedication to *Hero and Leander,* which Chapman completed from Marlowe's unfinished translation, Chapman suggests he had been "drawne by strange instigation" to finish what Marlowe had started, and that in the third section of the same piece, he speaks of communing with spirits.

Unfortunately, the case for Chapman was about to be invaded by the kind of creed that responded to ridicule with ever more books and articles, until it skewered the argument in the direction its author wanted to go. In the end, not only was Chapman the Rival Poet, he was part of a classicists' conspiracy bent on humiliating Shakespeare with these private poems. The arch-exponent of this new heresy was one Arthur Acheson, who began writing books about Shakespeare and the sonnets in 1903 and did not stop for a quarter of a century.

The Acheson schism, which defined and redefined itself according to the latest attack upon it, was stated in these terms in Acheson's final volume, *Shakespeare's Sonnet Story* (1922): "The sonnets were collected from their original recipients by John Florio and published by him in collusion with George Chapman and others in 1609 as an attack upon Shakespeare by making public the basis of the shadowed scandal in [the poem] *Willobie His Avisa*." Apparently, "the definite identification of the 'dark lady' [Anne Davenant] . . . from the finding of [Matthew] Roydon as the author of *Willobie His Avisa,* [had] put the identity of the other figures . . . for ever beyond conjecture."

Needless to say, in Acheson's singular scenario the sonnets' original recipient, though not their begetter, was the Earl of Southampton. Acheson was a Southamptonite through and through, sharing the *Fraser Magazine* correspondent's view that Shakespeare could never "have been so destitute of the sense of shame as to proclaim [the sonnets] to the world." Hence, Q's publication was all a plot on the part of Chapman, Florio, and friends.

The Southamptonites, in retreat ever since the Pembrokians stopped trying to align the Fair Youth with a specific Dark Lady, thus had a new scenario that centered upon John Florio. They recast Florio from the influential, well-connected scholar and translator of histories into a vindictive, spiteful snob who was incensed at Shakespeare for satirizing him as the character Holofernes, the pompous pedant in *Love's Labours Lost,* and annoyed at having to share the favors of Southampton with the young upstart. On Acheson's planet, the dedication in Florio's 1598 *A Worlde of Wordes*—"to your bounteous Lordship, most noble, most virtuous, and most Honourable Earl of Southampton . . . to whom I owe and vow the years I have to live"—was a conscious retort to Shakespeare's earlier, and equally demonstrative, *Lucrece* dedication.

In fact, Florio's connection with Henry Wriothesley was considerably stronger than any Shakespeare enjoyed. He had already lived for some years with the earl. He also enjoyed a friendship with William Herbert, to the extent that in his will, he left gifts to the Earl of Pembroke, on condition that he look after his second wife, Rose. As for connections with his literary contemporaries, he married the sister of sonneteer Samuel Daniel, and clearly enjoyed the friendship of Chapman and Jonson. Jonson sent him a copy of *Volpone,* one of the books Thorpe published on Jonson's behalf. Jonson inscribed it to his "loving father and worthy friend, Master John Florio," adding, "Ben Jonson seals this testimony of his friendship and love." Yet no specific link to Shakespeare, save for common patrons, has ever been found (though some like to imagine that this is where the Stratfordian learned some French and Italian).

For all the ridicule that rightly rained down on his highly suppositional sonnet-*expliqué,* Acheson had his advocates. J. Middleton Murry was among the first. In 1927, Murry found the key to the sonnets in Chapman's early poems, where the poet is "incessantly girding at a successful rival poet who has established himself in the favour of a nobleman by poems which Chapman condemns as sensual." It took another third of a century for Acheson to find his next acolyte, but Leona Rostenberg made up for lost time. Her article "Thomas Thorpe, Publisher of Shakespeare's Sonnets" in the *Proceedings of the Bibliographical Society of America* combined valuable new research on Thorpe's publishing practices with an unquestioning acceptance of the thesis of that "distinguished Shakespearean scholar," Arthur Acheson. Rostenberg recast Thorpe as a mere puppet on the end of strings pulled by this school of scholar-poets:

In a period of turbulent theatrical competition [1606–9] it seems
that Thorpe was the literary agent, if not the tool, of [a] particular
clique which sought to rival Shakespeare. . . . During these three
years, Thorpe met the young translator, John Healy. He also met
his guardian spirit, John Florio, who was not only a friend of Ed-
ward Blount, Marston, Jonson, and Chapman, but also an avowed
enemy of Shakespeare, as well as former tutor in Italian to the
Earls of Southampton and Pembroke. . . . [He was thus] the tool of
one man or a group, who wished to avenge their personal pique by
the exposure of material designed for circulation only among the
poet's "priuate friends."

A theory eccentric enough to come from an Oxfordian or Baconian,
the Florio-Chapman script stayed ripe enough for further retelling. Two
decades after Rostenberg, respected publisher Robert Giroux, with his
own money and imprint, published *The Book Known as Q* (1982), in
which Florio was again the surreptitious scribe of secret sonnets sent to
Southampton by Shakespeare.

This strategy had become a necessity because the Southamp-
tonites—across a century's worth of guesswork—had failed to make the
case for any "W.H." as the actual procurer of the sonnets. Initially, there
had been the forlorn expectation that they might, one day, identify the
person in question. But as of the death of Sidney Lee in 1926, they were
still waiting for a better suggestion than the one Malone had made back
in 1780—that "a line [in Q20: 'A man in hew all Hews in his controwl-
ing'] . . . inclines me to think that the initials W.H. stand for W. Hughes."
The simplicity of this notion—and Shakespeare's love of a good pun—
certainly convinced Oscar Wilde, who took the idea and ran wild with it,
writing the short story "A Portrait of Mr W.H."

But it didn't point Southamptonites in the direction of their favored earl, and was rejected accordingly. Drake had attempted to suggest that Thorpe had deliberately inverted the earl's own initials (Henry Wrio-thesley), as a purblind; but it didn't take Minto to point out, "If any blind was thought necessary, why have a dedication at all?" For a while, the Southamptonites allowed themselves to be distracted by other arguments concerning Pembroke and the Dark Lady, but in the 1860s they returned to "Mr W.H."

D. Barnstorff rebooted the debate in 1860 with a whimsical suggestion, offered "simply as a guess," that the letters W.H. "stand for the word William and Himself." Offensively simple, it prompted an almost immediate retort from Samuel Neil, who came forward with William Hathaway, Shakespeare's brother-in-law, born November 30, 1578. After Shakespeare retired to Stratford, he apparently "wished to give his brother-in-law a start, and so gave him the manuscripts of the sonnets to sell." At a going rate of between one and three pounds per literary manuscript, it wouldn't have been much of a start! Nor was it the beginning of a new consensus—save one that rubbished Neil's suggestion.

The next suggestion at least had legs. The impressively named Ebenezer Forsyth, in an 1867 monograph, expressed his belief that a printer's error in Q had transformed "W. HALL" into "W. H. ALL." William Hall was a member of the Stationers' Company, having begun his publishing career in 1606, so at least he was a credible candidate. And Sidney Lee, casting around for any kind of explanation that did not have Pembrokian connotations, latched onto this one with alacrity, suggesting that he was the same "W.H." who had previously published a neglected manuscript poem—"A Foure-fould Meditation"—by the Jesuit Robert Southwell. He theorized that "Thorpe gave Hall's initials only, because he was an intimate associate who was known by those initials to their common circle of friends."

What Lee doesn't explain is why Thorpe's previous dedication to a far more "intimate associate," Edward Blount, gave his full name. Nor does he resolve a question Schoenbaum later asked, on behalf of all Shakespeareans: "Why Hall, who in 1609 had his own press, should have procured the manuscript for another printer." (More plausible is a suggestion of Harold Love's, in his 1997 textbook on seventeenth-century scribal publications, that W.H. might be the name of the scribe who surreptitiously swiped a copy of the sonnets and brought them to Thorpe.)

Another suggestion, offered the same year as Forsyth's by the productive Gerald Massey, albeit more equivocally, lay unremarked upon for more than a century before A. L. Rowse decided to champion its cause. Having tentatively proposed the countess of Southampton's third husband, Sir William Hervey, Massey left it to Rowse to convince people that, because Sir William took a much younger bride in 1609 after the countess's death, he somehow wanted to unburden himself of any stray manuscripts he may have acquired, written to his ex-wife's son.

Of course, establishing the potential identity of the only procurer was only ever going to be a distraction from the real prize, one "of extraordinary value," according to Edwardian biographer Lytton Strachey: "nothing less than a true insight into the most secret recesses of the thoughts and feelings of perhaps the greatest man who ever lived." The focus of that investigation temporarily shifted, after 1886, from the identity of the two male figures in the sonnets, to the single female subject, the Dark Lady.

In part, this was because by the turn of the century, after William Archer and Thomas Tyler ganged up on Sidney Lee to put an end to his favored earl once and for all, the Southamptonites and Pembrokians had fought themselves to a standstill. Although their generally well-argued assault ensured that Lee's Southampton was never again able to put himself on the front foot, nor did Archer and Tyler deliver the knock-out blow.

More pertinently, the Dark Lady's newfound vogue stemmed from finding a name that seemed, at least for a while, to fit all the facts: Mary Fitton. Those facts, though, tended to change depending on which of the sonnets were applied to the lady. The Dark Lady continued to confound critics. The difficulties of identification were compounded by the scattershot way "her" sonnets lay distributed among the "disordered appendix" that succeeds the Fair Youth sonnet-sequence (Q127–54). It may have been this that had convinced the likes of Malone, Steevens, Boswell, Dyce, and Collier to evince no curiosity as to her identity.

Given the fact that Malone's division has gone largely unchallenged for two centuries or more, one might even imagine that the sonnets in this group follow a pattern similar to that of the previous 126. However, they do nothing of the sort. Of the twenty-eight sonnets that succeed the "envoi" to the Fair Youth sequence (Q126), at least seven have nothing to do with the lady in question (128–29, 145–46, 151, 153–54), while just nine can with confidence be assigned to her (127, 130, 132, 137, 141, 144, 147–48, 150). The others remain up for grabs. The design that seems to bind the preceding poems has been abandoned, whether by Shakespeare or by Thorpe.

If we address only the sonnets that describe the Dark Lady's characteristics with any specificity, we must prune the list further. The one sonnet on which almost her entire profile has been constructed by critics (Q130) is, first and foremost, a satire on other sonneteers. Yet, such is the literalness that can infuse the sonnet-debate that the arguments for and against Fitton at the end of the nineteenth century were ultimately "decided" by the fact that a portrait of the lady was produced that seemed to suggest that she was fair-haired, and therefore incapable of being "black as hell, as dark as night" (Q147.14).

Before Fitton's staged entrance, sonnet-speculators had spent most of the century building up an identikit portrait based entirely on the poems—and, for Ludwig Tieck, the plays. In 1826, Tieck argued that her personae was reflected in Rosalind, Rosaline, Beatrice, Juliet, and even Venus, though he made no attempt to give her a name.

At the same time critics found a way to ensure that the lady's profile was regularly boosted. This was by making her trials and tribulations a part of the main sonnet-sequence, to see her visage reflected in and by the Fair Youth poems. Many found her fingerprints all over Q40–42— which are primarily concerned with unfaithfulness on the part of the Fair Youth. As early as 1829, one fan fatally infected with the romance virus, Anna Jameson (*Memoirs of the Loves of the Poets*), had put her down for eleven more of the Fair Youth sonnets (though not 40–42).

Jameson proved to be positively restrained, though, compared with some of her late Victorian successors. Hermann Conrad, a fervent "disintegrationist" (a reorderer of Q), gave the lady sixty-six sonnets, divided into nine sections: Approach, Love, Slight Shadows, Separation, Second Meeting, Disturbances, Jealousy, Estrangement, and Backward Glances. M. J. Wolff used his 1907 biography to heap another twenty-nine on the pile.

The conscious gender-blurring adopted by Shakespeare, and announced in dramatic fashion with Q20, perhaps to save his own skin, made such a process awfully tempting to adopt, and impossible to refute. But for all the rearranging and reassigning, the one thing the Victorians lacked, until 1884 anyway, was a credible Dark Lady who might leap from the pages of history and color in a second sonnet narrative.

Shortly before this candidate emerged, Frederick Furnivall found himself summarizing her traits in a couple of sentences: Shakespeare "had become involved in an intrigue with a married woman who threw him over for his friend Will. She was dark, had beautiful eyes, and was a fine musician, but false." Meanwhile, Edward Dowden convinced himself, "We shall never discover the name of that woman who for a season could sound . . . the instrument in Shakespeare's heart."

It was in 1884 that Thomas Tyler, that "specialist in pesimmism,"[14] began to mount his case for Mary Fitton, first in a couple of lectures, then in an 1886 introduction to a facsimile of Q, and eventually in an 1890 edition dedicated largely to proving his argument. From the very first, Fitton's candidacy was tied to the Pembroke cause, largely because it was by her June 1600 assignation with the would-be earl that he decided we should know her. It was a connection devoutly to be wished by anyone looking to make a *ménage à trois* out of the sonnets, but it played fast and loose with the facts.

Fitton, who came from minor Cestrian nobility, had become one of the queen's maids of honor in 1595, serving her faithfully until one moonlit night in June 1600, when she gave up her virtue to the young, thrusting Herbert. At this juncture, the facts of Fitton's life were sacrificed in favor of the "fictional" sonnet-story. Tyler and his subscribers cast her as the mistress to the lusty lord, though there is no evidence she was anything of the sort. Her revelation that she was with child sent Pembroke south, to Fleet prison, at the queen's command, and herself north, to the Cheshire family home.

According to Tyler, "a great scandal . . . cause[d] the father and daughter to 'steal' off from London and into Cheshire, and to lead her friends to cease from the efforts they had been making on her behalf." One suspects that this scandal was not her pregnancy, but rather the evidence that she had seduced, and not *been* seduced by, the young lad. Either way, her days at court were over, as was her virtue, and in the next six years she bore two more bastards to one Richard Leveson, before marrying a captain in 1607. All straight out of a torrid romance novel, yet minus the necessary parallels to the pithy portrait that Furnivall had previously sketched.

Nonetheless, the Fitton-Herbert thesis was given "vigorous support" by the likes of W. A. Harrison and William Archer, and the intermittent endorsement of a confused Furnivall. Charlotte Stopes, though, was not convinced—as the author of a biography of Southampton, perhaps not surprisingly—and marshaled her arguments accordingly. According to Stopes, Fitton was neither a brunette, nor ugly; she was widely loved; there is no evidence she knew Shakespeare; and, finally, she was not married when(ever) the sonnets were written. But it was an examination of two portraits of Fitton held at Arbury Hall, first by Furnivall, then by C. G. O. Bridgeman, that really put paid to Tyler's attempt to tilt at windmills; and by the turn of the century, the Dark Lady had returned to the shadows from whence such a "singing fiction" had first come.

But the plight of Fitton had gripped some particularly imaginative souls, and her name was destined to live on, not in the scholar's tracts or among the bard's biographies, but in fictional accounts of Shakespeare's life (and loves) that were becoming many a writer's response to the dearth of detail in bardic biography. Even though he expressed a "disbelief in her alleged connection with Shakespeare," Bernard Shaw still made Fitton the focus of his 1910 playlet, *The Dark Lady of the Sonnets.* He even provided his own literary *caveat emptor* as a preface to the play:

> Shakespear rubbed in the lady's complexion in his sonnets mercilessly; for in his day black hair was as unpopular as red hair was in the early days of Queen Victoria. Any tinge lighter than raven black must be held fatal to the strongest claim to be the Dark Lady. And so, unless it can be shewn that Shakespear's sonnets exasperated Mary Fitton into dyeing her hair and getting painted in false

colors, I must give up all pretence that my play is historical. . . .
[Yet] I was, in a manner, present at the birth of the Fitton theory.
Its parent [i.e., Tyler] and I had become acquainted; and he used
to consult me on obscure passages in the sonnets, on which, as far
as I can remember, I never succeeded in throwing the faintest
light, at a time when nobody else thought my opinion, on that or
any other subject, of the slightest importance. I thought it would
be friendly to immortalize him . . . much as Shakespear immortal-
ized Mr W.H.

Another, obscurer literary heavyweight from the first half of the twen-
tieth century, who wrote and lectured on Shakespeare well and often,
was Oxford University Press editor Charles Williams, who in 1928, fol-
lowing Shaw's example, wrote a playlet. In *A Myth of Shakespeare,* Mary
Fitton appeared alongside Southampton—not Pembroke—displaying
a ready wit much like the one given the Dark Lady in her sonnets:

SHAKESPEARE: *God save the Queen, and give the Queen her will.*
MARY FITTON: *Isn't that you, Will Shakespeare, the Queen's Will?*
SHAKESPEARE: *Queen's Will because the Queen's will made me will*
     No other Will to serve the Queen so well.
SOUTHAMPTON: *God save your willship then, worshipful Will!*
MARY FITTON: *And keep your will-self from wilfulness.*
RALEIGH: *Lest willy-nilly you be 'wildered, Will.*
SOUTHAMPTON: *Truce, truce, he fails! The joke falls down at last.*

Such was the Dark Lady's hold on the romantic imagination—whether
she was Fitton, or someone else who was made to fit—that she not only
featured in AE's (George W. Russell's) long poem *House of the Titans*
(1934), and received a passing mention in James Joyce's *Ulysses,* but

also served as the key love interest in an early fictional account of Shakespeare's life, *Gentleman of Stratford* (1939), by John Brody. Brody calls her Mistress Nell, but in all other senses, he says, she "conforms to what Shakespeare tells us of the dark woman in the Sonnets." Fiction, from this point forward, continued to favor her in the face of an ongoing lack of facts about the sonnets' author—let alone their ostensible subject matter.

But whatever the imaginations of twentieth-century novelists, poets, and playwrights managed to conjure out of sonnets 127–54, it was as nothing to what the once-respected writer of autobiography, verse, and Elizabethan history, A. L. Rowse, constructed when he attempted, in 1973, to present, in all scholastic seriousness, his own candidate for the Dark Lady: Emilia Lanier, a musician of Italian descent.

Lacking the merest *soupçon* of a connection between this lady and our poet, Rowse chose to be bold. No mere footnote to a lifetime of research was enough for Emilia. Instead, he announced his "discovery" with a fanfare of which the four horsemen of the Apocalypse would have been proud. On January 29, 1973, *The Times* ran a full-page article by Rowse, entitled "Revealed at Last, Shakespeare's Dark Lady," in which he accused all previous theorists of "barking up the wrong tree" and compared his own revelation with Newton's discovery of gravity and Ventris's of Linear B. But his case for Emilia was riddled with holes, especially as he managed to misread "brown" for "brave" in Simon Forman's journals, his primary source for details about Emilia, thus describing Lanier as "exceptionally dark" when all Forman meant was that she had suffered many hardships.

Paraphrases and summaries of Rowse's speculation soon sprouted up in journals the world over. Not content, Rowse rushed out a rather bland, revised edition of the sonnets, provocatively and presumptuously entitled *Shakespeare's Sonnets: The Problems Solved.* A historian who refused to learn from history, Rowse found his theories rounded up and put in the same ring of ridicule previously frequented by those the likes of George Chalmers, Thomas Tyler, and Arthur Acheson once expounded. If Rowse's thesis proved to be the product of an overactive imagination, the sonnets had been preying on overactive imaginations ever since Malone's restoration had allowed them to work their magic anew. Not surprisingly, some of the more eccentric inspirations came from poets themselves. In 1925, Robert Graves adopted the more dubious parts of Samuel Butler's and Arthur Acheson's crackpot theories. As such, he made "W.H. with the assistance, probably, of a rival playwright and the Dark Lady, [lay] a trap for Shakespeare, inviting him to a rendezvous . . . [where he] arranged for Shakespeare to be surprised and assaulted when about to compromise himself grotesquely." Then, in 1609, according to Graves, W.H. "allowed Thorpe to publish a collection of sonnets, both those addressed to himself and those addressed to the Dark Lady. Revenge for this piratical publication . . . seems to me one of the chief motives for the writing of *The Tempest*," apparently an attempt to get back at the likes of Chapman.

W. H. Auden—who held Graves, but not his theories, in high regard—subsequently suggested that the sonnets represented a different kind of test, being "the best touchstone I know of for distinguishing . . . those who love poetry for its own sake . . . from those who only value poems . . . because they express feelings or beliefs of which the reader happens to approve." Similarly, Ralph Waldo Emerson had previously claimed these poems as the exclusive property of poets: "Shakespeare's Sonnets are readable only by poets, and it is a test of poetic apprehension, the value which a reader attached to them."

Half a century after Wordsworth provided a key of sorts to the sonnets, the pugnacious Robert Browning tried to change the lock. In his 1871 poem "House," Browning derided the pastoral poet's entire premise. "'With this same key / Shakespeare unlocked his heart,' once more! / Did Shakespeare? If so, the less Shakespeare he!" fumed Browning, the anti-personalist, appalled at the idea of Shakespeare filling his poems with personal detail.

For the anti-personalists, the sonnets themselves were a fiction, but for others they were a rich source of fiction. And so, at the same time that Emerson and Browning were busy trying to depersonalize the debate, Oscar Wilde, at his impish best, had come up with the perfect amalgam of fact and fiction: a short story, "A Portrait of W.H.," that made the case for a new candidate to "onlie begetter" status, while at the same time lampooning the very notion itself (he even has his prosaic proselytizer, Cyril Graham, shoot himself when his friend demands evidence).

The inspirations for Wilde's story were twofold. Taking a century-old idea from Malone—that the line "in hew all Hews in his controlling" (Q114.8) was a deliberate pun on W.H.'s name, Hughes—he adapted it to a suggestion tossed out by Minto, in his 1874 volume on the characteristics of English poets: "The representation of women's parts on the stage by boys may have fostered to an unusual degree the sentimental admiration of beautiful youths. This last influence could hardly but have affected Shakespeare, seeing that he acted up to boys in that character."

The appeal to Wilde's own proclivities was obvious. He set about writing a short story about a young boy in Shakespeare's theater troupe named Willie Hughes, and, inevitably, the more he wrote the story, the more convinced he became that he might be on to something. So the narrator goes from stating, "I am [un]likely to be converted to any new idea. The matter has ceased to be a mystery to any one," to arguing heatedly with his friend, Erskine, that he should "give to the world his marvellous interpretation of the Sonnets—the only interpretation that thoroughly explained the problem."

In a July 1889 letter to W. E. Henley, Wilde even rhapsodized about his discovery of "the real Mr W.H." And he seems to have convinced his nemesis, Lord Alfred Douglas, because many years later Douglas (like C. A. Brown before him) felt compelled to write his own *True History of Shakespeare's Sonnets* (1933). And even after *Blackwood's Magazine* ran Wilde's story, shortly after his letter to Henley, the playwright reworked the material, writing a version that was more expansive, and arguing the case for Willie Hughes with yet more vim.

But even in the flush of full enthusiasm, Wilde recognized the pitfalls of his theory. At the end of the story he cannot resist letting the first-person narrator turn the argument on its head: "However it came about . . . there was no doubt that Willie Hughes suddenly became to me a mere myth, an idle dream, the boyish fancy of a young man who, like most ardent spirits, was more anxious to convince others than to be himself converted." It was a classically Wildean way of having his critical cake and eating it, too. Having argued his case for two dozen pages, he suddenly suggested he was just playing devil's advocate. What a wit.

Wilde's Malone-Minto amalgam, though, was too enticing a notion to end up the same way as his anti-hero, Graham; and forty years later, Willie Hughes lived again, as a character in George Sylvester Viereck's *My First Two Thousand Years.* Here, the Wandering Jew meets Willie as he is playing the part of Juliet for the first production of *Romeo & Juliet* by the Chamberlain's Men. But Viereck did not share Wilde's bent, and so he turned the idea around, making Hughes a girl who is disguised as a boy in order to act in the theater. Viereck's Shakespeare—who duly dedicates his sonnets to his sweet Willie—willingly lets the "scandal" set tongues wagging although he knows the truth.

Thus was Shakespeare redeemed from the stain of sodomy, and the key to the sonnets given another unexpected twist. Viereck was another writer who took a personal delight in presenting a novel thesis under the canopy of fiction, and unlike Wilde, he left it at that. But such was the appeal of this simple idea—Mr W.H. really being Miss W.H., resolving all those concerns about Q20's "master-mistress" which had troubled Victorians deep into the night—that Willie demanded another revival.

As Gwynneth Paltrow, a.k.a. Lady Viola, the noble lady who yearns to be a lowly player, in the Hollywood blockbuster *Shakespeare in Love* (1998), he got his wish. Of course, scriptwriter Tom Stoppard, author of the daringly unoriginal *Rosencrantz and Guildenstern Are Dead,* was far too astute to make his debt to Viereck (and Wilde) obvious. Although Paltrow's character does at one point in the film receive Sonnet 18—the very sonnet that announces the Fair Youth sonnet-sequence—from the lovelorn young William, the connection between Stoppard's script and Viereck's premise is never acknowledged. In Hollywood, there was not going to be anything latent about the playwright's sexual leanings.

Wilde's whimsical novella marked a sea change in how many liberals viewed the sonnets—both challenging the homophobia that drove many a Victorian to champion the anti-personalist agenda, and finding that making fiction from "fact" was perhaps a sounder approach than making a fiction of the facts. The one strand of sonnet-speculation still left dangling in the wind, as they marched Wilde off to Reading gaol was that of the disintegrationists, for whom the order of the sonnets was the real riddle in need of unraveling.

CHAPTER EIGHT

1841–2007

"THE DIVISION AND SUMMING OF THE CHAPTERS"

*It is a sad day for a man when he becomes entangled...
in the problem of the order of Shakespeare's sonnets.
His happiness is departed; his mind is no longer his
own. He is in the condition of those who set them-
selves to work out a system of breaking the bank at
Monte Carlo.*
—*Times Literary Supplement,* NOVEMBER 26, 1925

*The division and summing of the Chapters was not of
[the poet's] doing, but adventured by the over-seer of
the print, for the more ease of the Readers.*
—WILLIAM PONSONBY, PREFACE TO SIR PHILIP
SIDNEY'S *Arcadia,* 1590

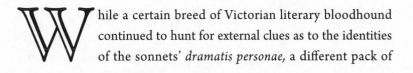hile a certain breed of Victorian literary bloodhound
continued to hunt for external clues as to the identities
of the sonnets' *dramatis personae,* a different pack of

culture-vultures turned to the sonnets themselves, hoping to pick apart evidence that had eluded all previous comers. Increasing in number as the external trail dried up, and as the battle-weary exponents-of-earls called a truce, these unsatiated souls endlessly reexamined the order and contents of Q itself.

The first "disintegrationist" to challenge the order as published was Charles Knight, who in 1841, six decades after Malone, published the sonnets within his eight-volume *Pictorial Edition of the Works of Shakspere.* As the son of a printer-bookseller, and a former journalist, Knight had set himself up as an independent publisher of almanacs, pictorial histories, and the like. Another of those amateur antiquarians the era effortlessly produced, Knight unambiguously asserted that Q was printed "without the cognizance of the author, [included] all the Sonnets which could be found attributed to Shakspere; [and therefore] some of these formed a group of continuous poems . . . some were detached . . . [but only] accident has arranged them in the form in which they first were handed down to us."

It was a necessary challenge to contemporary thinking, which had settled on Malone's implicit acceptance of Q as largely, if accidentally, authoritative. This Knight of the realm demanded an altogether more critical approach to the text as published. And though he refrained from printing the sonnets in the order he supposed correct, sticking to Q, his "preferred" order printed as an appendix represented a radical reorganization of Thorpe's, beginning with Q105–24, and ending with the very sonnet that began the Fair Youth sequence, Q18.

Compiling this edition when he was just starting his own, somewhat fanciful life of "Shakspere," Knight refrained from applying names and dates to his narrative, but nonetheless assigned most of the Fair Youth sonnets to a category he called "Confiding Friendship." He also, as Rollins wrote, "started a game that promises never to end. If our wives do not write novels . . . they are likely on no provocation at all to malarrange Shakespeare's lyrics."

Of the Victorian Shakespeareans, ladies and gentlemen alike, who examined the contents of Q anew, few followed Knight in addressing the history of Q itself. Most simply took up where Knight left off, dispensing with Thorpe's order in its entirety. Victor Hugo—who in his 1857 French translation recast the sonnets into seven parts to "reveal" a scandal involving Southampton, Shakespeare, and a married woman—accused Thorpe of being complicit in a conscious attempt to disguise the "real" story.

It was almost invariably Southamptonites who wanted to disintegrate Q, attempting, in Archer's choice phrase, "to explain away an improbability" through the art of reorganization. Of these, perhaps the most persistent was Gerald Massey, who divided the sonnets in his 1866 edition into twenty-five sections, primarily concerned with the relationships of Southampton, Elizabeth Vernon, and Shakespeare, save for the Dark Lady sonnets, which apparently addressed William Herbert's passion for Lady Rich! Six years later, Massey republished his edition with a new, snappier title, *The Secret Drama of Shakespeare's Sonnets Unfolded, with the Characters Identified.* But by 1888 he had rejected his original order, devising a largely new structure that still gave center stage to Southampton.

It took until 1904 for Charlotte Stopes to supersede Massey's twenty-five divisions. At least her twenty-seven sections, by her own admission, did not pretend "to better Shakespeare, but to find out what he means, and to get behind Thomas Thorpe." And, like Knight, she only offered her rearrangement as an appendix to her edition of Q. A Southamptonite in sheep's clothing, she wrapped her categories in generalities ("Personal Affection develops"; "After return sees the Lady"; "Gossip concerning Friend") that ended, happily, with the "Triumph of Love over Time."

But if Stopes was almost apologetic about the way she related the son-
nets' internal story to the life of the poet, she was a rare Southamptonite.
The year before her edition appeared, Arthur Acheson inflicted the first
of his fanciful impositions on events of the Elizabethan era, *Shakespeare
and the Rival Poet.* Over another two decades he honed his theories in the
vacuum-sealed world of A. Acheson. By 1922, when he published *Shake-
speare's Sonnet Story, 1592–1598,* this narrative totalled 676 pages, with a
chapter devoted to each of the seven books into which he reorganized
the sonnets. His motivation was betrayed by his subtitle: *Restoring the
Sonnets written to the Earl of Southampton to their original books and corre-
lating them with personal phases of the Plays of the Sonnet period; with docu-
mentary evidence identifying Mistress [Anne] Davenant as the Dark Lady.*

The oddity of the theory, though, need not directly correlate with the
kind of radical reorganization Acheson's ilk favored. For sheer eccen-
tricity, aligned with unswerving self-assurance, Samuel Butler's intro-
duction to his 1899 edition, in which he explained how he had
memorized the poems, then cut them out of his copy, and rearranged
them until he felt he had arrived at "their original order," probably takes
the cookie. And yet Butler's reorganization of the sonnets themselves
was hardly dramatic (1–32 and 63–138 he left entirely alone), believing
as he did that Q had "every appearance of having intentionally pre-
served the order in which the Sonnets were written. . . . For this mercy
we should be grateful, for had the order been irrecoverably disturbed
the Sonnets would have been a riddle beyond all reading."

Less intuitive souls preferred to examine the sonnets as published,
taking a more measured view, recognizing signs of both order and disor-
der in Q. Some even saw indications of authorial intent in the way cer-
tain sonnets were soldered together by word associations and rhymes.
Others proffered the possibility that Thorpe had published the material
"faithfully," but that it came to him already disorganized. Robert

Shindler, in an 1892 article, thought he recognized an intermediary process between author and publisher; hence, the "signs of continuity, [with] numbers which clearly stand together, but the breaks and gaps, the omissions and the wrong arrangements, are just as clear. . . . [Because] Thorpe . . . could only print the Sonnets just as they stood in his ms., those that . . . stood together he printed together, and so produced those traces of orderly arrangement which we see."

Beeching, too, in his intelligent 1904 edition, while generally accepting of the way the sonnets had been organized, suspected "some few are misplaced; 36–39, if they are rightly placed, do not explain their position; 75 would come better after 52; 77 and 81 interrupt the series on the Rival Poet." And E. K. Chambers concurred with his illustrious predecessor, suggesting, "The unity of the sonnets is [largely] one of atmosphere. The thread of incident is a frail one. Each sonnet is generally self-contained. A few are linked. . . . [But] there is occasionally a jar in the continuity, which may [well] suggest misplacement."

Another, more troublesome thesis threatened an alternative explanation for such breaks in continuity—the impositions of an impostor. After all, the logical outcome of a critical attitude to the order of Q was to doubt the actual contents of Q—as a fair few already had, casting scorn and doubt on the long narrative that occupied its end-sheets, "A Lover's Complaint." Those who began to doubt the authenticity of at least a handful of the sonnets were hardly confined to the outer fringes of Shakespeareans. J. W. Mackail—while mounting a solid case for Shakespeare's non-authorship of the long poem—threw in another suggestion as a footnote: "[Q]153 and 154 are pretty certainly not by Shakespeare, 128 and 145 are very doubtful, and a plausible case can be made out against 135, 136 and 143."

In fact, Q153 and 154 have proven particularly problematic to every Shakespearean who favors the order and contents of Q. Both patently derive from an epigram by Marianus Scholasticus, a lawyer poet from the sixth century, that was included in the so-called Palatine Anthology. Concerned with a myth about a sleeping Cupid whose torch is stolen by a virgin nymph, who quenches it in a cold well that becomes imbued with curative properties, the two sonnets—printed as one by Benson—serve as a highly curious coda to the (second) sequence. Malone felt that Shakespeare "hardly could have intended to send them both into the world," whereas Auden seized on their inclusion as proof of Q's unauthorized status: "Any writer with an audience in mind knows that a sequence of poems must climax with one of the best. Yet the sequence as we have it concludes with two of the worst of the sonnets, trivial conceits about, apparently, going to Bath to take the waters."

Even Duncan-Jones was obliged to address the anomalous position of these sonnets. Required to argue that they had been put there at Shakespeare's behest, she suggests that "several other authors used similar 'Anacreontic' [a long-winded synonym for 'erotic'] verses to divide off their collections of sonnets from the continuous lyric or complaint which followed." She does not, however, explain why Shakespeare should indulge in such overt repetition. Nor can she explain away the formulaic triteness with which "he" handles the "trivial conceits," or the lack of any obvious Shakespearean stamp to either lyric. Malone, equally disturbed by the use of "the very same thoughts differently versified," felt they must have been "early essays of the poet." Unfortunately for that theory, James Hutton demonstrated in 1941 that the earliest English translation of Scholasticus's Greek original was in 1603, which would place the poems at the tail-end of any credible composition-date—if they were Shakespeare's.

Alternatively, these could be stray sonnets, added as an epilogue at the conclusion of the two sonnet-sequences, as Dante Gabriel Rossetti suggested in his Recollections (1882). But if so, they must have been put there by a man with no poetic soul, such as Thomas Thorpe, which again serves to debunk the presumption, made increasingly often, that the 154 sonnets told a story, and that every lyric was part of a greater whole.

In large part, such a thesis was considered desirable because the other great sonnet-sequences of the period had an order to them, even if it was not readily apparent on its original, piratical publication, as was the case with Sidney's *Astrophil & Stella*. Indeed, disintegrationists of Q tended to treat Thorpe as another Newman. Yet many of the Elizabethan sonneteers were disintegrators of their own work. Drayton's *Ideas Mirrour* went through at least five revisions, and Daniel could not leave *Delia* alone, try as he might.

The literary legions were attempting to provide Thorpe's edition with something it appeared to be missing—evidence of the structural sophistication one would have expected of Shakespeare if he had intended to produce a publishable sonnet-sequence. It was this very absence of a clearly delineated order which convinced Auden that "the one hundred and fifty-four sonnets as we have them . . . are not in any kind of planned sequence. The only semblance of order is a division into two unequal heaps."

There remained something fundamentally unsatisfactory about Thorpe's sonnet-sequence which no reorganization could sate. Perhaps it was meant to be that way. A lesser poet, Denys Bray, writing between the wars, decided that these seemingly intractable problems bore all the marks of another Jacobethan disintegrationist: "In the end . . . [Shakespeare] broke the chain and disarranged the flowing whole, either in artistic dissatisfaction with it, or, more probably, to ensure that whatever the future had in store, the heart that he had unlocked in his own inner chamber should not lie exposed for daws to peck at."

Of course, Bray himself still managed to crack the code with a simple phonetic trick—"the mechanical coupling of sonnet to sonnet by

rhyme-link." As a result, he produced his own nine-tiered tower, totter-
ing between "Adoration" (I) and "The Dark Lady" (IX), with interme-
diate parts that included "Reproaches for the Breaking of a Twofold
Truth, Hers and His" and "Triumph of Love over Silence and Separa-
tion." It took E. K. Chambers to point out that Bray's strict reliance on
rhyme-links resulted in the loss of as many links as his method found:
"Intent upon his continuous chain of formal links, he has rent asunder
many sense-links . . . clearly apparent in Thorpe's text."

Thus did the rays of reason reenter the debating hall, but not for long.
Chambers had postulated a view, based on the evidence, that pointed to
an unauthorized text at least one remove from Shakespeare's autograph
copy(s). And that just wouldn't do. Nor was Rollins's titanic compilation
of every nuanced notion ever expended on the sonnets, which made up
volume two of his 1946 variorum edition, enough to still those who de-
manded Q be taken at face value. He had argued that "there can be no as-
surance [Q] represents with any degree of accuracy [the author's] own
classification of the poems. Yet exactly the opposite assumption . . . un-
derlies the arguments of most defenders of the existing order."

And in 1983, those "defenders of the existing order" found a new
champion in the shape of Katherine Duncan-Jones, a Cambridge pro-
fessor of English with a profound distaste for inconvenient truths. For
her, "The origins of the widespread belief that Q is unauthorized lie . . .
in deep anxieties felt by British scholars . . . in the aftermath of the infa-
mous 'Labouchere amendment' of 1885, which criminalized homosex-
ual acts between consenting adult males." Actually, the likes of Malone,
Hazlitt, and Knight had cast doubt on such a thesis long before
Labouchere laid down the law and Wilde got all profound.

Duncan-Jones certainly had her work cut out for her. Not only did
she have to rehabilitate the maverick Thorpe, recasting him as a misun-
derstood lover of literature, but she had to explain away every inconsis-

tency and oddity in the thin quarto of sonnets (and, as we have seen, these were not confined to the mere order in which they were published); the sloppy way the book was produced; and the lack of any authorial preface or dedication. Finally, she had to argue not only that the sequence was Shakespeare's, but that the long, labored narrative poem that appeared at the end of the volume—which was uncredited on the title page and had no Stationers' Company registration—was his, too.

Fortunately for this career academic, after a century and a half of disintegration the time seemed right for a spot of revisionist thinking. Rather than arguing about unresolvable issues of happenstance, academics returned to the poems themselves, treating them as an aesthetically satisfying unit of authorial integrity to which the full apparatus of New Criticism could be brought to bear. That it flew in the face of all logic—and the precious few facts—was an issue easily sidestepped with an "op. cit. Duncan-Jones."

Thus a serious scholar like Helen Vendler—by her own admission "inclined to believe Katherine Duncan-Jones's argument that the Sonnets may have been an authorized printing"—looking for symmetry in her superbly subjective *The Art of Shakespeare's Sonnets* (1997), found it. But even she knew that she must construct an explanation for the poems' "variation in aesthetic success" (or just plain badness). So she suggested "that some sonnets . . . were inserted *ad libitum* for publication." Quite how an artist as mature and measured as Shakespeare was in 1609 could have thought two parodic paeans to Cupid would be a good way to round things off, Vendler fails to address.

At least by steering well clear of "A Lover's Complaint," Vendler concentrated on a set of unequivocally Shakespearean poems. Duncan-Jones proved less discriminating. Having been commissioned to edit an Arden edition of the sonnets on the back of her disconcertingly influential 1983 article—"Was the 1609 *Shake-speares Sonnets* Really

Unauthorized?"—she elected to include "A Lover's Complaint." Her new edition was published ahead of Vendler's monumental critique.

By the time Duncan-Jones gave her endorsement to this "sensuous poem with an astonishingly complex narrative structure," the tide had truly turned. Indeed, it was sometimes hard to remember that William Hazlitt, the dean of literary criticism, had proclaimed his doubts about the poem's authenticity 180 years before this, and that it had been largely disparaged or disregarded ever since. Even when the likes of Lee and Mackail examined the language of this long poem, during the Edwardian Indian summer which ushered in a new age, they found little worth lingering upon.

Lee was utterly dismissive, describing its tone as too conventional, its language strained, while "the far-fetched imagery exaggerates the worst defects of Shakespeare's *Lucrece*, [while] a very large number of words which are employed in the poem are found nowhere else in Shakespeare's work. Some of these seem invented for the occasion to cover incapacity of expression. The attribution . . . to Shakespeare may well be disputed. It was probably . . . circulated like the sonnets in written copies, and was assigned to Shakespeare by an enterprising transcriber." Two years later, G. W. Hadow similarly struggled to get past "the strangeness of the vocabulary," and he rejected it from his own edition of the sonnets.

By 1912, J. W. Mackail had decided to examine the poem thoroughly to see if it genuinely bore the stamp of Shakespeare. He forced himself to get beyond his first, damning impression "that this [poem] is highly mannered, and that the mannerism is not daring or even inventive, but rather laboured and tortuous." His next observation immediately moved the debate forward. "A Lover's Complaint," he said, "is not the work of a beginner. Its style, alike in its good and its bad points, is formed and even matured. . . . It is either a work of his later and matured period, or not a work of his at all." Placing the poem in the seventeenth century put an even greater strain on those who wanted it to be William's, but it was hard to argue with Mackail's reasoning (no one on either side of the fence ever has).

Tackling, in order, the vocabulary, syntax, and phrasing of the poem, Mackail posited a thesis disturbing to the poem's few advocates: "What we do find habitually is a forcing of phrase, which follows a fashion of the period, but follows it as a servant, does not sway it as a master. Sometimes this forcing of phrase appears due to pedantry, to the artificiality of a contracted and ill-digested scholarship; sometimes to mere clumsiness, what Lee aptly calls incapacity of expression."

Rather than arguing that the poem was simply not "Shakespearean," Mackail methodically moved toward a thesis that the poem was conceived as self-consciously "Shakespearean" in an act "of what may be called stylistic impersonation." Unable to reconcile the highs and lows of diction and insight in "A Lover's Complaint" with an artist at the height of his artistic powers, he decided it was "easier to believe that a rival poet could catch, here and there, some reflection of Shakespeare's genius, than to believe that Shakespeare would deliberately and with no visible reason write down to the level of a rival's style."

It was a brilliant analysis, and—as we saw in Chapter 4—it held the critical consensus for fully fifty years. But, as we know, rarely do things stay in stasis in the world of Shakespearean studies. By 1964–65, it was no longer enough to suggest that "A Lover's Complaint" was too god-awful to be part of the canon. MacDonald P. Jackson and Kenneth Muir, on opposite sides of the world, set about challenging Mackail's attribution of the poem to "a rival poet."

Muir went first, focusing on the "Shakespearean" nature of the poem's language. But it was New Zealand scholar Jackson who really made the case for this "Complaint" as the work of William—and, in keeping with most Shakespearean scholars who have built their arguments on linguistic quicksand, he did so unequivocally: "The large number of new words, the nature of these coinages, and the many links with the verbal habits of Shakespeare's middle and late periods point unmistakably to Shakespearian authorship at a date that can scarcely be earlier than 1600." Even his few qualifications, such as, "I do not for a moment suppose that parallel passages necessarily imply identity of authorship," are promptly requalified in favor of his thesis: "But the ease with which parallels between 'A Lover's Complaint' and the whole range of the Shakespearean canon may be found makes Shakespeare's responsibility for the poem the simplest hypothesis."

No one had told Jackson that the "simplest hypothesis" need not necessarily be the most persuasive. And so Jackson went out of his way to sidestep Mackail's central conclusion—that the author of "A Lover's Complaint" was trying to emulate and imitate Shakespeare—even though these "parallel passages" fit his thesis just as easily as they did Jackson's. Belatedly, Jackson realized this. And so, in 2004, he set out to make a second, more persuasive case for Shakespeare's authorship, which did address other claimants, and even took account of the publishing history of Q.

In the interim, there had been dissenting voices, albeit ones that were largely drowned out by the considerable clout that Duncan-Jones and Kerrigan carried. In 1992, John Roe described the poem as "a good deal less readable, artistically less assured, than Shakespeare's other verse narratives," but still paid lip service to the New Consensus by including it in his Cambridge University Press edition of the *Poems*.

Meanwhile, nascent technological advances had started to challenge these "authorial" advocates. In 1987, Russian scholar Marina Tarlinskaja had run a series of sophisticated computer tests based on "quantitative prosody," using the canonical plays and the poems of Shakespeare, and decisively rejected his authorship of the "Complaint." A decade later, the poem's diction was again tackled by linguistic technicians Ward Elliott and Robert Valenza, who "applied to the poem a series of stylometric tests which had been validated in previous research into Shakespeare's poems" [BV]. Fourteen stylometric tests were found to be usable on both the plays and the poems, and none of the 3,000 word blocks of text that were undisputedly Shakespearean failed more than two of them. Most failed none. "A Lover's Complaint" failed six of them.

It was in such a climate that Jackson set out to restore the poem's reputation, and his own, in an article for the 2004 *Shakespeare Studies* (published in the fall of 2003). In the intervening period, presumably under the influence of advocates like John Kerrigan, who in 1991 devoted an entire volume to the poem, Jackson's opinion of the poem's qualities had come on in leaps and bounds. Back in 1964, he had owned up to the poem's "numerous defects" and admitted that the treatment itself was "hackneyed." Now he thought that, "at its best," the poem was "very fine." Not only was the "Complaint" an "adaptation of Shakespeare's most condensed mature style to nondramatic poetry," but it had apparently been conceived as "the third movement in a sonata-like structure" within Q, which "preserves Shakespeare's own arrangement of his sonnets."

In this brave new world, Jackson used the familiar "op. cit." to suggest that the debate about Q's authorized status was all but done and dusted. Recognizing that "a spurious 'A Lover's Complaint' would undermine trust in Thorpe's volume; [whereas] a Shakespearean 'A Lover's Complaint' tends to authenticate it," he examined the phraseology of every Jacobethan playwright in the Chadwyck-Healy LiOn (Literature Online) database, with specific emphasis on George Chapman, the one candidate advocated by those who accepted Mackail's thesis (principally by John Robertson in his 1917 tome, *Shakespeare and Chapman: A Thesis on Chapman's Authorship of 'A Lover's Complaint'*).

What Jackson found was what he expected to find, that the "phrasal links to plays of 1590–1610 are . . . overwhelmingly with Shakespeare," at the expense of the likes of Chapman, Jonson, Marston, and Heywood, whose combined score amounted to barely half of Shakespeare's. Having seemingly closed the door on further debate, Jackson concluded that "unless . . . some alternative candidate . . . shows even more points of contact with the poem . . . Thorpe's unambiguous ascription should stand."

But barely had Jackson put down his laptop, when another expert in authorship studies, Professor Brian Vickers, began to voice concerns about Jackson's methodology. Fresh from flattening another Thorpe-authenticated text fleetingly attributed to Shakespeare (in *Counterfeiting Shakespeare: Evidence, Authorship and John Ford's Funerall Elegye* [2001]), Vickers preferred to refer to a different aspect of the same database, *English Poetry 900–1900*. He was looking for rival poets, not fellow playwrights. Picking three odd words and two peculiar phrases that appear in the "Complaint," but nowhere (else) in Shakespeare—"maund," "forbod," "affectedly," "rocky heart," and "fell rage"—he found just one (other) contemporary writer who had used all five expressions: John Davies of Hereford.

As Davies' entry in the most up-to-date *Dictionary of National Biography (DNB)* makes clear, this "writing-master" was "one of the most voluminous didactic poets of the age; he was also one of the most tedious." The idea that he was also the author of "an astonishingly complex narrative structure" like "A Lover's Complaint" seemed, on the face of it, faintly risible. But, thanks to the magnificent work of the Reverend Alexander Grossart, who had edited a number of subscriber-only volumes of poetry by Shakespeare's contemporaries in the late Victorian era, Davies' collected works had been preserved in a two-volume edition (utilized by Chadwyck-Healy); and because Davies was nothing if not prolific, Vickers now had a lot to work with.

Wasting no time, Vickers announced his initial conclusions, and essential thesis, in an article in the *Times Literary Supplement* in December 2003. He set out to remind his fellow Shakespeareans that the text is the thing, and that "the issue can only be decided on the internal evidence, since the single external witness, Thomas Thorpe, is notoriously unreliable." A lot more comfortable analyzing the written word than investigating the interactions of the Jacobean literary community, Vickers preferred to posit that "in an age of intense copying and circulating of poetry, manuscripts of Davies's work could easily have become mixed up with Shakespeare's."

Even after previous demolitions of false attributions, Vickers knew that his fellow Shakespearean scholars would take a lot of convincing, especially those with entrenched positions. Professor Duncan-Jones quickly reminded readers of a popular Shakespeare blog[!] that "on the case for the Sonnets as an authorized publication, I first argued for this, with a good deal of evidence [*sic*], in a longish article in *The Review of English Studies* as long ago as 1983. I also gave evidence for the inclusion of 'A Lover's Complaint' as a designed part of the whole." Actually, her entire thesis was tethered to the authenticity of this poem, which she saw as forming "part of the same structural unit as the Sonnets." It would take a lot more than mere evidence to get a *mea culpa* here.

It took Vickers until 2007 to fulfill his self-imposed brief, but he finally delivered an impressive 330-page case study in attribution and authorship issues, *Shakespeare, A Lover's Complaint and John Davies of Hereford.* His case, though, differed little from the one outlined in the *TLS;* only the weight of evidence he now summoned to bolster the argument

had changed. And he still spent just six pages directly addressing the is-
sue of how the poem had ended up in Q, even though Mackail had
thought the problem of attribution intrinsically bound up with "the
problem of the Sonnets, and more particularly, that part of the problem
which deals with the way in which they reached Thorpe's hands . . . and
the circumstances of their publication."

Vickers preferred to look at Davies' chameleon-like capacity to as-
sume other poetic styles, arguing that his "ability to imitate other poets'
voices as easily as he could write many different hands . . . makes it im-
possible to define his own 'normal' verse style." This was an important
part of his thesis because there were no other examples in Davies' volu-
minous *ouevre* of him either attempting a narrative poem in the "female
complaint" genre, or using the rhyme-royal favored by Shakespeare.

At his side, he had not just Grossart's edition of Davies' work, but also
the Victorian prelate's detailed introduction, in which he championed
the relative worth of Davies' output. Admitting that Davies "occasion-
ally potters among the dust and chaff when he should soar," Grossart
also found "luminous flashes and sudden darts of insight and real
'singing,' not saying." There was one characteristic of this part-time poet
that Grossart was especially keen to emphasize: his capacity for "terse,
compacted couplets, stanzas, half-stanzas, lines and half-lines, which . . .
cleave to the memory."

Imagery that soars high and sinks low was one characteristic of the
"Complaint" that had been drawing comment since the days of Malone
and Steevens (the latter explicitly doubted that Shakespeare would use a
formulaic phrase like "forme receive" not once, but twice, for the sake of
a rhyme [lines 239/41; 306–7]). It was also a concern of Grossart's
friend Algernon Swinburne, the poet, who felt that "A Lover's Com-
plaint" "contains two of the most exquisitely Shakespearean verses ever
vouchsafed to us by Shakespeare, and two of the most execrably eu-

phuistic or dysphuistic lines ever inflicted on us by man." (Advocates of the poem's authenticity often quote the former, rarely the latter part of the poet's critique.)

Swinburne was in the rare position of knowing something of Davies' works, being among the hundred subscribers to Grossart's 1878 edition,[15] though he perhaps never made it all the way through the dust and chaff. But he probably made it through his friend's lengthy Preface, in which the reverend unwittingly highlighted Davies' tendency to appropriate his imagery from his betters. In quoting one of Davies' "surpassingly fine and pathetic metaphor[s]"—"my Ship, through Fate's crosse waue / Now grates vpon the Grauell of my Graue"—Grossart promptly realized that it had already been put to superior use by martyred poet Robert Southwell, in "The full of your spring-tide is now fallen, and the stream of your life waneth to a low ebb; your tired bark beginneth to leak, and grateth oft upon the gravel of the grave."

This is precisely the kind of "phrasal resemblance"—to use Jackson's choice phrase—that the "Complaint" poet reapplied to Shakespeare's plays. Jackson cites a number of them, but one example will suffice. To him, "the grounds and motives of her woe" [line 63] is an irresistible reminder of Hamlet's words, "the motive and the cue for passion." Unfortunately, it has none of its acuity. Nor were these phrasal resemblances confined to the plays. Jackson also found parallels in the sonnets themselves, a fact which had led Mackail to suppose, a century ago, "that if the author of 'A Lover's Complaint' was not the author of the sonnets, he had read them, or some of them, when he wrote the poem." The significance of this supposition, if it could be supported by the facts, was not immediately apparent.

The intractable problem for any advocate of authenticity is the sheer clumsiness with which the author of "A Lover's Complaint" sometimes executes his exercise in obfuscation. As Vickers persuasively argues,

"Shakespeare's affinities were with Sidney, Daniel and Drayton, whose syntax was much closer to the 'playne and easye composition' desired by Thomas Wilson" than the poet responsible for this rhyming narrative.

In fact, the "Complaint" poet's way with words more closely resembles Grossart's depiction of Davies, whose vocabulary, "if not marked by culture, is suggestive of considerable and out-o'-the-way reading. . . . Some of his words—since worn and familiar—flash out finely, e.g. translucent, refulgent, purple, diaphanal, accloy, adamantine, attone, coact, empery, and abundant others." Unfortunately, Davies was equally inclined to make neologisms for novelty's sake, or to satisfy a rhyme. In one attributed poem, he rhymed the word "gander" with "wander," then added in the margin, "for the Rime's necessity."

Paucity of imagination is not a flaw one would usually lay at Shakespeare's door. And yet, when, at the end of line 297, the "Complainer" needs a rhyme for "craft," he made the past tense of "doff" (as in "to doff a cap") into "daffed," which is plain daft. Vickers cites "another [such] enforced neologism when recording the woman's self-defence of having capitulated to her tempter—'Who young and simple would not be so loverd'—the rhyme scheme he had chosen [having] already given him 'coverd' and 'hoverd.'" It would be one thing to accuse the Midlander of having little Latin or Greek, another to suggest that Shakespeare could ever have stooped so low with the language he used better than anyone before or since.

Rhymes are a constant minefield to the man behind this curious "Complaint." Rather than displaying the fluidity of a man who had two dozen powerful plays, a couple of accomplished narrative poems, and a complex sonnet-sequence under his belt, this anonymous *auteur* uses a cliched triple rhyme like wind/find/minde (86–89) (and, as Vickers points out, exactly the same rhyme occurs in Davies's *Humours Heav'n on Earth*); while in another stanza, he is "forced to use a rhyme-word twice, 'takes,' 'makes,' 'takes' (107–10)." He also recycles rhymes like the world is running out of words. Find/minde (88–89) turns up again less than fifty lines later, as mind/find (135/137), and within a further fifty lines, again as mind/find (184/187).

As Vickers tellingly observes, the "Complaint" poet "displays a lack of invention of which . . . Shakespeare was never guilty." And yet, when he published his verified view in the summer of 2007, he found no shortage of dissenters. In the *TLS,* the role of reviewer devolved to Harold Love, author of *The Culture and Commerce of Texts: Scribal Publication in 17th Century England,* an ideal recipient. And Love partly embraced Vickers's thesis, feeling convinced "personally that Shakespeare was not the author of the Complaint," but he felt there was something missing, something the author could have found in Mackail if he'd looked closely enough: "Internal evidence of the kind that is given pride of place in this study should ideally be supplemented by external evidence; but here there is still much uncertainty. In order to establish his case, Vickers [really] has . . . to revisit the publishing history of the Sonnets."

A wise old bird, Love had nailed the one hole in Vickers's thesis. In fact, Vickers had stopped short of the one supposition that could have led him where he needed to go, even when briefly revisiting "the publishing history of the Sonnets" in the six pages he devoted to "Thomas Thorpe and the 1609 *Sonnets.*" Rather than expending much of his undoubted brain-power on how "A Lover's Complaint" ended up in Q, Vickers posited four possible scenarios, three of which made Thorpe culpable in some way for misleading his readers:

> Given the vast flood of poetry in circulation at any time, honest mistakes could and did occur . . . but several other scenarios are possible. (1) Thorpe did not know the author of the poem, but added Shakespeare's name. . . . (2) The manuscript that reached

Thorpe was written in the same hand as the Sonnets, so Thorpe concluded that the Complaint was also by Shakespeare. (If so, why was it not mentioned either in the Stationers' Register or on the title page?) (3) Thorpe knew that the Complaint was by John Davies of Hereford, but . . . substituted a more famous name. (4) Thorpe . . . knew Davies and actually commissioned the poem from him in order to round off his volume. Honoured by the invitation, Davies obliged, adopting the stanza form of . . . *The Rape of Lucrece,* and trying to adopt a Shakespearean idiom.

But there was a fifth possibility that Vickers failed to consider, one which could provide the kind of "external evidence" needed to turn a mere possibility into a strong probability. Perhaps Thorpe was an innocent dupe and it was John Davies of Hereford who *deliberately* passed the poem off as Shakespeare's, deceiving the publisher, who took the poem at face value because it came from the very same "source" who had provided him with the sonnets. Indeed, the manuscript that reached Thorpe may well have been written in the same hand as the sonnets that he had (probably already) received precisely because it was Davies who wrote "A Lover's Complaint," though only after first copying out his favorite poet's sonnets, which he'd acquired some time ago.

CHAPTER NINE

2007–2008

"TOO WORTHIE FOR A COUNTERFEIT?"

I, desirous to delighte each minde,
Haue made an hotch-potch heere, of euery kinde.
—JOHN DAVIES OF HEREFORD,
Scourge of Folly, 1611

If the author of A Lover's Complaint *was not the*
author of the Sonnets, he had read them, or some of
them, when he wrote the poem.
—J. W. MACKAIL, 1912

We would have to assume . . . that he had read them
in manuscript. This is not impossible, but . . . there are
virtually insurmountable obstacles to believing in
such a Shakespearean imitator.
—MACDONALD P. JACKSON, 1965

The rebuttal to Vickers's views came soon enough, and from a not entirely unexpected quarter. Duncan-Jones was given two and a half columns in the *TLS*, a fortnight after Love's review appeared, to mount her counteroffensive. She did so by firing off a series of questions, all presumably unanswerable. Naturally, she threw in the odd red herring: a claim that "Thorpe was doing careful work for . . . Jonson," when their association had already ceased; and that Thorpe had no reason to "risk the wrath of" Shakespeare by publishing something under his name that was not by him—i.e., exactly what Jaggard, Pavier, and Eld had previously done without the slightest repercussion. But it was her three main charges that were designed to stymie the non-attributionists once and for all:

> [i] If someone other than Shakespeare penned the Complaint, how did that person come to be deeply familiar with the as yet unpublished Sonnets, with which the Complaint has numerous thematic and verbal links? . . . [ii] What possible motive could [Thorpe] have had for appending an inauthentic item to Shakespeare's long-awaited Sonnets, a collection already of sufficient length? . . . And to dally momentarily with unnecessary surmise, why should John Davies of Hereford have penned such a poem? Though prolific, Davies was not celebrated for the genre of "female complaint." Shakespeare was, both in his dramatic and nondramatic writings. [iii] And even though Davies's cultural networks were extensive, they do not appear to have included Thomas Thorpe.

The answer to her first challenge was simple enough—Davies had indeed read the sonnets in manuscript. Not only were there no "insurmountable obstacles" to such a premise, but there is growing evidence that the reading of fellow writers' work in manuscript verged on the norm in Jacobean London. And the one type of work we know for a fact Shakespeare passed around privately were his "sugred sonnets." As for Davies, Vickers had already addressed the issue of his connections, clearly and lucidly: "As a hard-working scribe moving in London literary and theatrical circles, Davies was well situated to take part in the copying and exchanging of manuscripts which played such a large part in English Renaissance culture.... [And certain] debts [in his own poems] suggest that Davies had access to Shakespeare's Sonnets in manuscript, not an unlikely suggestion given ... the contacts he seems to have cultivated with other literary figures."

Those contacts were extremely wide-ranging, intersecting with Shakespeare's literary contemporaries and his circle of patronage at every turn. Davies was a networker par excellence. Those writers and potential patrons he didn't know personally, he knew all about; and Shakespeare was no exception. In fact, Davies appears to have been something of a life-long fan, precisely the sort of "other poet [who] steeped himself in Shakespeare's poems and sonnets" whom Kenneth Muir had failed to find, thus attributing the "Complaint" to a Shakespeare who simply "wrote a poem with a number of feeble lines."

When, in 2004, Jackson still doubted the existence of "a non-Shakespearean poet writing in deliberate response to [the sonnets, because] the mind of such a man [would have] to be saturated with the phraseology and diction of Shakespeare's plays," he had not even considered the candidacy of Davies. And yet, obscure as Davies deservedly became, he did publish a still-famous epigram "To our English Terence Mr. Will: Shake-speare" (note the hyphen—as per Q) a year after the Sonnets' appearance:

> SOME say good Will (which I, in sport, do sing)
> Had'st thou not plaid some Kingly parts in sport,

> *Thou hadst bin a companion for a King;*
> *And, beene a King among the meaner sort.*
> *Some others raile; but raile as they thinke fit,*
> *Thou hast no rayling, but, a raigning Wit:*
> *And honesty thou sow'st, which they do reape;*
> *So, to increase their Stocke which they do keepe.*

Actually, allusions to Shakespeare, direct and indirect, come thick and fast
in Davies' canon. In a 546-line poetic satire he appended to *The Scourge of
Folly* (1611), he again acknowledged the man's greatness, while admon-
ishing him for "making lewd Venus, with eternall Lines, / To tye Adonis
to her loues designes: / Fine wit is shew'n therein: but finer twere / If not
attired in such bawdy Geare." Like the "Complaint" poet, Davies became
something of a prude, imagining that with a little decorum he might im-
prove on Shakespeare's model. He certainly would have approved of the
winsome couplet in "A Lover's Complaint" (ll. 146–47), in which the
brute takes her virtue: "Threw my affections in his charmed power, / Re-
serv'd the stalke and gave him al my flower." Here, writ small, was the po-
etic equivalent of those B-movie scenes where crashing waves serve as a
coquettish visual metaphor for the act of lovemaking.

Davies' love of Shakespeare's work must have been mighty strong if
he was prepared to visit those theatrical dens of iniquity, to see his
plays—and him perform—which he explicitly says he did, and probably
quite often. In his second published collection, *Microcosmos* (1603),
Davies sought to contrast the worth of what Shakespeare and his men
produced with baser elements of the theaters, on which he had already
expended four bilious verses:

> *Players, I loue yee, and your Qualitie,*
> *As ye are Men, that passtime not abus'd :*

And some I loue for painting, poesie,

And say fell Fortune cannot be excus'd,

That hath for better uses you refus'd :

Wit, Courage, goodshape, good partes, and all good,

As long as al these goods are no worse us'd,

And though the stage doth staine pure gentle bloud.

Yet generous yee are in minde and moode.

He expels any doubt that he is referring to the King's Men by one of his marginal notes, where the initials W.S.R.B. are etched alongside the third line, i.e., William Shakespeare and the actor Richard Burbage (who fancied himself a painter). He repeats these initials in a note to a later poem on "Fortune." What is less clear is whether Davies and Shakespeare had a direct relationship. Vickers doubts there was anything stronger than a passing acquaintance, noting that although Davies "celebrated in verse Sidney, Donne, Drayton, Shakespeare, Marston, [only] Drayton reciprocated, so Davies was probably a hanger-on in these circles."

The one piece of evidence that suggests more than a passing acquaintance was mentioned by Grossart in the introduction to his 1878 edition of Davies' poetry, where he interprets lines from "Speculum Proditori" (1616) as referring to an earlier depiction of Shakespeare as someone who "plaid some Kingly parts in sport." In the epigram in question, Davies claims he "knew a Man, unworthy as I am, / And yet too worthie for a counterfeit, / Made once a king . . . " The choice of "knew," at a time when Shakespeare had retired to Stratford, implies a direct association.

Those with long memories may also recall that, before Grossart published his edition of the work, a certain Henry Brown had advocated Davies as a potential "rival poet," though not as the "better spirit" Shakespeare had railed against in the sonnets (Q78–86). Katharine M. Wilson, in *Shakespeare's Sugared Sonnets* (1974), also thought Shakespeare was parodying one of the "amorous" sonnets (XXIV) that form the first section of Davies' *Wittes Pilgrimage* (1605) in Q151 ("Love is too young to know what conscience is"). She also speculated that in Q148 he was mocking imagery that Davies had adopted at the end of his sonnet XXII (where he is "blinded by the light of his lady's sun"). The two lines in Q148 are: "The sun itself sees not, till heaven clears / Oh cunning love, with tears thou keep'st me blind."

At no point does Wilson consider the possibility that the direction of the debt went from Shakespeare to Davies, and that far from parodying his predecessor, Davies was attempting to emulate him. That could only have happened if he had, at the very least, secured a copy of the Dark Lady sonnets. This is hardly impossible. There is an obvious connection, one that could well put Davies in the frame for partial Rival Poet status (even if Jonathan Bate stretches the textual meaning to breaking point in his new life of Shakespeare). Davies had close connections with the Pembroke family—so strong that, Grossart argues, the Pembrokes "were evidently more than mere patrons." "In many a Sonnet," the editor points out, "he addresses parents and children alike in unembarrassed and familiar terms."

The first time Davies' credentials as a writing-master crop up are in 1599, when he was at Wilton, working on a presentation copy of *The Psalms* of David for Queen Elizabeth at the behest of the countess. And then, when he makes it to London and publishes his first set of poems, *Mirum in Modum* (1602), he dedicates it "To the most noble, judicious, and my best beloued Lorde, William Earle of Pembrooke," to whom he will also later dedicate *A Select Second Husband for Sir Thomas Overburie's Wife.* Meanwhile, William's brother, Phillip, would receive the dedication for *Wittes Pilgrimage,* while William and his mother got their own, obsequious poems in the collection itself. There is even a distinct possibility that Davies taught William Herbert the art of writing, as he later did Lord Percy's son.

But the younger Herberts would hardly have provided Davies with his only opportunity to access any privately circulating poems of the playwright making the rounds of potential patrons. Personal references, epigrams, and dedications to the likes of Sir Philip Sidney, Pembroke, Montgomery, Essex, Southampton, Lady Rich, Sir Thomas Lucy, Lord Percy, and Alice, Countess of Derby litter Davies' published works. And through the Pembroke circle of patronage, in particular, he made several important literary contacts. According to Brian Vickers: "Of the poets and dramatists patronized by William Herbert and Mary, Countess of Pembroke, Davies addressed epigrams 'to my worthily disposed friend' Samuel Daniel, 'to my well-accomplished friend' Ben Jonson, and 'To myne honest and loving friend Mr Michaell Drayton.'"

Through Drayton, Davies extended his tendrils further still, attaching himself to another important Jacobean playwright, Francis Beaumont, and the acerbic poet George Wither, whose dedication to *Abuses Stript and Whipt* (1613) seemed to send up Thorpe's own in Q. If his contacts were wide, his interest in literary contemporaries knew no bounds. George Chapman was one such figure to whom he dedicated a poem, though he admitted, "I know thee not (good George) but by thy pen." In fact, as the entry on Davies in the *DNB* avers, "He addresses many of the 292 epigrams [in *The Scourge of Folly* (1610)] to the greatest writers ... of the period: Francis Bacon, Sir John Davies, Fulke Greville, Thomas Campion, Samuel Daniel, Ben Jonson, William Shakespeare, John Fletcher, John Marston . . . Francis Beaumont, Michael Drayton and George Chapman."

However, as Duncan-Jones likes to reminds us, "Even though Davies's cultural networks were extensive, they do not appear to have included Thomas Thorpe." Well, if his "cultural networks" didn't extend there, they came pretty damn close. In fact, it would be incredible if he did not know Thorpe. Unlike Shakespeare—who had no documented contacts in publishing, save the still-active master-printer Richard Field, but still apparently alighted on the obscure, impoverished publisher Thorpe as the perfect publisher for his "sugred sonnets"—Davies was known to a bewildering retinue of publishers and printers.

Of the four stationers who had a hand in Q, Davies definitely knew and worked with three of them. He had known William Aspley since at least 1602, when the bookseller shared the act of publishing Davies' first collection, *Mirum in Modum,* while George Eld and John Wright actually worked in tandem to produce Davies' *The Muses Teares* (1613). The lad from Hereford had even worked with the brigand William Jaggard, who printed and published *Summa Totalis* in 1607. In any given period, at every turn, we find associations between "publishers of Shakespeare" and John Davies of Hereford. At the very least, we can probably assume he took advantage of these associates to acquire the many Shakespeare quartos, good and bad, that rolled off Jacobean printing presses (Vickers puts the total at forty-nine by 1609, comprising some fifteen plays, including *Hamlet* and *King Lear*).

Clearly, the "Complaint" poet, if he was not the author of these plays, had access to many of these quartos. And yet it is a large part of Jackson's thesis that such a thorough knowledge of Shakespeare's plays—in particular the Jacobean tragedies—was almost inconceivable from any contemporary figure save the author, even though half the plays of the period appeared in quarto form. The most problematic of these—for both sides—is *Pericles,* which was registered to Thorpe's old friend Edward Blount in May 1608, but did not appear in print until the following year, and then under the imprint of Henry Gosson.

And yet, in "A Lover's Complaint," there are three distinctive expressions that are found also in *Pericles,* one of which the "Complaint" author alludes to quite self-consciously. The use of "sister" as a verb and "rubied" as an adjective might suggest either common authorship or "stylistic impersonation," but would Shakespeare really have used the collocation "sleided silk" twice within such a short period? One of two possibilities thus arises: that the "Complaint" poet was either Shakespeare, or someone who had seen a text of *Pericles* ahead of Gosson's edition. Perhaps from Blount? Or, why not in transit to Blount?

Lest we forget, Davies' contemporary renown centered on his credentials as a "writing master," not as a poet. This aptitude would have been known to any printer, scrivener, or publisher, and may even, in times of financial stringency, have led Davies to use his gift for writing lucidly and with alacrity on a publisher's behalf. One line of inquiry that has gone unexplored is the possibility that Davies was himself a producer of "stolen reports"—the oral transcripts of plays to which most "bad" quartos and some "good" ones have been attributed. We know that Davies was a frequenter of the plays of Shakespeare, and presumably those of other contemporaries, and that he had an abiding interest in the playwright's art. We also know that he had a great facility (renowned throughout the land) for speed-writing. And we know that the author of "A Lover's Complaint" repeatedly used words undocumented outside the remit of a Shakespeare play (the nub of both Jackson's and Muir's theses).

And at the precise period we are addressing, there were two surprisingly good quartos of recent Shakespeare plays that nevertheless appear to have originated not from "foul papers" or "play scripts" but from "stolen reports": *King Lear* and *Pericles*. Both quartos are very similar in their presentation—often drifting into prose when the rhythms of blank verse have been lost—and both suggest "a report, possibly with the aid of shorthand" [EKC]. The art of shorthand was a relatively new science, dating to Timothy Bright's 1588 volume, *Characterie; An Arte of Shorte,*

Swifte and Secrete Writing by Character. But it would surely have been beholden to a writing-master to know its rudiments.

Pericles was actually registered to Edward Blount on the same day as *Antony & Cleopatra*—another play the "Complaint" poet appears to have known, given his use of the word "pelleted "(l. 18), meaning formed of water, a usage known only from that particular play and poem. Yet no published text of *Pericles* appeared ahead of Q.[16] Nor did Blount end up publishing either play, or asserting his copyright, though the previously unpublished First Folio text of *Antony & Cleopatra,* which contains its fair share of verbal corruptions, may well have come directly from Blount (who was a junior member of the syndicate responsible).

Just why Blount surrendered *Pericles* to Gosson, and refrained from publishing *Antony & Cleopatra,* is unclear. Most likely, he was bought off—just as James Roberts had been back in 1603, when the King's Men began to be proactive about protecting their plays. But if Blount knew Davies, he would be the fourth potential conduit to Thorpe within Davies' wide circle of publishing contacts.

Davies also had another potential connection to Thorpe. They were both members of a club whose membership dare not speak its name: Each was a Catholic. In Davies' case, we know this because of a passing comment made by one of his pupils, Arthur Wilson, whose memoir later appeared in Francis Peck's *Desiderata Curiosa* (1732–35). In it, Wilson wrote of a time when he "could not write the Court and Chancerie hands. So my father left me for halfe a year (this was about 1611) with Mr. John Davies, in Fleet Street (the most famous writer of his time) to learne those hands. Who, being also a Papist . . . gave growth to my opinions."

Thorpe's religious leanings remained a secret for a while longer. Only in 1963 did Albert J. Loomie publish the findings of a May 1597 *inquisition post mortem* into the affairs of Sir Francis Englefield, who had died the previous year in Spain. A Thomas Thorpe, identified as a "stationer," testified at the inquest that he had been at "Englefield's house in Madrid" at the time, "by the meanes of Father Parsons," presumably the well-known Jesuit Robert Parsons. As J. W. Bennett concludes, "The testimony of the inquisition . . . strongly suggests that Thorpe was a Catholic and that he was in the employ of the English government, [which] would explain why, in his old age, he found asylum in the royal almshouse at Ewelme."

Thorpe and Davies also seem to have shared another common experience—the ongoing struggle to make ends meet. As the *DNB* records, "If his incessant complaints are to be trusted, Davies was not richly rewarded for his teaching." Those complaints reached a crescendo the year before Q's appearance. When a tax-assessment in 1608 seemed somewhat at odds with his true net worth—assessed at £10 "in lands," whereas Davies claimed it was closer to £3—he used one of his powerful friends, Lord Ellesmere, to pull some strings on his behalf (successfully, it would appear, because the assessment was reduced from 26/8d to 5/-).

Davies subsequently sent Ellesmere a copy of his latest tome, *The Holy Roode* (1609), as a thank-you gift, along with a letter acknowledging his help. He also later published a poem on the subject, in *Scourge of Folly*, which proclaimed, "Had they weigh'd my gaines in commonsence / They might have weigh'd my purse but not my pence." To such a man, a few pounds for a scribal copy of somebody else's poems might have been awfully tempting. At least, it would have been prior to February 6, 1609, when his wide circle of patronage again paid dividends, and he began to tutor the young Lord Percy "to write, for a year," for which he received the altogether more princely sum of £20. By then, Thorpe had presumably secured his manuscript, and was in the process of raising the costs of printing it. Davies, meanwhile, had poems of his own to produce, perhaps including one he now slipped to Thorpe as the work of William Shakespeare.

With such a penchant for pastiche, and a keen admiration for more praised peers, one would expect Davies, if he'd already had the opportunity to study the sonnets, to have slipped the odd common image into any narrative poem "inspired" by their edifying example. "A Lover's Complaint" contains more than enough sonnet-links to have convinced Mackail that its author "had read them . . . when he wrote the poem." He personally cites six examples, all from the Fair Youth sequence(s), the most persuasive of which can be found at line 194 of the long poem, "Harm have I done to them but n'er was harmed," which finds its parallel in Q94's "They that have power to hurt and will do none."

MacDonald P. Jackson was himself convinced that the two experiments in poetics consciously shared a dialogue, albeit from the one mind. He considers that one of the most effective couplets in the "Complaint"—"but, spite of heaven's fell rage / Some beauty peep'd through lattice of sear'd age"—knowingly drew upon an image first found in Q3, "So through windows of thine age shalt see / Despite of wrinkles this thy golden time." He does not, however, address the issue of whether Shakespeare's febrile imagination might not have chafed at using such a similar turn of phrase when it was generally allowed to run riot.

In accepting that the "Complaint" poet had the sonnets to inspire him leads one to wonder how long he had been so inspired. If, as has been widely assumed, the full sonnet-sequence was completed before the author became one of the King's Men, then these private papers sat for some time in somebody's casket. Any association Davies had with the Pembroke family—if they were indeed the source, unwitting or not, of some or all of Q—seems to have enjoyed its heyday in the period up to 1605. Surely, any copy of Q so acquired would be reflected in Davies' own work of the period. With a personality like his, he would be bound to leave clues trailing.

In fact, in *Wittes Pilgrimage*, a volume published at the end of 1605, Davies made an obvious attempt to "emulate" the kind of sonnet-sequence Shakespeare had so masterfully executed.[17] This volume, which the *DNB* misdates to 1610–11, contains "a sonnet sequence about a frustrating love affair that is much superior to his religious poetry. Unfortunately it was written at a moment nearly saturated with dazzling Petrarchan sonnet sequences." Duncan-Jones herself notes that *Wittes Pilgrimage* "totals 152 sonnets, the same number as Shakespeare's sequence if we except the two Diana/Cupid sonnets at the end." This uncharacteristic act from Davies, writing an entire sonnet-sequence along nondidactic, nondedicatory lines, smacks of some external impetus—like a recently acquired set of love sonnets from his favorite poet-playwright.

Not surprisingly, this sonnet-sequence drew very little attention until Vickers reexamined it, but when he did, he found plentiful parallels to support his supposition. One such sonnet (XXVII) Davies began "in the vein of Donne, before modulating to something very close to Shakespeare." Another (XXXIV), addressing his mistress, Vickers thought "distinctly Shakespearean," specifically citing Q87 as a point of comparison. Yet another sonnet (V) uses the Shakespearean trick of reserving "the personal pronouns for the concluding couplet." There are doubtless others, awaiting a more forensic analysis from some hardy textual scholar.

Having dealt with opportunity, we turn now to Davies' motive for writing such an intricate, carefully wrought narrative as "A Lover's Complaint," knowing from the start that he would accrue no credit from it for a few centuries. After all, as Duncan-Jones reminds us, "Though prolific,

Davies was not celebrated for the genre of 'female complaint.' Shake-speare was, both in his dramatic and nondramatic writings." This re-quires us to glean something of Davies' personality from his plentiful poetic output.

To do this, we must wade through the thick foliage of self-deprecation and obsequious fawning that bestrews Davies' work—along with almost every other poet of the age—to get to the undergrowth of honest opin-ion beneath. Once there, we find that, for all his protestations of unwor-thiness—specimen 1, "Some say they wonder how so well I write, / (Although my lines to no greate wonders stretch)"; specimen 2, "Accept this Scumme of Wit, that flyes before / The breath of Laughter . . . "— there beat the heart of a poetaster with delusions of grandeur. Thus, in a sonnet to George Chapman, "Father of English poets," he has the temer-ity to put himself in Chapman's notoriously exacting literary company:

> George, thou wert accurst, and so was I
> To bee of that most blessed company;
> For if they most are blest that most are crost,
> Then poets (I am sure) are blessed most.
> Yet wee with rime and reason trimme the times,
> Though they giue little reason [i.e., recompense] for our rimes.

The bitterness that starts to suffuse his work with this 1611 collection (*The Scourge of Folly*) suggests that he no longer enjoyed the patronage of the great (as does a particular couplet from his last volume, *A Scourge of Paper-Persecutors*, "Away with patronage, a plague upon't / That hideous word is worse than Termagent."). Nor had he received the recognition of his peers. Yet he clearly believed that his "works" would live on after him. He even alludes to burying his own work in someone else's "notebooks" as early as 1605, in one of the *Wittes Pilgrimage* sonnets:

> *(Silke worm like) Ile worke me in my Tombe,*
> *Where, though I, poor Worme, from my Labours rest*
> *My Works well wou'n by some more dextrous Witt*
> *May line perhapps the Note-books of the best.*

As to Davies' inclination for adding to the endpapers of poetry books, we have two examples of him adding poems by hand to printed editions of his own work. In one, *Coryat's Crudities,* he has added a short poem; and in the so-called "Grenville" copy of *The Muses Sacrifice* (1612) in the British Library, he has added a full ten pages of autograph verses addressed to Henry Percy, his former pupil. If Eld faithfully printed what Thorpe had given him, there is another clue that the manuscript copy may well have come from Davies. In "A Lover's Complaint," he prints the word "particular" with an "e" ("perticular"). The only other time a Jacobean poet used the same peculiar spelling was in 1607, when Davies published his *Summa Totalis.*

Ignored or patronized by those one aspired to impress, what better jape than to reinvent oneself as a Welsh Shakespeare, and see if anyone could tell peer from peerless? Whether Davies concocted such a scheme when the opportunity presented itself, or had already turned his hand to emulating Shakespeare's narrative poems, adding a smattering of Spenser for good measure, it is impossible to know. But that the "Complaint" poet set out to "complete" a trilogy that to date featured the "lewd" *Venus & Adonis* and *The Rape of Lucrece,* in rhyme-royal, seems indisputable.

As Mackail pointed out back in 1912, the opening couplets to the "Complaint" and *Lucrece* even have "the same grammatical and rhetorical evolution." And Vickers has counted some thirty-five instances where the "rhymes shared between 'A Lover's Complaint', *Venus & Adonis* and *The Rape of Lucrece* were not re-used by Shakespeare," resemblances that he believes were "due to an admiring imitator who picked up words, phrases, rhymes and larger units of sense from other poets," and who went by the name of John Davies of Hereford.

The main problem for Davies was not the one that concerns Duncan-Jones—his novice-status in the "female complaint" department—but the rhyme scheme itself. The rhyme-royal stanza (*ababbcc*) would have been an intrinsic part of such an exercise, being the very scheme used in *Lucrece,* but as Vickers pointed out in his original *TLS* article, "The ['Complaint'] poet seems to have had difficulty with his rhyme scheme. He [even] made unmotivated changes between past and present tense in his narrative (the Seducer's hair 'did hang in crooked curls', but the wind 'their silken parcels hurls') in order to rescue a rhyme ... [and] when all else failed ... was ready to distort the English language to yield a rhyme, turning the past participle 'seen' into 'sawn' (to rhyme with 'drawn')."

Davies simply had no experience of using such an "intricate" rhyme-scheme. He was a simple rhymester of the old school, sticking almost invariably to *abab* or *aabb*. Even then, he was "often stumped for a rhyme" [BV]. Nevertheless, he pulled off a 329-line poem with enough "terse, compacted couplets, stanzas, half-stanzas, lines and half-lines, which ... cleave to the memory," to convince a fair few modern Shakespearean critics that what Mackail called "some reflection of Shakespeare's genius" was actually the real thing.

Whether he did this to dine out on the story, to ensure that at least one of his "works ... may line perhapps the Note-books of the best," or for his own private satisfaction, is a mystery lost to the ages. Whatever his motivation, Davies would hardly have been the first or last wannabe poet who produced a work in another's name (or no name) in the hope that it would linger on after he "to all the world must die."

Indeed, the saga of this "Complaint" closely resembles another cause célèbre of literary fakery, perpetrated a hundred years later by the wife of a Scottish knight. Some time before 1719, Lady Wardlaw, widow to Sir Henry Wardlaw, wrote her own forty-four-stanza poem in the style of a traditional ballad, and arranged for it to be published as "Hardyknute, a fragment." A story was concocted in which the unimpeachable Sir John Bruce found the "original" "in a vault at Dunfermline . . . written on vellum, in a fair gothic character, but so much defaced by time . . . that the tenth part is not legible." And this story held for fifty years, until the lady was no longer around to face the charge (she had died in 1727).

Only in the 1760s was the identity of its author revealed by Lord Hailes, who conducted investigations on behalf of Bishop Percy, after the prelate had decided to include the poem as a genuine relic in that eighteenth-century publishing phenomenon, *Reliques of Ancient English* [sic] *Poetry* (1765)—thus reinforcing Allan Ramsay's attribution of it, in *The Ever Green* (1724), as another "Scots Poem" written "by the ingenious before 1600."

But the story did not end there. In 1859, the eminent Scottish antiquarian Robert Chambers published a monograph in which he claimed, on the basis of her authorship of "Hardyknute," that Lady Wardlaw had in fact written many of the great Scottish ballads, notably the inestimably ancient "Sir Patrick Spens." Only after a couple of systematic rebuttals of Chambers' thesis from other ballad scholars of the era was the Wardlaw heresy laid to rest.

In the pre-Romantic era, attribution of authorship had nothing like the allure it acquired once it became attendant upon the cult of personality, so Davies (and Wardlaw) doubtless enjoyed putting their acts of poetic homage into the world. As for Thorpe, I suspect he should be exonerated from any complicity in the deception, though at the expense of his literary credentials. I doubt he would have noticed the difference in craftsmanship between the poet-playwright and the poetaster, so anxious was he to put his name to some of Shakespeare's poems. And anyway, I must agree with Jackson, that "Thorpe could have had no commercial motive for fraudulently adding 'A Lover's Complaint' to a volume that would have sold just as well without it." I just cannot share the professor's belief that "he was, in any case, a reputable publisher." He was, and always would be, a chancer.

CHAPTER TEN

2009

THE LITTLE
RED NOTEBOOK

[It is] not euill ... to publish, to the honor of the
Englishe tong ... those workes which the ungentle
hoorders up of such treasure haue heretofore
[d]enuied thee.
— PREFACE TO TOTELL'S *Miscellany*, 1557

Although it be oftentimes imprisoned in Ladyes casks,
& the president bookes of such as cannot see without
another man's spectacles, yet at length it breakes
foorth in spight of his keepers.
— THOMAS NASHE, PREFACE TO *Astrophil & Stella*,
1ST QUARTO, 1591

Though much has changed in the past 400 years concerning the aesthetic appreciation of a poet's art—most such changes being at the expense of a rhetorical style and the strict subject-matter of your average Elizabethan sonneteer—the one thing that has

remained steadfast is the psychology of the collector. The parallels be-
tween the Jacobethan collecting and book-publishing nexus and the ac-
tivities of modern (i.e., rock music) bootleggers of the 1970s—not
perhaps immediately obvious to most literary scholars—are quite strik-
ing. The sharp practices, the way material circulates and is ultimately
passed to "professionals" and utilized by them, the petty rivalries, even
the way texts are acquired, are the same whether the transactions are
taking place in London in 1609, or Los Angeles in 1969–78. (I refer in-
terested readers to my history of this subject, *Bootleg: The Rise and Fall
of the Secret Recording Industry*, 2003.)

In booklegging and bootlegging, everything seems to be done behind
closed doors, or down dark alleys, making rumor and innuendo by-
words of the business. And without the fan(zine)s that have docu-
mented these latter-day bookleggers—now equally consigned to
history-books by the technology of cyberspace—we would know as lit-
tle about them as their seventeenth-century predecessors, whose story
scholars are only now starting to piece together. For, at almost exactly
the same time I started investigating modern collecting circles—in the
mid-1990s—three important studies of the Jacobethan literary manu-
script culture appeared in close order: Harold Love's *The Culture and
Commerce of Texts: Scribal Publications in 17th Century England* (1993);
Arthur Marotti's *Print and the English Renaissance Lyric* (1995); and H.
R. Woudhuysen's *Sir Philip Sidney and the Circulation of Manuscripts,
1558–1640* (1996).

None of these noble scholars did, or indeed could, concentrate, on
Shakespearean manuscripts for the simple reason that not a single con-
temporary ms. has survived (save for less than 150 lines of the play *Sir
Thomas More,* if Hand D is actually his). Marotti at least addressed some
of the issues the sonnets raised, and wisely concluded, "There is no text
of the Sonnets, in either manuscript or print, that can be shown to repre-

sent the ideal of old-fashioned textual critics, the 'author's final inten-
tions,'" a riposte to all those who wanted Q to be authorized, but not
one many heeded.

Yet these works have illuminated the publishing history of these po-
ems far more than textual scholars of the sonnets whose tomes have ap-
peared on library shelves next to theirs. In particular, by demonstrating
the often incestuous relationship between the writers, themselves inter-
ested parties and manuscript-collectors, and the printers and publishers
who fed off their scraps, they have demonstrated that this was no one-
way series of transactions.

Thus Thomas Nashe, whose acid tongue and wanton turn of phrase
made it hard for him to attract patronage, was prepared to dedicate a
bookleg edition of Sidney's *Astrophil & Stella* (1591) to the author's sis-
ter, the countess—at publisher Newman's behest—even though he be-
rated those who left such gems "imprisoned in Ladyes casks." However,
when the shoe was on the other foot—as apparently became the case
when his *Terrors of the Night* (1594) fell into the wrong hands, thanks to
a careless "kinde frend of mine"—Nashe was quick to insist, in another
preface, that he alone reap the rewards:

> A long time since hath it line suppressed by mee; until the urgent
> importunitie of a kinde frend of mine (to whom I was sundrie
> waies beholding) wrested a Coppie from me. That Coppie pro-
> gressed from one scriueners shop to another, & at length grew so
> common, that it was readie to bee hung out for one of their
> signes.... Wheruppon I thought it as good for mee to repeape the
> frute of my owne labours.

Such protestations bestrew the scant literary records of the era.
When, in 1609, the well-known clergyman Richard Stock found that a

sermon he'd delivered three years earlier was about to appear in print, he registered it himself. He then prefaced his own edition with an explanation of its belated appearance:

> Some men for their gaine . . . having copies of this slender labour of myne . . . might happely some have passed and beene speedily printed before I should have had notice of it, and that with such imperfections as would have bene small to my credit and as little to thy contentment. Wherefore I resolved . . . to seeke forth my owne copie.

The relationship between writers and publishers was a fraught one precisely because it was so incestuous. George Withers didn't make any attempt to pull his prosaic punches in *The Schollers Purgatory* (1624), where he warned of how a bookseller, if he "gett any written Coppy into his powre, [that is] likely to be vendible; whether the Author be willing or no, he will publish it." Yet he still liked to boast of how his earlier Wither's Motto—*Nec habeo, nec careo, nec curo* (Latin for "I have not, I want not, I care not")—had sold some 30,000 copies in a matter of months.

Seventeenth-century prefatory pleas and polemics should invariably be taken with a pinch of sodium. In Jacobethan times there were a number of reasons for preferring such an exclusive means of dissemination as manuscript. And one was to create a groundswell of interest in a work, as a means of (re-)establishing a reputation in literary circles, with a view to finding a willing publisher who would publish the work in its entirety. An example of this would be Thomas Watson's *Booke of Passionate Sonnetes*, which was circulated in manuscript for at least two years before its 1582 publication. When it was published, it carried on the title page the legend, "published at the request of certaine Gentlemen his very frendes."

At the other end of the era, when Edmund Waller published his *Poems* (1645), the "Advertisement to the Reader" claimed that they had been previously "pass'd up and downe through many hands amongst persons of the best quality, in loose imperfect Manuscripts."

Another poet whose influence on Shakespeare's sonnets is a matter of record made similar protestations when he published the sequence that turned the fad into a craze: Samuel Daniel's *Delia*. According to Daniel, the appearance of twenty-four of his own sonnets alongside Sidney's great sonnet-sequence, *Astrophil & Stella*, came about because he had been "betraide by the indiscretion of a greedie Printer." H. R. Woudhuysen posits another, more credible scenario:

> On his return to England during 1591, Daniel got hold of a manuscript of *Astrophil & Stella* and determined to make a risky bid for the Countess of Pembroke's patronage, which would at the same time announce his own arrival on the literary scene. He approached [the publisher] Newman . . . [who] agreed to publish the manuscript of Sidney's sequence and to include other poems in the volume, most notably a collection of Daniel's sonnets. . . . Feigning shock and horror at what had happened, Daniel revised his sonnets, which he had now seen in print, and dedicated them to the Countess with an obsequious but quite untrue explanation for their earlier appearance . . . next to her brother's poems.

Nor should we consider such disingenuous ingenuity the sole prerogative of Jacobethan poets. Many a 1970s' rock artist ensured that a tape fell into a bootlegger's hands in order to bask in the kudos that comes with bootleg status.

But by 1598, when Francis Meres made his fabled remark that fixed the sonnets in time, Shakespeare would have had no need to play coy with his poetic output. Despite being the author of plays as popular as *Romeo & Juliet* and *Love's Labours Lost,* he was still best known among contemporaries for the two narrative poems published in his name in 1593–94.

Indeed, when chancing upon contemporary references to the man from Stratford during the second half of the 1590s, one discovers they almost invariably pertain to these poems, rather than the plays. And when, in 1600, two popular miscellanies affirmed Shakespeare's literary status—Robert Allott's *England's Parnassus* and John Bodenham's *Belvedere*—the majority of quotations came from these published poems (some 65 from 95 instances in the former, 125 out of 213 for the latter).

However, fame itself did not lead a poet inexorably into the publishers' clutches, precisely because even with success and sales, the author stood to make more from the patronage of the good and the great than by any publishing "advance"—and could still preserve exclusivity into the bargain. The populist Michael Drayton, one contemporary who was widely published, even complained in a 1612 collection that, "Verses are wholly deduc't to Chambers, and nothing esteem'd in this lunatique Age, but what is kept in Cabinets, and must only passe by Transcription."

And anyone who wonders where William preferred to place his hat should recall the fact that "the earliest known reference to the existence of any collection of sonnets by Shakespeare indicates that he followed the fashion in writing them exclusively for private audiences" [SL]. And with good reason. As one astute historian recently remarked, "The attraction of manuscript circulation lay in the medium's social status, its personal appeal, relative privacy, freedom from government control, its cheapness, and its ability to make works quickly available to a select audience" [HRW].

That freedom also afforded the opportunity for ongoing revision of its contents, order, and language. Such a process was exercised in print by the likes of Daniel and Drayton, but as Love reveals, "The scribal author-publisher [was] able both to polish texts indefinitely and to personalize them to suit the tastes of particular recipients." He could also decide how wide the circle of recipients would be, and which feathers he would ruffle by his rhetorical speculations.

Thus, when John Donne wrote *Biathanatos,* circa 1607–8, a poem on the subject of suicide that seemed to suggest there were circumstances where it need not be deemed a sin, he was extremely cautious about whom he would allow to see it. In a 1619 letter to Sir Robert Ker, Donne wrote, "No hand hath passed upon it to copy it, nor many eyes to read it; onely to some particular friends in both Universities." He nonetheless entrusted a copy to Ker, with the following instruction: "Reserve it for me, if I live, and if I die, I only forbid it the Presse, and the Fire: publish it not, but yet burn it not; and between those, do what you will with it."

Ben Jonson showed an altogether more blasé attitude when it came to his stray lines in an epigram to Lady Digby, imagining, "What reputations to my lines, and me, / When hee shall read them at the Treasurers bord, / The knowing Weston, and that learned Lord / . . . Then, what copies shall be had, / What transcripts begg'd?"

Sometimes, though, circulation was risky. For this reason, it strikes me as unlikely that Shakespeare treated his main sonnet-sequence with the same blithe regard that he did certain "sugred sonnets." Of course, the most risky type of private literature was the kind that was, or that could be interpreted as being, politically or religiously sensitive. Punishments could be arbitrary and severe. For posting a libel against the Dutch in 1593—signed "Tamberlaine"—on the door of a foreigner who was "lykewyse a scrivenar on the other syde the exchange, ovar agaynst

s. bartlelmews churche wall," the stationer Shore was given a hefty fine, pilloried for three days, and jailed for four years.

Shakespeare himself was far too shrewd to use the form to express any socially subversive thoughts. The one apparent reference to a political event in the entire 2,155 lines—"The mortall moon hath her eclipse endur'd" (Q107.5), a clear reference to Elizabeth I—is so obtuse that four centuries later no one can agree about whether it refers to events in 1579, 1588, or any year between 1592 and 1603 (with the exception of 1597, for some reason).

Whatever his earlier political inclinations, Shakespeare learned to steer clear of controversy after sailing a little too close to the winds of change in February 1601—when his own company, the Chamberlain's Men, were convinced with gold to perform a long-forgotten play of his, *Richard II,* which depicted the deposition and murder of a king, for the Earl of Essex's men on the eve of their ill-fated rebellion. Though the queen saw fit not to read too much into the performance, actually allowing the troupe to entertain her on the eve of Essex's execution, it cannot have helped Shakespeare in his endeavors to gain favor with the court.

And by 1603 there was a king on the English throne who knew only too well the potential impact of a poem or song, passed around in order to destabilize a reigning monarch. After all, it was he, as James VI of Scotland, who had fled Edinburgh in 1592, after the murder of James Stewart, second Earl of Moray, by George Gordon, sixth earl of Huntly, had resulted in "common rhymes and songs [that] kept in recent detestation" the king and Huntly; and which implicitly accused the Scottish king of orchestrating the earl's death because of a supposed affair with the queen. (At least one of these "common rhymes," "The Bonnie Earl of Moray," is still sung to this day.)

Shakespeare wasn't about to let any views expressed in haste come back and bite him. All political points, if they ever were a part of his private poems, were expunged or obscured. Thus, though the reference to "art made tongue-tied by authority" (Q66.9) could refer to the restraint on playing imposed by the state in July 1597, it hardly demands such a specific application.

But there was little he could do about the "Greek" element of his Fair Youth sonnets—save ensure the poems stayed private. It is unlikely he thought he could get away with a published edition, even if he considered one, especially after the Bishop of London's June 1599 "recall" (see Chapter 2). After all, as he doubtless knew, the Stationers' Company had been founded with the primary purpose of making publishers and printers accountable for the works they published—i.e., to impose censorship, political and moral, and to suppress "seditious, schismaticall, and *scandalous* [my italics] Bookes and Pamphlets" ("A Proclamation against Disorderly Books," 1623).

Copyright was a mere by-product of registration. In an age of ostensible religiosity and Old Testament morality—yet with that streak of loose morals beneath its veneer that provided such a rich source for many a Jacobethan playwright—there were widely known works whose publication would have been quite impossible as long as the Stationers' Company held sway. It is unlikely that Sidney's *Astrophil & Stella* could have appeared in his lifetime, given its celebration of an adulterous love for the wife of Lord Rich, Penelope (or, indeed, the *Old Arcadia,* with its combination of "transvestism, adultery, pre-marital sex, attempted rape, suicide, and regicide in a combination which might have offended many readers" [HRW]).

Other, more populist examples also spring to mind: a lyric like "The Sea Crabb," for one, which can be found in the most invaluable seventeenth-century manuscript of songs, poems, and ballads, the Percy Folio, compiled shortly after the English Civil War, largely from earlier manuscript sources. In this charming tale, a woman sits down on a bucket to relieve herself—"The good wiffe, she went to doe as shee was wont"—unaware that her husband has put a live sea-crab in there, intended for dinner: "Up star[t] the Crabfish, & catcht her by the Cunt." The song went unpublished for another two centuries, but like the Crabfish it continued to live and thrive in oral tradition.[18]

Shakespeare, though, was no oral poet—he was reliant on the preservation of the written word for the survival of his poems. And the slender evidence that exists for the life of the sonnets in manuscript suggests that, from their very creation, there were degrees of privacy that Shakespeare applied selectively to this material. As Dover-Wilson suggests, "Thorpe [probably] had at his disposal transcripts of two distinct classes of sonnets: (a) what we may call portfolio sonnets, namely the 'sugred sonnets' known to Meres in 1599; and (b) what we may call secret or private sonnets."

Dover-Wilson himself was convinced that the latter group were "those connected with the Dark Woman." I think not. It seems to me that the Dark Lady sonnets fall into the former category, his "portfolio sonnets." Not only do they "bewail and bemoan the perplexities of Love," like the ones that Meres described, but two of them passed from somebody's poetical miscellany into the greedy clutches of William Jaggard as early as 1599 (and, as Harold Love notes, "The most characteristic mode through which verse was circulated to [Jacobethan] readers was the miscellany containing work by a number of writers"—the era's equivalent of the iPod).

The "secret or private sonnets" surely were the Fair Youth sonnets (Q18–126), from which just a single sniff of a copy transcribed from manuscript has survived, and then, only if we consider that the one seventeenth-century manuscript text of Q106, preserved in a couple of corrupt texts—the *Holgate Commonplace Book,* circa 1650, and the Rosenbach manuscript—does not derive from Q, but traveled independently (if so, it acquired at least two clear corruptions, "mine" for "rime" and "pleasant" for "present"). The title the sonnet was given in both manuscripts, "On His Mistress' Beauty," certainly suggests that its transmission was some way removed from any autograph copy, and that the person responsible had never seen other sonnets in the same sequence, or even read this sonnet with any diligence.

The four (other) sonnets that we can, with a degree of confidence, surmise were in circulation as manuscripts in the 1590s or early 1600s (Q2, 8, 138, 144) do not contain even a whiff of impropriety with a male member of the nobility. This might explain why they met with such miscellaneous approbation, in a way that, say, Sonnet 20 or 26 would not have. But it seems more likely that the former sonnets were disseminated, in manuscript and print, precisely because they were among the "less private" of the sonnets that Shakespeare felt inspired to write at this time—to satirize a fad, to immortalize a friend, to demonstrate a deep affection, to exercise his poetic skills, and/or simply to pass the time (which, we know, was ever on his mind).

We know that Shakespeare did circulate certain sonnets "among his private friends," while keeping the order and contents of a more ambitious sequence to himself. It otherwise beggars coincidence that none of the four "pre-Q" sonnets should come from the central sequence, even though it accounts for over two-thirds of Q's contents. Unfortunately, accepting this, we remove the one solid historical ballast that might anchor the Fair Youth sonnets to a specific date or period in the poet's life.

As for the others, I tend to think they circulated in two sets, one by Shakespeare—as Meres suggests—the other probably not. The ones that passed "quickly" into print came from the first set, the so-called Dark Lady sonnets, though this really is a misnomer. They are a miscellany, as they were intended to be—Shakespeare showing off for friends and other strangers. I personally doubt that they ever included the two

Cupid sonnets (Q153–54), but elsewhere they handsomely display Shakespeare's singular wit, even when in the pit of amorous despair.

Though the ones in the other set, 1–17, appear to have a direct relationship with the Fair Youth sonnets, they smack of a commission from a wealthy patron seeking to use the power of poetic persuasion for an immediate purpose—to convince a young lord to marry. If this was indeed the case, the sonnets became the property of the patron, to do with as s/he willed. As Shakespeare suggests in his seemingly extravagant 1594 Lucrece dedication to the Earl of Southampton, "What I have done is yours."

The youth himself, delighted by these sonnets, if not persuaded by them, may well have shown them to acquaintances. But the fact that Q2 and probably Q8 had an alternate path to posterity does rather suggest that they received a discreet circulation of their own, along avenues separate from those by which Jaggard acquired his booty (given similar concerns expressed in *Passionate Pilgrim*, we can be confident that Jaggard would have utilized any "marriage" sonnets that had come his way).

The central series of sonnets, though, bears all the marks of a "real" sonnet-sequence, and a private one at that. Replete with all the thematic connections, rhyme-links, sense-links, and forward motion of a narrative, it has that fragile unity one would expect from a sequence "written over three or more years, as an autobiographical one, following the ups and downs of an emotional relationship" [EKC]. The other parts of Q, i.e., the prefatory "marriage" sonnets and the "disordered appendix," do not. The marriage sonnets have thematic integrity, but as a group they are entirely static, whereas the "disordered appendix" lacks a consistent seriousness of tone. The Fair Youth sonnets, in contrast, are bejewelled by both that seriousness and that structure—which Shakespeare signposted by his selection of 108 poems.

Ironically, Katherine Duncan-Jones is the first modern academic to identify these 108 sonnets as a sequence unto themselves, and to suggest they reflect "many elements of thematic and structural coherence . . . which commentators have failed to recognize." (Ironic because she also finds such elements where they are largely absent, i.e. in sonnets 1–17 and 127–54.) Despite sharing this common ground with Duncan-Jones, I reach a quite different conclusion. Believing that Shakespeare did indeed construct this sequence after 1598—and that Q generally adhered to its authorial "integrity" because the structure of the central sequence lent itself to being kept that way—I find no such "structural coherence" in the organization, editing, or presentation of the other sonnets in Q.

Yet it took Duncan-Jones to demonstrate that Shakespeare's Fair Youth sequence "conforms to the precedent set by Sidney in *Astrophil & Stella,* which in the authoritative 1598 text, overseen by his sister, has 108 sonnets [plus an envoi]." "In totalling 108/9," Duncan-Jones writes, Shakespeare "must surely have intended to label his sequence as belonging in some sense to the august tradition established by Sidney." Nor, to an Elizabethan, would the numerical significance of 108 have been simply confined to this poetic precedent. Equally importantly, 108 was a number divisible into units of two, three, four, six, nine, and twelve.

Northrop Frye may well be right to posit that the sequence "revolves around the youth in a series of three cycles, each of which apparently lasts for a year and takes him through every aspect of his love." But Shakespeare's sequence seems subtler still. With each year comprising four seasons, the sequence that Frye divides into units of thirty-six further devolves down to units of nine—and then three. Chambers, positing his own theory about the sonnets' organization in 1943, was one who saw triplets at every turn:

> Many contiguous sonnets were clearly written, if not at one time,
> at any rate under a common impulse, and fall naturally into pairs
> or triplets or even larger groups. . . . Sometimes there is a definite
> grammatical connection . . . through which argument flows on.
> Sometimes it is merely a matter of a continuous theme, as in . . .
> the nine which complain that he has found another poet. Often . . .
> the sense-linking of a group is emphasized by a definite stylistic
> device . . . the constant repetition of significant words and also . . .
> of rhyme-sounds, in sonnets so related.

And such sophistication would not be lost on an Elizabethan, particularly a well-read one, to whom such sets of sonnets "were far from being collections of miscellaneous poems. [His] readers would be accustomed to sonnet series in some such form, and would expect to find groups where each new sonnet said the same thing a little differently, or else carried forward the theme of the previous one" [KW]. Thankfully, such a sophisticated sequence retained its Shakespearean self because the procurer, not the publisher, took real care with the material.

Which brings us back, somewhat circuitously, to the activities of our friend from Hereford, the redoubtable Mr. Davies. The fact that Davies frequented the houses of nobles is a matter of record, and we know that he was an acquirer of literary manuscripts. Opportunities to transcribe any poems addressed to a pupil of his would certainly have arisen. That Davies would have been up to the task, and would have seized such opportunities, fits with what we know about his personality. When it came to the marriage sonnets, one would have thought all he had to do was ask. But what about a longer, more private sonnet-sequence?

Described by Thomas Fuller, in *England's Worthies* (1662), as "the greatest master of the pen that England in her age beheld," Davies was equally renowned "for Fast-writing, so incredible [was] his expedition." Whenever it was that such an opportunity arose, we can assume his interest in such displays of Shakespeare's "wit" had already been piqued, aligned to his documented interest in literary manuscripts. (At one point he refers to having seen Greville's *Mustapha* in manuscript, "as it is written, not printed," while, according to Vickers, he imitated Donne's "The Flea"—which he can only have seen as a manuscript—long before it was published.)

It is even possible that Davies was asked to transcribe Shakespeare's sonnets by one of his patrons, and took a copy for himself. At this time, any secretary (and therefore, presumably, any writing-master), "if his master was a writer, or a collector of others' writings, he would expect to do regular turns at transcription in addition to his other duties, and to serve as a point of relay for documents circulating through author and user publication" [HL]. The Pembrokes fit such a remit. So do others in Davies' circle. And we have at least one extant example of a set of poems transcribed by a secretary for his employer, the manuscript of John Donne's poems that Rowland Woodward copied for his employer Francis Fane, first Earl of Westmorland.

However, if Davies, or the unknown scribe who chanced upon Q18–126, was working from an autograph copy, it would appear that the script itself was problematic. In particular, the idiosyncratic use of italics in Q suggests a confusion at source, probably as a result of the autograph copy being in what would be called the "Secretary" hand. As Love outlines, in his invaluable history of seventeenth-century scribal publications:

> Secretary was a derivative of the 15th century "gothic" hand of the same name. Those who used it as their regular hand would often use italic for proper names and headings or interpolated passages that required to be distinguished in some way. . . . Both the

problems and advantages [of the script] are on display in the sec-
tion of BL Harleian MS 7368 . . . [which] use two or more forms
for single letters . . . [like] a, b, g, h, p, s and t, [and] the impression
may have been even stronger if the writer had not been so sparing
in his use of capitals.

The section of Manuscript 7368 under discussion is the part of *Sir
Thomas More* believed to be in the handwriting of a certain William
Shakespeare. Davies, as a professional writing-master, would have been
able to write in at least two hands, the native secretary and the imported
italic. We can be fairly certain that he would have faithfully transcribed
an autograph manuscript, but one doubts that such respect would have
been given by the compositor of Q. As Joseph Moxon clearly states in
his Caroline textbook, *Mechanik Exercises on the Whole Art of Printing*
(1683), it is "a task and duty incumbent on the Compositor . . . to dis-
cern and amend the bad Spelling and Pointing of his Copy." In fact,
we can probably assume that two compositors worked on the central
sonnet-sequence, which was divided equally between them. Hence, the
fourteen instances in sonnets 18–71 where the one compositor has mis-
taken "their" for "thy," but just a single instance in the second half of the
sequence.

Though it is perfectly possible that Davies, or the anonymous pro-
curer, received a third party's scribal copy (or copies) when he acquired
the less private sonnets (Q1–17, 127–52), it seems unlikely that he
would have had the permanent loan of the prized Fair Youth sonnets,
even if his acquisition of them was not in some way underhanded.
(Needless to say, I do not subscribe to the view of some scholars that
the Fair Youth sequence must have been acquired from "one of three
persons"—Shakespeare, the Fair Youth, or the Dark Lady.)

As Harold Love has shown, a number of "the better-known poets, Alexander Brome, Sir John Davies, Donne, Harington, the two Herberts, King, Marvell and Katherine Philips, all seem to have taken a supervisory role in the production and circulation of copies of their works." Shakespeare surely supervised the distribution of such a sensitive sequence closely, hoping to keep it, for at least a time, "within a closed circle of readers, on the understanding it is not to be allowed to go beyond the circle." In this, he probably relied "upon their primary audience's knowledge of the particular circumstances that generated [the sonnets]" [AM]. But he did not count on the collector mentality, because he was not one himself. Or he would never have left such a nonexistent paper trail behind him.

Over the years, much has been made of the scholar-poets and their supposed "spat" with Shakespeare the populist. What is intriguing about any such dynamic is how it has been built upon the suspicion that Shakespeare was always at least a single step removed from many of his contemporaries—unlike, say, Jonson, who seems to have enjoyed the full gamut of rivalries, animosities, and friendships with his peers. No Shakespearean presentation copies, foul papers, autograph manuscripts, or even personal dedications to fellow playwrights and poets have survived the centuries. Shakespeare, I suspect, didn't care about such things.

Yet for many of his contemporaries and near-contemporaries, the world of scribal manuscripts was a refreshing medium of propagation and dissemination, free of censorship, and grasping printers. Sadly, we know almost nothing of the way that William's work circulated privately, but H. R. Woudhuysen's attempt "to build up a picture of a group of men and women interested in Sidney's work, eager to obtain copies of his poems," can probably be applied equally to his successor. And though, by his own admission, Woudhuysen "may not be able to [ex-actly] define this scribal community . . . the links which can be forged among the earlier owners of Sidney's works in manuscript"—and, I dare say, Shakespeare's—"are often powerful ones."

If I am right, then the minor poet John Davies of Hereford and the major playwright Richard Brome were both associate members of the equivalent collecting-circle. As presumably was Francis Meres; and, we can probably safely assume, Ben Jonson. Unfortunately, this circle rarely seems to have crossed with the far more active circle that seems to have built up around the poetry of John Donne, whose work circulated extremely widely in the period immediately after Shakespeare's death. And some things that passed between members of the bardic circle—the fabled play of *Cardenio*, for one—are long gone.

Such a tantalizing tragedy raises issues that resound even to this day. The issue of artistic control has now become the preserve of lawyers and managers; but the collecting mentality, and its close cousin, the impulse to bootleg, has endured. I still wonder what would happen if there was, out in the world today, an intrinsically private work like Shakespeare's sonnets, as resonant, as "desirable," as essential to an understanding of a truly great wordsmith, just waiting to be discovered.

As it happens, there is, and I have followed its trail closely. *The Blood on the Tracks* notebook, the "little red notebook," contains some seventeen lyrics in the handwriting of Bob Dylan—dare I suggest, the Shakespeare of his day?—written in the summer of 1974. Ten of these he subsequently recorded for the album of the same name, seven of them he didn't. Here are the lyrics, public and private, that record the passionate affair that threatened a previously strong marriage, along with a Wild West fantasy, a valedictory to an earlier affair, and a night he spent with a prostitute in 1962 (really!).

What the artist elected to use of this material appeared the following January, and sold in the millions—just think, a work of this rich artistic quality actually becoming a number one album on both sides of the Atlantic. It is still selling tens of thousands of copies a year, in digital formats that weren't even invented when the record was made; for it, too, is destined to endure "so long as men can breathe." But the album is not the notebook, which is so much more personal an artifact—if you like, Dylan's "sugred sonnets."[19]

Such a notebook, to a fan, would be priceless. To a collector, it would be extremely valuable. Its author knew that, and he held on to it. However, a couple of decades later, it went missing, then turned up in the house of a Brooklyn merchant-banker, becoming the crown jewel of the largest collection of Dylan manuscripts in the world. (Twenty years after it was used to record the album, I was privileged to inspect the notebook at the home of its then-owner.) But then Dylan himself heard of its reemergence, and—being powerful enough to reclaim what was once his—set the wheels in motion to remove the notebook from prying eyes. Eventually, it was agreed that the notebook would be donated to the Morgan Library, in New York, and that access would be restricted only to those who had the blessing of Dylan's office.

In the meantime, not surprisingly, the notebook had become a "holy grail" to Dylan collectors. Rumors of at least one copy made during its fleeting passage from Dylan to procurer to collector continued to abound (prompting an editorial in the *New York Observer* by Ron Rosenbaum, in the Francis Meres role, who later wrote his own book on the original bard, *The Shakespeare Wars*). And, sure enough, such a copy was made, along with a "scan" of the notebook made on behalf of the Brooklyn collector, prior to its return to its rightful owner—and author.

And yet still the contents of the notebook have stayed outside the public domain, accessible only to a handful of fortunate souls. Rest assured, though, that should the original go up in flames tonight, if lightning should strike the Morgan Library out of shape, the collecting mentality has already ensured its contents will be preserved for the ages. Because sometimes a work of art is just too damn important to be entrusted to the artist. Sometimes it takes a brigand with a piratical disposition to say, "Screw the consequences, let's put this out."

So perhaps we should remind ourselves that, for all his dubious business practices, Thomas Thorpe did the world a huge favor when he obtained, bound, and published the secret sonnets of Shakespeare. These supreme sonnets that remind us of the fleeting nature of true passion, and the impermanence of even the written word. Not one scrap remains from the handful of copies of these sonnets that were passed around in manuscript. Not even a copy of a copy, assuming, as I do, that such a thing once existed. John Davies of Hereford's papers are long gone, as are Richard Brome's. Only the booklegger, with his disregard for the niceties of authorial rights, and disdain for any poetic sensibilities he might upset, saved the sonnets, and alone ensured that they shall live on "so long as men can breathe."

A SELECT BIBLIOGRAPHY

Note: Initials in square brackets mean that this particular source is utilized and so identified in the main text.

Modern Editions of the Sonnets Consulted

Burto, William, ed. *The Sonnets and Narrative Poems* (Everyman, 1992).

Duncan-Jones, Katherine, ed. *Shakespeare's Sonnets* (Arden, 1997).

Kerrigan, John, ed. *The Sonnets and A Lover's Complaint* (Penguin, 1986).

Seymour-Smith, Martin, ed. *Shakespeare's Sonnets* (Heinemann, 1963).

West, David. *Shakespeare's Sonnets* (Duckworth Overlook, 2007).

Other Works Consulted

Acheson, Arthur. *Shakespeare's Sonnet Story, 1592–98* (Bernard Quaritch, 1922).

Arber, Edward. *Transcript of the Registers of the Company of Stationers of London, 1554–1640* (London, 1876–94).

Archer, William. "Shakespeare's Sonnets: The Case against Southampton," *Fortnightly Review* 78, December 1, 1897.

Auden, W. H. "Introductory essay," in *The Sonnets,* ed. William Burto (New American Library, 1964).

Ayscough, Rev. Samuel. *An Index to the Remarkable Passages and Words Made Use of by Shakspeare* (London, 1790).

Bate, Jonathan. *Soul of the Age: The Life, Mind and World of William Shakespeare* (Viking, 2008).

Beeching, H. C. *Shakespeare's Sonnets* (Athenaeum Press, 1904) [HCB].

Bell, Ilona. "That Which Thou Hast Done," in *Critical Essays on Shakespeare's Sonnets,* ed. James Schiffer (Garland Publishing, 1999).

Bennett, H. S. *English Books and Readers, 1558–1603* (Cambridge University Press, 1965).

———. *English Books and Readers, 1603–1640* (Cambridge University Press, 1970).

Bennett, J. W. "The Alleged Piracy of Shakespeare's Sonnets and of Some of Jonson's Works," *Studies in Bibliography* (1973) [JWB].

Boaden, James. "To What Person the Sonnets of Shakespeare Were Actually Addressed," *Gentlemen's Magazine*, 1832.

———. *On the Sonnets of Shakespeare* (AMS Press, 1972; orig. ed., 1837).

Booth, Stephen, ed. *Shakespeare's Sonnets* (Yale University Press, 1977).

Bray, Denys. *The Original Order of Shakespeare's Sonnets* (Methuen, 1925).

Brooke, Tucker. *Shakespeare's Sonnets* (Oxford University Press, 1936).

Brophy, John. *Gentleman of Stratford* (Collins,1939).

Brown, Charles Armitage. *Shakespeare's Autobiographical Poems* (James Bohn, 1838) [CAB].

Butler, Martin. "Richard Brome," in *Dictionary of National Biography* (Oxford University Press, 2000).

Butler, Samuel. *Shakespeare's Sonnets* (London, 1898) [SB].

Chambers, E. K. *A Study of Facts and Problems,* 2 vols. (Oxford: Clarendon Press, 1930).

———. *Shakespearean Gleanings* (Oxford University Press, 1943) [EKC].

Child, Francis. *English and Scottish Popular Ballads,* vol. 2 (Houghton-Mifflin, 1886).

Conrad, Hermann (formerly Hermann Isaac). "Der Freund der Shakspereschen Sonette," *Preussische Jahrbücher* 177 (1919).

Crystal, Ben, and David Crystal. *The Shakespeare Miscellany* (Overlook Press, 2005) [BDC].

De Grazia, Margreta. "The Scandal of Shakespeare's Sonnets," in *Critical Essays on Shakespeare's Sonnets,* ed. James Schiffer (Garland Publishing, 1999).

Dover-Wilson, J. *Shakespeare's Sonnets: An Introduction for Historians and Others* (Cambridge University Press, 1963).

Drake, Nathan. *Shakespeare and His Times,* 2 vols. (London, 1817).

Dubrow, Heather. "Incertainties Now Crown Themselves Assur'd," in *Critical Essays on Shakespeare's Sonnets,* ed. James Schiffer (Garland Publishing, 1999).

Duncan-Jones, Katherine. "Was the 1609 *Shake-Speares Sonnets* Really Unauthorized?" *Review of English Studies* 34, no. 134 (1983) [KDJ].

————. "Letter to the editor," *Times Literary Supplement,* July 20, 2007.

Finkelpearl, P. J. "John Davies of Hereford," in *Dictionary of National Biography* (Oxford University Press, 2000).

Fowler, Alastair. *Triumphal Forms: Structural Patterns in Elizabethan Poetry* (Cambridge University Press, 1970).

Frost, David. *The School of Shakespeare* (Cambridge University Press, 1968).

Frye, Northrop. "How True a Twain," in *New Essays on Shakespeare's Sonnets,* ed. Hilton Landry (AMS Publishing, 1976).

Furnivall, Frederick, and John Hales. *Bishop Percy's Folio Manuscript: Loose and Humorous Songs* (London, 1867).

Gillet, Louis. *Shakespeare* (Grasset, 1931).

Giroux, Robert. *A Book Known as Q: A Consideration of Shakespeare's Sonnets* (Weidenfeld and Nicholson, 1982).

Gittings, Robert, ed.. *Letters of John Keats* (Oxford University Press, 1970).

Graves, Robert. *Poetic Unreason and Other Studies* (Cecil Palmer, 1925).

Greg, W. W. "The Copyright of Hero and Leander," *The Library* 24, 4th series (1944).

————. *The Gipsies Metamorphosed* (Oxford University Press, 1952).

————. *A Companion to Arber* (Clarendon Press, 1967).

Grossart, Rev. Alexander, ed.. *The Complete Works of John Davies of Hereford,* 2 vols. (privately printed, 1878).

Herford, C. H., Percy Simpson, and Evelyn Simpson. *Ben Jonson,* vol. 7 (Oxford University Press, 1941).

Hubler, Edward. "The Sonnets and the Commentators," in *New Essays on Shakespeare's Sonnets,* ed. Hilton Landry (AMS Publishing, 1976).

Ives, Edward. *The Bonny Earl of Murray: The Man, the Murder, the Ballad* (Tuckwell Press, 1997).

Jackson, MacDonald P. *Shakespeare's "A Lover's Complaint": Its Date and Authenticity* (University of Auckland, 1965).

————. "A Lover's Complaint Revisited," *Shakespeare Studies* 32 (January 2004).

Kermode, Frank. *Shakespeare's Language* (Allen Lane, 2000).

Knight, Charles. *The Works of William Shakespeare* (London, 1852).

Lavin, J. A. "The First Two Printers of Sidney's *Astrophil & Stella*," *The Library*, Series 5, 1971.

Lee, Sidney. "William Shakespeare," in *Dictionary of National Biography* (1898).

———. "Shakespeare and the Earl of Pembroke," *Fortnightly Review* 374, February 1, 1898.

———. *Shake-speares Sonnets* [Facsimile edition of Q] (London, 1905) [SL-F].

———. *A Life of William Shakespeare* (John Murray, 1916) [SL].

Lewis, C. S. *English Literature in the Sixteenth Century* (Oxford University Press, 1954).

Love, Harold. *The Culture and Commerce of Texts: Scribal Publication in 17th Century England* (University of Massachusetts Press, 1998) [HL].

———. "Hallow the Shallow," *Times Literary Supplement*, July 6, 2007.

Lynch, Jack. *Becoming Shakespeare* (Constable, 2008).

Mackail, J. W. "A Lover's Complaint," *Essays and Studies* 3 (1912).

Maidment, James. *Scottish Ballads and Songs: Historical and Traditionary* (Edinburgh, 1868).

Malone, Edmund, ed. *The Plays and Poems*, vol. 16 (London, 1790).

Malone, Edmund, and Boswell, James. *The Plays and Poems*, vol. 20 (London, 1821).

Marcham, Frank. *Thomas Walkley and the Ben Jonson "Works" of 1640* (The Library, 1931).

Marotti, Arthur F. "Shakespeare's Sonnets as Literary Property," in *Soliciting Interpretation*, ed. E. D. Harvey and K. E. Maus (Chicago University Press, 1990) [AM].

Massey, Gerald. *The Secret Drama of Shakespeare's Sonnets Unfolded* (London, 1872).

Minto, William. *Characteristics of English Poets* (William Blackwood, 1873).

Morrison, Paul G. *Index of Printers, Publishers and Booksellers in Short-Title Catalogue* (Bibliographical Society of the University of Virginia, 1950).

Muir, Kenneth. "A Lover's Complaint: A Reconsideration," in *Shakespeare, 1564–1964: A Collection of Modern Essays*, ed. E. Bloom (Brown University Press, 1964).

Nicholl, Charles. *The Lodger: Shakespeare on Silver Street* (Allen Lane, 2007).

Nichols, Bowyer. *Little Book of English Sonnets* (London, 1903).

Percy, Bishop. *Reliques of Ancient English Poetry* (London, 1775).

Phelps, W. L. "Notes on Shakespeare," *Proceedings of the American Philosophical Society* 81 (1939).

Poisson, Rodney. "Unequal Friendship," in *Critical Essays on Shakespeare's Sonnets*, ed. James Schiffer (Garland Publishing, 1999).

Pollard, A. W., and G. R. Redgrave. *A Short Title Catalogue of Books Printed in England, . . . 1475–1640* (Oxford University Press, 1950).

Robertson, J. M. *The Problems of the Shakespeare Sonnets* (Routledge, 1926).

Rollins, Hyder Edward. *The Poems: A New Variorum Edition* (Lippincott, 1938).

————. *The Sonnets: A New Variorum Edition*, 2 vols. (Lippincott, 1944) [HR].

Rostenberg, Leona. "Thomas Thorpe, Publisher of Shakespeares Sonnets" (Bibliographical Society of America, 1960).

Rowse, A. L. "Revealed at Last, Shakespeare's Dark Lady," *The Times* (London), January 29, 1973.

————. *Shakespeare's Sonnets: The Problems Solved* (Macmillan, 1973).

Schiffer, James. "Reading New Life into Shakespeare's Sonnets," in *Critical Essays on Shakespeare's Sonnets*, ed. James Schiffer (Garland Publishing, 1999).

Schlegel, A. W. von. *A Course of Lectures on Dramatic Art and Literature*, trans. John Black and A. J. W. Morrison (London, 1815).

Schoenbaum, Samuel. *William Shakespeare: A Documentary Life* (Oxford University Press, 1975).

————. *Shakespeare's Lives* (Oxford University Press, 1991).

Seymour-Smith, Martin. "Shakespeare's Sonnets 1–42: A Psychological Reading," in *New Essays on Shakespeare's Sonnets*, ed. Hilton Landry (AMS Publishing, 1976) [MSS].

Sharon-Zisser, Shirley, ed. "Introduction," in *Critical Essays on Shakespeare's "A Lover's Complaint"* (Ashgate, 2006).

Shaw, G. B. *Misalliance: The Dark Lady of the Sonnets & c.* (London, 1914).

Swinburne, A. C. *A Study of Shakespeare* (London, 1879).

Taylor, Gary. "Some Manuscripts of Shakespeare's Sonnets," *Bulletin of the John Rylands Library*, 1985–86.

————. *Reinventing Shakespeare* (Hogarth Press, 1990) [GT].

Tyler, Thomas. *The Herbert-Fitton Theory of Shakespeare's Sonnets: A Reply* (David Nutt, 1898).

Vendler, Helen. *The Art of Shakespeare's Sonnets* (Harvard University Press, 1999).

Vickers, Brian. *Counterfeiting Shakespeare: Evidence, Authorship and John Ford's "Funerall Elegye"* (Cambridge University Press, 2002).

————. "A Rum 'Do': The Likely Authorship of 'A Lover's Complaint,'" *Times Literary Supplement,* December 5, 2003.

————. *Shakespeare, "A Lover's Complaint" and John Davies of Hereford* (Cambridge University Press, 2007) [BV].

Wells, Stanley, and Gary Taylor. *William Shakespeare: The Complete Works* (Oxford University Press, 1988).

Wilde, Oscar. *A Portrait of Mr W.H., Now First Printed from the Original Enlarged Manuscript* (New York, 1921).

Williams, Charles. *A Myth of Shakespeare* (Oxford University Press, 1929).

Wilson, Katharine M. *Shakespeare's Sugared Sonnets* (Allen and Unwin, 1974) [KW].

Woudhuysen, H. R. *Sir Philip Sidney and the Circulation of Manuscripts, 1558–1640* (Oxford University Press, 1996) [HRW].

NOTES

1. The rights were assigned to Vicars in November 1624, qv. *Short Title Catalogue,* #17415. Thorpe appears to have registered his last new work in 1621, *A Sermon* by John Andrewes.

2. The full text for Watson's poem reads as follows:

> *Harke you that list to heare what sainte I serve:*
> *Her yellow locks exceede the beaten goulde;*
> *Her sparkeling eyes in heav'n a place deserve;*
> *Her forehead high and faire of comely moulde;*
> *Her wordes are music all of silver sounde;*
> *Her wit so sharpe as like can scarce be found;*
> *Each eyebrow hanges like Iris in the skies;*
> *Her Eagle's nose is straight of stately frame;*
> *On either cheeke a Rose and Lily lies;*
> *Her breath is sweete perfume, or hollie flame;*
> *Her lips more red than any corall stone;*
> *Her necke more white than aged swans yt mone;*
> *Her brest transparent is, like cristall rocke;*
> *Her fingers long, fit for Apollo's lute;*
> *Her slipper such as Momus dare not mocke;*
> *Her virtues all so great as make me mute:*
> *What other partes she hath I neede not say,*
> *Whose face alone is cause of my decaye.*

3. *Ideas Mirrour* went through some eleven new issues between its first publication in 1594 and the author's death in 1631. The issues of 1599, 1600, 1602, 1605, and 1619 were all new editions, with new sonnets included and old ones rearranged.

4. For almost her entire reign, Elizabeth I had been equated with Diana, the chaste goddess of the moon.

5. The critic in question was Bowyer Nichols, in the introduction to his *Little Book of English Sonnets* (1903).

6. Robert Greene, in his *Groatsworth of Wit* (1592), called Shakespeare "an upstart crow, beautified with our feathers," and it may be that the charge stung. The publisher later issued an apology of sorts "to divers play-makers," but Greene was probably not alone in his opinion.

7. Brian Vickers asserted the candidacy of John Ford. Lisa Hopkins has subsequently suggested that the poem may actually be by Ford's relative and acolyte William Stradling, thus justifying the initials attributed by Eld and/or Thorpe.

8. W. W. Greg suggests this was often the case, in "The Copyright of Hero and Leander," *The Library* 24, 4th series (1944).

9. See Josephine Waters Bennett [JWB], p. 246, note 38.

10. The one copy of Benson's edition of the gypsy masque resides in the Cambridge University Library (Syn.8.64.13).

11. James Knowles has suggested (in the *Times Literary Supplement*, February 7, 1997) that Brome took part in one of Jonson's masques, opening the New Exchange in The Strand in 1609.

12. There is no published version of "Willie o' Winsbury" from earlier than the nineteenth century, having been collected around 1770. However, one early collector thought the story of the ballad related to the early adventures of James V of Scotland. The reference to standing naked on a stone as a test of virginity is also decidedly medieval.

13. The editor was T. G. Tucker, in his 1924 edition of *The Sonnets*. He also rejected the possibility that the Dark Lady appeared in Q128, 129, 145, 146, 151, 153, and 154.

14. It was Bernard Shaw, in his 1910 Preface to *The Dark Lady of the Sonnets*, who described Tyler thus: "He was by profession a man of letters of an uncom-

mercial kind. He was a specialist in pessimism; had made a translation of Ecclesiastes of which eight copies a year were sold; and followed up the pessimism of Shakespear and Swift with keen interest."

15. Grossart published his various editions of Shakespeare's contemporaries in limited editions, for subscribers only. His two-volume edition of Davies' poetry lists the hundred subscribers, including Swinburne.

16. The pirate quarto of *Pericles,* though registered to Blount in May 1608, was not published until the following year, and then not by Blount. In the interim, George Wilkins published a novelized version.

17. The book was registered on September 27, 1605.

18. "The Sea Crabb" has been collected many times from oral tradition, though no version appeared in print until the early nineteenth century, when two Scottish collectors, Peter Buchan and Charles Kirkpatrick Sharpe, found versions, though only the latter published it at the time, in his *Ballad Book* (1823).

19. Dylan was inspired by at least one early sonneteer. The verses that "glowed like burning coal / Pouring off the page from me to you," in "Tangled Up in Blue," were the sonnets of Petrarch.

SHAKE-SPEARES SONNETS

I have herein retained Thorpe's numbering for the sonnets, though I have divided them into four sections, of which the second (XVIII-CXXVI) represents the primary sequence. The two Cupid sonnets (CLIII-CLIV), which I consider of questionable provenance, are still included last. For ease of use, I have here adopted modernized spelling, though in the text, when supporting my argument, I invariably quote something closer to the Q original.

The Marriage Sonnets (I–XVII)

I.

FROM fairest creatures we desire increase,
That thereby beauty's rose might never die,
But as the riper should by time decease,
His tender heir might bear his memory:
But thou, contracted to thine own bright eyes,
Feed'st thy light'st flame with self-substantial fuel,
Making a famine where abundance lies,
Thyself thy foe, to thy sweet self too cruel.
Thou that art now the world's fresh ornament
And only herald to the gaudy spring,
Within thine own bud buriest thy content
And, tender churl, makest waste in niggarding.
Pity the world, or else this glutton be,
To eat the world's due, by the grave and thee.

II.

When forty winters shall beseige thy brow,
And dig deep trenches in thy beauty's field,
Thy youth's proud livery, so gazed on now,
Will be a tatter'd weed, of small worth held:
Then being ask'd where all thy beauty lies,
Where all the treasure of thy lusty days,
To say, within thine own deep-sunken eyes,
Were an all-eating shame and thriftless praise.
How much more praise deserved thy beauty's use,
If thou couldst answer 'This fair child of mine
Shall sum my count and make my old excuse,'
Proving his beauty by succession thine!
This were to be new made when thou art old,
And see thy blood warm when thou feel'st it cold.

III.

Look in thy glass, and tell the face thou viewest
Now is the time that face should form another;
Whose fresh repair if now thou not renewest,
Thou dost beguile the world, unbless some mother.
For where is she so fair whose unear'd womb
Disdains the tillage of thy husbandry?
Or who is he so fond will be the tomb
Of his self-love, to stop posterity?
Thou art thy mother's glass, and she in thee
Calls back the lovely April of her prime:
So thou through windows of thine age shall see
Despite of wrinkles this thy golden time.
But if thou live, remember'd not to be,
Die single, and thine image dies with thee.

IV.

Unthrifty loveliness, why dost thou spend
Upon thyself thy beauty's legacy?
Nature's bequest gives nothing but doth lend,
And being frank she lends to those are free.
Then, beauteous niggard, why dost thou abuse
The bounteous largess given thee to give?
Profitless usurer, why dost thou use
So great a sum of sums, yet canst not live?
For having traffic with thyself alone,
Thou of thyself thy sweet self dost deceive.
Then how, when nature calls thee to be gone,
What acceptable audit canst thou leave?
Thy unused beauty must be tomb'd with thee,
Which, used, lives th' executor to be.

V.

Those hours, that with gentle work did frame
The lovely gaze where every eye doth dwell,
Will play the tyrants to the very same
And that unfair which fairly doth excel:
For never-resting time leads summer on
To hideous winter and confounds him there;
Sap check'd with frost and lusty leaves quite gone,
Beauty o'ersnow'd and bareness every where:
Then, were not summer's distillation left,
A liquid prisoner pent in walls of glass,
Beauty's effect with beauty were bereft,
Nor it nor no remembrance what it was:
But flowers distill'd though they with winter meet,
Leese but their show; their substance still lives sweet.

VI.

Then let not winter's ragged hand deface
In thee thy summer, ere thou be distill'd:
Make sweet some vial; treasure thou some place
With beauty's treasure, ere it be self-kill'd.
That use is not forbidden usury,
Which happies those that pay the willing loan;
That's for thyself to breed another thee,
Or ten times happier, be it ten for one;
Ten times thyself were happier than thou art,
If ten of thine ten times refigured thee:
Then what could death do, if thou shouldst depart,
Leaving thee living in posterity?
Be not self-will'd, for thou art much too fair
To be death's conquest and make worms thine heir.

VII.

Lo! in the orient when the gracious light
Lifts up his burning head, each under eye
Doth homage to his new-appearing sight,
Serving with looks his sacred majesty;
And having climb'd the steep-up heavenly hill,
Resembling strong youth in his middle age,
Yet mortal looks adore his beauty still,
Attending on his golden pilgrimage;
But when from highmost pitch, with weary car,
Like feeble age, he reeleth from the day,
The eyes, 'fore duteous, now converted are
From his low tract and look another way:
So thou, thyself out-going in thy noon,
Unlook'd on diest, unless thou get a son.

VIII.

Music to hear, why hear'st thou music sadly?
Sweets with sweets war not, joy delights in joy.
Why lovest thou that which thou receivest not gladly,
Or else receivest with pleasure thine annoy?
If the true concord of well-tuned sounds,
By unions married, do offend thine ear,
They do but sweetly chide thee, who confounds
In singleness the parts that thou shouldst bear.
Mark how one string, sweet husband to another,
Strikes each in each by mutual ordering;
Resembling sire and child and happy mother
Who all in one, one pleasing note do sing:
Whose speechless song, being many, seeming one,
Sings this to thee: 'thou single wilt prove none.'

IX.

Is it for fear to wet a widow's eye
That thou consumest thyself in single life?
Ah! if thou issueless shalt hap to die.
The world will wail thee, like a makeless wife;
The world will be thy widow and still weep
That thou no form of thee hast left behind,
When every private widow well may keep
By children's eyes her husband's shape in mind.
Look, what an unthrift in the world doth spend
Shifts but his place, for still the world enjoys it;
But beauty's waste hath in the world an end,
And kept unused, the user so destroys it.
No love toward others in that bosom sits
That on himself such murderous shame commits.

X.

For shame! deny that thou bear'st love to any,
Who for thyself art so unprovident.
Grant, if thou wilt, thou art beloved of many,
But that thou none lovest is most evident;
For thou art so possess'd with murderous hate
That 'gainst thyself thou stick'st not to conspire.
Seeking that beauteous roof to ruinate
Which to repair should be thy chief desire.
O, change thy thought, that I may change my mind!
Shall hate be fairer lodged than gentle love?
Be, as thy presence is, gracious and kind,
Or to thyself at least kind-hearted prove:
Make thee another self, for love of me,
That beauty still may live in thine or thee.

XI.

As fast as thou shalt wane, so fast thou growest
In one of thine, from that which thou departest;
And that fresh blood which youngly thou bestowest
Thou mayst call thine when thou from youth convertest.
Herein lives wisdom, beauty and increase:
Without this, folly, age and cold decay:
If all were minded so, the times should cease
And threescore year would make the world away.
Let those whom Nature hath not made for store,
Harsh featureless and rude, barrenly perish:
Look, whom she best endow'd she gave the more;
Which bounteous gift thou shouldst in bounty cherish:
She carved thee for her seal, and meant thereby
Thou shouldst print more, not let that copy die.

XII.

When I do count the clock that tells the time,
And see the brave day sunk in hideous night;
When I behold the violet past prime,
And sable curls all silver'd o'er with white;
When lofty trees I see barren of leaves
Which erst from heat did canopy the herd,
And summer's green all girded up in sheaves
Borne on the bier with white and bristly beard,
Then of thy beauty do I question make,
That thou among the wastes of time must go,
Since sweets and beauties do themselves forsake
And die as fast as they see others grow;
And nothing 'gainst Time's scythe can make defence
Save breed, to brave him when he takes thee hence.

XIII.

O, that you were yourself! but, love, you are
No longer yours than you yourself here live:
Against this coming end you should prepare,
And your sweet semblance to some other give.
So should that beauty which you hold in lease
Find no determination: then you were
Yourself again after yourself's decease,
When your sweet issue your sweet form should bear.
Who lets so fair a house fall to decay,
Which husbandry in honour might uphold
Against the stormy gusts of winter's day
And barren rage of death's eternal cold?
O, none but unthrifts! Dear my love, you know
You had a father: let your son say so.

XIV.

Not from the stars do I my judgment pluck;
And yet methinks I have astronomy,
But not to tell of good or evil luck,
Of plagues, of dearths, or seasons' quality;
Nor can I fortune to brief minutes tell,
Pointing to each his thunder, rain and wind,
Or say with princes if it shall go well,
By oft predict that I in heaven find:
But from thine eyes my knowledge I derive,
And, constant stars, in them I read such art
As truth and beauty shall together thrive,
If from thyself to store thou wouldst convert;
Or else of thee this I prognosticate:
Thy end is truth's and beauty's doom and date.

XV.

When I consider every thing that grows
Holds in perfection but a little moment,
That this huge stage presenteth nought but shows
Whereon the stars in secret influence comment;
When I perceive that men as plants increase,
Cheered and check'd even by the self-same sky,
Vaunt in their youthful sap, at height decrease,
And wear their brave state out of memory;
Then the conceit of this inconstant stay
Sets you most rich in youth before my sight,
Where wasteful Time debateth with Decay,
To change your day of youth to sullied night;
And all in war with Time for love of you,
As he takes from you, I engraft you new.

XVI.

But wherefore do not you a mightier way
Make war upon this bloody tyrant, Time?
And fortify yourself in your decay
With means more blessed than my barren rhyme?
Now stand you on the top of happy hours,
And many maiden gardens yet unset
With virtuous wish would bear your living flowers,
Much liker than your painted counterfeit:
So should the lines of life that life repair,
Which this, Time's pencil, or my pupil pen,
Neither in inward worth nor outward fair,
Can make you live yourself in eyes of men.
To give away yourself keeps yourself still,
And you must live, drawn by your own sweet skill.

XVII.

Who will believe my verse in time to come,
If it were fill'd with your most high deserts?
Though yet, heaven knows, it is but as a tomb
Which hides your life and shows not half your parts.
If I could write the beauty of your eyes
And in fresh numbers number all your graces,
The age to come would say 'This poet lies:
Such heavenly touches ne'er touch'd earthly faces.'
So should my papers yellow'd with their age
Be scorn'd like old men of less truth than tongue,
And your true rights be term'd a poet's rage
And stretched metre of an antique song:
But were some child of yours alive that time,
You should live twice; in it and in my rhyme.

The "Fair Youth" Sonnet-Sequence (XVIII–CXXVI)

XVIII.

Shall I compare thee to a summer's day?
Thou art more lovely and more temperate:
Rough winds do shake the darling buds of May,
And summer's lease hath all too short a date:
Sometime too hot the eye of heaven shines,
And often is his gold complexion dimm'd;
And every fair from fair sometime declines,
By chance or nature's changing course untrimm'd;
But thy eternal summer shall not fade
Nor lose possession of that fair thou owest;
Nor shall Death brag thou wander'st in his shade,
When in eternal lines to time thou growest:
So long as men can breathe or eyes can see,
So long lives this and this gives life to thee.

XIX.

Devouring Time, blunt thou the lion's paws,
And make the earth devour her own sweet brood;
Pluck the keen teeth from the fierce tiger's jaws,
And burn the long-lived phoenix in her blood;
Make glad and sorry seasons as thou fleets,
And do whate'er thou wilt, swift-footed Time,
To the wide world and all her fading sweets;
But I forbid thee one most heinous crime:
O, carve not with thy hours my love's fair brow,
Nor draw no lines there with thine antique pen;
Him in thy course untainted do allow
For beauty's pattern to succeeding men.
Yet, do thy worst, old Time: despite thy wrong,
My love shall in my verse ever live young.

XX.

A woman's face with Nature's own hand painted
Hast thou, the master-mistress of my passion;
A woman's gentle heart, but not acquainted
With shifting change, as is false women's fashion;
An eye more bright than theirs, less false in rolling,
Gilding the object whereupon it gazeth;
A man in hue, all 'hues' in his controlling,
Much steals men's eyes and women's souls amazeth.
And for a woman wert thou first created;
Till Nature, as she wrought thee, fell a-doting,
And by addition me of thee defeated,
By adding one thing to my purpose nothing.
But since she prick'd thee out for women's pleasure,
Mine be thy love and thy love's use their treasure.

XXI.

So is it not with me as with that Muse
Stirr'd by a painted beauty to his verse,
Who heaven itself for ornament doth use
And every fair with his fair doth rehearse
Making a couplement of proud compare,
With sun and moon, with earth and sea's rich gems,
With April's first-born flowers, and all things rare
That heaven's air in this huge rondure hems.
O' let me, true in love, but truly write,
And then believe me, my love is as fair
As any mother's child, though not so bright
As those gold candles fix'd in heaven's air:
Let them say more than like of hearsay well;
I will not praise that purpose not to sell.

XXII.

My glass shall not persuade me I am old,
So long as youth and thou are of one date;
But when in thee time's furrows I behold,
Then look I death my days should expiate.
For all that beauty that doth cover thee
Is but the seemly raiment of my heart,
Which in thy breast doth live, as thine in me:
How can I then be elder than thou art?
O, therefore, love, be of thyself so wary
As I, not for myself, but for thee will;
Bearing thy heart, which I will keep so chary
As tender nurse her babe from faring ill.
Presume not on thy heart when mine is slain;
Thou gavest me thine, not to give back again.

XXIII.

As an unperfect actor on the stage
Who with his fear is put besides his part,
Or some fierce thing replete with too much rage,
Whose strength's abundance weakens his own heart.
So I, for fear of trust, forget to say
The perfect ceremony of love's rite,
And in mine own love's strength seem to decay,
O'ercharged with burden of mine own love's might.
O, let my books be then the eloquence
And dumb presagers of my speaking breast,
Who plead for love and look for recompense
More than that tongue that more hath more express'd.
O, learn to read what silent love hath writ:
To hear with eyes belongs to love's fine wit.

XXIV.

Mine eye hath play'd the painter and hath stell'd
Thy beauty's form in table of my heart;
My body is the frame wherein 'tis held,
And perspective it is the painter's art.
For through the painter must you see his skill,
To find where your true image pictured lies;
Which in my bosom's shop is hanging still,
That hath his windows glazed with thine eyes.
Now see what good turns eyes for eyes have done:
Mine eyes have drawn thy shape, and thine for me
Are windows to my breast, where-through the sun
Delights to peep, to gaze therein on thee;
Yet eyes this cunning want to grace their art;
They draw but what they see, know not the heart.

XXV.

Let those who are in favour with their stars
Of public honour and proud titles boast,
Whilst I, whom fortune of such triumph bars,
Unlook'd for joy in that I honour most.
Great princes' favourites their fair leaves spread
But as the marigold at the sun's eye,
And in themselves their pride lies buried,
For at a frown they in their glory die.
The painful warrior famoused for fight,
After a thousand victories once foil'd,
Is from the book of honour razed quite,
And all the rest forgot for which he toil'd:
Then happy I, that love and am beloved
Where I may not remove nor be removed.

XXVI.

Lord of my love, to whom in vassalage
Thy merit hath my duty strongly knit,
To thee I send this written embassage,
To witness duty, not to show my wit:
Duty so great, which wit so poor as mine
May make seem bare, in wanting words to show it,
But that I hope some good conceit of thine
In thy soul's thought, all naked, will bestow it;
Till whatsoever star that guides my moving
Points on me graciously with fair aspect
And puts apparel on my tatter'd loving,
To show me worthy of thy sweet respect:
Then may I dare to boast how I do love thee;
Till then not show my head where thou mayst prove me.

XXVII.

Weary with toil, I haste me to my bed,
The dear repose for limbs with travel tired;
But then begins a journey in my head,
To work my mind, when body's work's expired:
For then my thoughts, from far where I abide,
Intend a zealous pilgrimage to thee,
And keep my drooping eyelids open wide,
Looking on darkness which the blind do see
Save that my soul's imaginary sight
Presents thy shadow to my sightless view,
Which, like a jewel hung in ghastly night,
Makes black night beauteous and her old face new.
Lo! thus, by day my limbs, by night my mind,
For thee and for myself no quiet find.

XXVIII.

How can I then return in happy plight,
That am debarr'd the benefit of rest?
When day's oppression is not eased by night,
But day by night, and night by day, oppress'd?
And each, though enemies to either's reign,
Do in consent shake hands to torture me;
The one by toil, the other to complain
How far I toil, still farther off from thee.
I tell the day, to please them thou art bright
And dost him grace when clouds do blot the heaven:
So flatter I the swart-complexion'd night,
When sparkling stars twire not thou gild'st the even.
But day doth daily draw my sorrows longer
And night doth nightly make grief's strength seem
　　stronger.

XXIX.

When, in disgrace with fortune and men's eyes,
I all alone beweep my outcast state
And trouble deaf heaven with my bootless cries
And look upon myself and curse my fate,
Wishing me like to one more rich in hope,
Featured like him, like him with friends possess'd,
Desiring this man's art and that man's scope,
With what I most enjoy contented least;
Yet in these thoughts myself almost despising,
Haply I think on thee, and then my state,
Like to the lark at break of day arising
From sullen earth, sings hymns at heaven's gate;
For thy sweet love remember'd such wealth brings
That then I scorn to change my state with kings.

XXX. ✓

When to the sessions of sweet silent thought
I summon up remembrance of things past,
I sigh the lack of many a thing I sought,
And with old woes new wail my dear time's waste:
Then can I drown an eye, unused to flow,
For precious friends hid in death's dateless night,
And weep afresh love's long since cancell'd woe,
And moan the expense of many a vanish'd sight:
Then can I grieve at grievances foregone,
And heavily from woe to woe tell o'er
The sad account of fore-bemoaned moan,
Which I new pay as if not paid before.
But if the while I think on thee, dear friend,
All losses are restored and sorrows end.

.

XXXI.

Thy bosom is endeared with all hearts,
Which I by lacking have supposed dead,
And there reigns love and all love's loving parts,
And all those friends which I thought buried.
How many a holy and obsequious tear
Hath dear religious love stol'n from mine eye
As interest of the dead, which now appear
But things removed that hidden in thee lie!
Thou art the grave where buried love doth live,
Hung with the trophies of my lovers gone,
Who all their parts of me to thee did give;
That due of many now is thine alone:
Their images I loved I view in thee,
And thou, all they, hast all the all of me.

XXXII.

If thou survive my well-contented day,
When that churl Death my bones with dust shall cover,
And shalt by fortune once more re-survey
These poor rude lines of thy deceased lover,
Compare them with the bettering of the time,
And though they be outstripp'd by every pen,
Reserve them for my love, not for their rhyme,
Exceeded by the height of happier men.
O, then vouchsafe me but this loving thought:
'Had my friend's Muse grown with this growing age,
A dearer birth than this his love had brought,
To march in ranks of better equipage:
But since he died and poets better prove,
Theirs for their style I'll read, his for his love.'

XXXIII.

Full many a glorious morning have I seen
Flatter the mountain-tops with sovereign eye,
Kissing with golden face the meadows green,
Gilding pale streams with heavenly alchemy;
Anon permit the basest clouds to ride
With ugly rack on his celestial face,
And from the forlorn world his visage hide,
Stealing unseen to west with this disgrace:
Even so my sun one early morn did shine
With all triumphant splendor on my brow;
But out, alack! he was but one hour mine;
The region cloud hath mask'd him from me now.
Yet him for this my love no whit disdaineth;
Suns of the world may stain when heaven's sun staineth.

XXXIV.

Why didst thou promise such a beauteous day,
And make me travel forth without my cloak,
To let base clouds o'ertake me in my way,
Hiding thy bravery in their rotten smoke?
'Tis not enough that through the cloud thou break,
To dry the rain on my storm-beaten face,
For no man well of such a salve can speak
That heals the wound and cures not the disgrace:
Nor can thy shame give physic to my grief;
Though thou repent, yet I have still the loss:
The offender's sorrow lends but weak relief
To him that bears the strong offence's cross.
Ah! but those tears are pearl which thy love sheds,
And they are rich and ransom all ill deeds.

XXXV.

No more be grieved at that which thou hast done:
Roses have thorns, and silver fountains mud;
Clouds and eclipses stain both moon and sun,
And loathsome canker lives in sweetest bud.
All men make faults, and even I in this,
Authorizing thy trespass with compare,
Myself corrupting, salving thy amiss,
Excusing thy sins more than thy sins are;
For to thy sensual fault I bring in sense—
Thy adverse party is thy advocate—
And 'gainst myself a lawful plea commence:
Such civil war is in my love and hate
That I an accessary needs must be
To that sweet thief which sourly robs from me.

XXXVI.

Let me confess that we two must be twain,
Although our undivided loves are one:
So shall those blots that do with me remain
Without thy help be by me be borne alone.
In our two loves there is but one respect,
Though in our lives a separable spite,
Which though it alter not love's sole effect,
Yet doth it steal sweet hours from love's delight.
I may not evermore acknowledge thee,
Lest my bewailed guilt should do thee shame,
Nor thou with public kindness honour me,
Unless thou take that honour from thy name:
But do not so; I love thee in such sort
As, thou being mine, mine is thy good report.

XXXVII.

As a decrepit father takes delight
To see his active child do deeds of youth,
So I, made lame by fortune's dearest spite,
Take all my comfort of thy worth and truth.
For whether beauty, birth, or wealth, or wit,
Or any of these all, or all, or more,
Entitled in thy parts do crowned sit,
I make my love engrafted to this store:
So then I am not lame, poor, nor despised,
Whilst that this shadow doth such substance give
That I in thy abundance am sufficed
And by a part of all thy glory live.
Look, what is best, that best I wish in thee:
This wish I have; then ten times happy me!

XXXVIII.

How can my Muse want subject to invent,
While thou dost breathe, that pour'st into my verse
Thine own sweet argument, too excellent
For every vulgar paper to rehearse?
O, give thyself the thanks, if aught in me
Worthy perusal stand against thy sight;
For who's so dumb that cannot write to thee,
When thou thyself dost give invention light?
Be thou the tenth Muse, ten times more in worth
Than those old nine which rhymers invocate;
And he that calls on thee, let him bring forth
Eternal numbers to outlive long date.
If my slight Muse do please these curious days,
The pain be mine, but thine shall be the praise.

XXXIX.

O, how thy worth with manners may I sing,
When thou art all the better part of me?
What can mine own praise to mine own self bring?
And what is 't but mine own when I praise thee?
Even for this let us divided live,
And our dear love lose name of single one,
That by this separation I may give
That due to thee which thou deservest alone.
O absence, what a torment wouldst thou prove,
Were it not thy sour leisure gave sweet leave
To entertain the time with thoughts of love,
Which time and thoughts so sweetly doth deceive,
And that thou teachest how to make one twain,
By praising him here who doth hence remain!

XL.

Take all my loves, my love, yea, take them all;
What hast thou then more than thou hadst before?
No love, my love, that thou mayst true love call;
All mine was thine before thou hadst this more.
Then if for my love thou my love receivest,
I cannot blame thee for my love thou usest;
But yet be blamed, if thou thyself deceivest
By wilful taste of what thyself refusest.
I do forgive thy robbery, gentle thief,
Although thou steal thee all my poverty;
And yet, love knows, it is a greater grief
To bear love's wrong than hate's known injury.
Lascivious grace, in whom all ill well shows,
Kill me with spites; yet we must not be foes.

XLI.

Those petty wrongs that liberty commits,
When I am sometime absent from thy heart,
Thy beauty and thy years full well befits,
For still temptation follows where thou art.
Gentle thou art and therefore to be won,
Beauteous thou art, therefore to be assailed;
And when a woman woos, what woman's son
Will sourly leave her till she have prevailed?
Ay me! but yet thou mightest my seat forbear,
And chide thy beauty and thy straying youth,
Who lead thee in their riot even there
Where thou art forced to break a twofold truth,
Hers by thy beauty tempting her to thee,
Thine, by thy beauty being false to me.

XLII.

That thou hast her, it is not all my grief,
And yet it may be said I loved her dearly;
That she hath thee, is of my wailing chief,
A loss in love that touches me more nearly.
Loving offenders, thus I will excuse ye:
Thou dost love her, because thou knowst I love her;
And for my sake even so doth she abuse me,
Suffering my friend for my sake to approve her.
If I lose thee, my loss is my love's gain,
And losing her, my friend hath found that loss;
Both find each other, and I lose both twain,
And both for my sake lay on me this cross:
But here's the joy; my friend and I are one;
Sweet flattery! then she loves but me alone.

XLIII.

When most I wink, then do mine eyes best see,
For all the day they view things unrespected;
But when I sleep, in dreams they look on thee,
And darkly bright are bright in dark directed.
Then thou, whose shadow shadows doth make bright,
How would thy shadow's form form happy show
To the clear day with thy much clearer light,
When to unseeing eyes thy shade shines so!
How would, I say, mine eyes be blessed made
By looking on thee in the living day,
When in dead night thy fair imperfect shade
Through heavy sleep on sightless eyes doth stay!
All days are nights to see till I see thee,
And nights bright days when dreams do show thee me.

XLIV.

If the dull substance of my flesh were thought,
Injurious distance should not stop my way;
For then despite of space I would be brought,
From limits far remote where thou dost stay.
No matter then although my foot did stand
Upon the farthest earth removed from thee;
For nimble thought can jump both sea and land
As soon as think the place where he would be.
But ah! thought kills me that I am not thought,
To leap large lengths of miles when thou art gone,
But that so much of earth and water wrought
I must attend time's leisure with my moan,
Receiving nought by elements so slow
But heavy tears, badges of either's woe.

XLV.

The other two, slight air and purging fire,
Are both with thee, wherever I abide;
The first my thought, the other my desire,
These present-absent with swift motion slide.
For when these quicker elements are gone
In tender embassy of love to thee,
My life, being made of four, with two alone
Sinks down to death, oppress'd with melancholy;
Until life's composition be recured
By those swift messengers return'd from thee,
Who even but now come back again, assured
Of thy fair health, recounting it to me:
This told, I joy; but then no longer glad,
I send them back again and straight grow sad.

XLVI.

Mine eye and heart are at a mortal war
How to divide the conquest of thy sight;
Mine eye my heart thy picture's sight would bar,
My heart mine eye the freedom of that right.
My heart doth plead that thou in him dost lie—
A closet never pierced with crystal eyes—
But the defendant doth that plea deny
And says in him thy fair appearance lies.
To 'cide this title is impanneled
A quest of thoughts, all tenants to the heart,
And by their verdict is determined
The clear eye's moiety and the dear heart's part:
As thus; mine eye's due is thy outward part,
And my heart's right thy inward love of heart.

XLVII.

Betwixt mine eye and heart a league is took,
And each doth good turns now unto the other:
When that mine eye is famish'd for a look,
Or heart in love with sighs himself doth smother,
With my love's picture then my eye doth feast
And to the painted banquet bids my heart;
Another time mine eye is my heart's guest
And in his thoughts of love doth share a part:
So, either by thy picture or my love,
Thyself away art resent still with me;
For thou not farther than my thoughts canst move,
And I am still with them and they with thee;
Or, if they sleep, thy picture in my sight
Awakes my heart to heart's and eye's delight.

XLVIII.

How careful was I, when I took my way,
Each trifle under truest bars to thrust,
That to my use it might unused stay
From hands of falsehood, in sure wards of trust!
But thou, to whom my jewels trifles are,
Most worthy of comfort, now my greatest grief,
Thou, best of dearest and mine only care,
Art left the prey of every vulgar thief.
Thee have I not lock'd up in any chest,
Save where thou art not, though I feel thou art,
Within the gentle closure of my breast,
From whence at pleasure thou mayst come and part;
And even thence thou wilt be stol'n, I fear,
For truth proves thievish for a prize so dear.

XLIX.

Against that time, if ever that time come,
When I shall see thee frown on my defects,
When as thy love hath cast his utmost sum,
Call'd to that audit by advised respects;
Against that time when thou shalt strangely pass
And scarcely greet me with that sun thine eye,
When love, converted from the thing it was,
Shall reasons find of settled gravity,—
Against that time do I ensconce me here
Within the knowledge of mine own desert,
And this my hand against myself uprear,
To guard the lawful reasons on thy part:
To leave poor me thou hast the strength of laws,
Since why to love I can allege no cause.

L.

How heavy do I journey on the way,
When what I seek, my weary travel's end,
Doth teach that ease and that repose to say
'Thus far the miles are measured from thy friend!'
The beast that bears me, tired with my woe,
Plods dully on, to bear that weight in me,
As if by some instinct the wretch did know
His rider loved not speed, being made from thee:
The bloody spur cannot provoke him on
That sometimes anger thrusts into his hide;
Which heavily he answers with a groan,
More sharp to me than spurring to his side;
For that same groan doth put this in my mind;
My grief lies onward and my joy behind.

LI.

Thus can my love excuse the slow offence
Of my dull bearer when from thee I speed:
From where thou art why should I haste me thence?
Till I return, of posting is no need.
O, what excuse will my poor beast then find,
When swift extremity can seem but slow?
Then should I spur, though mounted on the wind;
In winged speed no motion shall I know:
Then can no horse with my desire keep pace;
Therefore desire of perfect'st love being made,
Shall neigh—no dull flesh—in his fiery race;
But love, for love, thus shall excuse my jade;
Since from thee going he went wilful-slow,
Towards thee I'll run, and give him leave to go.

LII.

So am I as the rich, whose blessed key
Can bring him to his sweet up-locked treasure,
The which he will not every hour survey,
For blunting the fine point of seldom pleasure.
Therefore are feasts so solemn and so rare,
Since, seldom coming, in the long year set,
Like stones of worth they thinly placed are,
Or captain jewels in the carcanet.
So is the time that keeps you as my chest,
Or as the wardrobe which the robe doth hide,
To make some special instant special blest,
By new unfolding his imprison'd pride.
Blessed are you, whose worthiness gives scope,
Being had, to triumph, being lack'd, to hope.

LIII.

What is your substance, whereof are you made,
That millions of strange shadows on you tend?
Since every one hath, every one, one shade,
And you, but one, can every shadow lend.
Describe Adonis, and the counterfeit
Is poorly imitated after you;
On Helen's cheek all art of beauty set,
And you in Grecian tires are painted new:
Speak of the spring and foison of the year;
The one doth shadow of your beauty show,
The other as your bounty doth appear;
And you in every blessed shape we know.
In all external grace you have some part,
But you like none, none you, for constant heart.

LIV.

O, how much more doth beauty beauteous seem
By that sweet ornament which truth doth give!
The rose looks fair, but fairer we it deem
For that sweet odour which doth in it live.
The canker-blooms have full as deep a dye
As the perfumed tincture of the roses,
Hang on such thorns and play as wantonly
When summer's breath their masked buds discloses:
But, for their virtue only is their show,
They live unwoo'd and unrespected fade,
Die to themselves. Sweet roses do not so;
Of their sweet deaths are sweetest odours made:
And so of you, beauteous and lovely youth,
When that shall fade, my verse distills your truth.

LV.

Not marble, nor the gilded monuments
Of princes, shall outlive this powerful rhyme;
But you shall shine more bright in these contents
Than unswept stone besmear'd with sluttish time.
When wasteful war shall statues overturn,
And broils root out the work of masonry,
Nor Mars his sword nor war's quick fire shall burn
The living record of your memory.
'Gainst death and all-oblivious enmity
Shall you pace forth; your praise shall still find room
Even in the eyes of all posterity
That wear this world out to the ending doom.
So, till the judgment that yourself arise,
You live in this, and dwell in lover's eyes.

LVI.

Sweet love, renew thy force; be it not said
Thy edge should blunter be than appetite,
Which but to-day by feeding is allay'd,
To-morrow sharpen'd in his former might:
So, love, be thou; although to-day thou fill
Thy hungry eyes even till they wink with fullness,
To-morrow see again, and do not kill
The spirit of love with a perpetual dullness.
Let this sad interim like the ocean be
Which parts the shore, where two contracted new
Come daily to the banks, that, when they see
Return of love, more blest may be the view;
Else call it winter, which being full of care
Makes summer's welcome thrice more wish'd, more rare.

LVII.

Being your slave, what should I do but tend
Upon the hours and times of your desire?
I have no precious time at all to spend,
Nor services to do, till you require.
Nor dare I chide the world-without-end hour
Whilst I, my sovereign, watch the clock for you,
Nor think the bitterness of absence sour
When you have bid your servant once adieu;
Nor dare I question with my jealous thought
Where you may be, or your affairs suppose,
But, like a sad slave, stay and think of nought
Save, where you are how happy you make those.
So true a fool is love that in your will,
Though you do any thing, he thinks no ill.

LVIII.

That god forbid that made me first your slave,
I should in thought control your times of pleasure,
Or at your hand the account of hours to crave,
Being your vassal, bound to stay your leisure!
O, let me suffer, being at your beck,
The imprison'd absence of your liberty;
And patience, tame to sufferance, bide each check,
Without accusing you of injury.
Be where you list, your charter is so strong
That you yourself may privilege your time
To what you will; to you it doth belong
Yourself to pardon of self-doing crime.
I am to wait, though waiting so be hell;
Not blame your pleasure, be it ill or well.

LIX.

If there be nothing new, but that which is
Hath been before, how are our brains beguiled,
Which, labouring for invention, bear amiss
The second burden of a former child!
O, that record could with a backward look,
Even of five hundred courses of the sun,
Show me your image in some antique book,
Since mind at first in character was done!
That I might see what the old world could say
To this composed wonder of your frame;
Whether we are mended, or whether better they,
Or whether revolution be the same.
O, sure I am, the wits of former days
To subjects worse have given admiring praise.

LX.

Like as the waves make towards the pebbled shore,
So do our minutes hasten to their end;
Each changing place with that which goes before,
In sequent toil all forwards do contend.
Nativity, once in the main of light,
Crawls to maturity, wherewith being crown'd,
Crooked eclipses 'gainst his glory fight,
And Time that gave doth now his gift confound.
Time doth transfix the flourish set on youth
And delves the parallels in beauty's brow,
Feeds on the rarities of nature's truth,
And nothing stands but for his scythe to mow:
And yet to times in hope my verse shall stand,
Praising thy worth, despite his cruel hand.

LXI.

Is it thy will thy image should keep open
My heavy eyelids to the weary night?
Dost thou desire my slumbers should be broken,
While shadows like to thee do mock my sight?
Is it thy spirit that thou send'st from thee
So far from home into my deeds to pry,
To find out shames and idle hours in me,
The scope and tenor of thy jealousy?
O, no! thy love, though much, is not so great:
It is my love that keeps mine eye awake;
Mine own true love that doth my rest defeat,
To play the watchman ever for thy sake:
For thee watch I whilst thou dost wake elsewhere,
From me far off, with others all too near.

LXII.

Sin of self-love possesseth all mine eye
And all my soul and all my every part;
And for this sin there is no remedy,
It is so grounded inward in my heart.
Methinks no face so gracious is as mine,
No shape so true, no truth of such account;
And for myself mine own worth do define,
As I all other in all worths surmount.
But when my glass shows me myself indeed,
Beated and chopp'd with tann'd antiquity,
Mine own self-love quite contrary I read;
Self so self-loving were iniquity.
'Tis thee, myself, that for myself I praise,
Painting my age with beauty of thy days.

LXIII.

Against my love shall be, as I am now,
With Time's injurious hand crush'd and o'er-worn;
When hours have drain'd his blood and fill'd his brow
With lines and wrinkles; when his youthful morn
Hath travell'd on to age's steepy night,
And all those beauties whereof now he's king
Are vanishing or vanish'd out of sight,
Stealing away the treasure of his spring;
For such a time do I now fortify
Against confounding age's cruel knife,
That he shall never cut from memory
My sweet love's beauty, though my lover's life:
His beauty shall in these black lines be seen,
And they shall live, and he in them still green.

LXIV.

When I have seen by Time's fell hand defaced
The rich proud cost of outworn buried age;
When sometime lofty towers I see down-razed
And brass eternal slave to mortal rage;
When I have seen the hungry ocean gain
Advantage on the kingdom of the shore,
And the firm soil win of the watery main,
Increasing store with loss and loss with store;
When I have seen such interchange of state,
Or state itself confounded to decay;
Ruin hath taught me thus to ruminate,
That Time will come and take my love away.
This thought is as a death, which cannot choose
But weep to have that which it fears to lose.

LXV.

Since brass, nor stone, nor earth, nor boundless sea,
But sad mortality o'er-sways their power,
How with this rage shall beauty hold a plea,
Whose action is no stronger than a flower?
O, how shall summer's honey breath hold out
Against the wreckful siege of battering days,
When rocks impregnable are not so stout,
Nor gates of steel so strong, but Time decays?
O fearful meditation! where, alack,
Shall Time's best jewel from Time's chest lie hid?
Or what strong hand can hold his swift foot back?
Or who his spoil of beauty can forbid?
O, none, unless this miracle have might,
That in black ink my love may still shine bright.

LXVI.

Tired with all these, for restful death I cry,
As, to behold desert a beggar born,
And needy nothing trimm'd in jollity,
And purest faith unhappily forsworn,
And guilded honour shamefully misplaced,
And maiden virtue rudely strumpeted,
And right perfection wrongfully disgraced,
And strength by limping sway disabled,
And art made tongue-tied by authority,
And folly doctor-like controlling skill,
And simple truth miscall'd simplicity,
And captive good attending captain ill:
Tired with all these, from these would I be gone,
Save that, to die, I leave my love alone.

LXVII.

Ah! wherefore with infection should he live,
And with his presence grace impiety,
That sin by him advantage should achieve
And lace itself with his society?
Why should false painting imitate his cheek
And steal dead seeing of his living hue?
Why should poor beauty indirectly seek
Roses of shadow, since his rose is true?
Why should he live, now Nature bankrupt is,
Beggar'd of blood to blush through lively veins?
For she hath no excheckr now but his,
And, proud of many, lives upon his gains.
O, him she stores, to show what wealth she had
In days long since, before these last so bad.

LXVIII.

Thus is his cheek the map of days outworn,
When beauty lived and died as flowers do now,
Before the bastard signs of fair were born,
Or durst inhabit on a living brow;
Before the golden tresses of the dead,
The right of sepulchres, were shorn away,
To live a second life on second head;
Ere beauty's dead fleece made another gay:
In him those holy antique hours are seen,
Without all ornament, itself and true,
Making no summer of another's green,
Robbing no old to dress his beauty new;
And him as for a map doth Nature store,
To show false Art what beauty was of yore.

LXIX.

Those parts of thee that the world's eye doth view
Want nothing that the thought of hearts can mend;
All tongues, the voice of souls, give thee that due,
Uttering bare truth, even so as foes commend.
Thy outward thus with outward praise is crown'd;
But those same tongues that give thee so thine own
In other accents do this praise confound
By seeing farther than the eye hath shown.
They look into the beauty of thy mind,
And that, in guess, they measure by thy deeds;
Then, churls, their thoughts, although their eyes
    were kind,
To thy fair flower add the rank smell of weeds:
But why thy odour matcheth not thy show,
The solve is this, that thou dost common grow.

LXX.

That thou art blamed shall not be thy defect,
For slander's mark was ever yet the fair;
The ornament of beauty is suspect,
A crow that flies in heaven's sweetest air.
So thou be good, slander doth but approve
Thy worth the greater, being woo'd of time;
For canker vice the sweetest buds doth love,
And thou present'st a pure unstained prime.
Thou hast pass'd by the ambush of young days,
Either not assail'd or victor being charged;
Yet this thy praise cannot be so thy praise,
To tie up envy evermore enlarged:
If some suspect of ill mask'd not thy show,
Then thou alone kingdoms of hearts shouldst owe.

LXXI.

No longer mourn for me when I am dead
Then you shall hear the surly sullen bell
Give warning to the world that I am fled
From this vile world, with vilest worms to dwell:
Nay, if you read this line, remember not
The hand that writ it; for I love you so
That I in your sweet thoughts would be forgot
If thinking on me then should make you woe.
O, if, I say, you look upon this verse
When I perhaps compounded am with clay,
Do not so much as my poor name rehearse.
But let your love even with my life decay,
Lest the wise world should look into your moan
And mock you with me after I am gone.

LXXII.

O, lest the world should task you to recite
What merit lived in me, that you should love
After my death, dear love, forget me quite,
For you in me can nothing worthy prove;
Unless you would devise some virtuous lie,
To do more for me than mine own desert,
And hang more praise upon deceased I
Than niggard truth would willingly impart:
O, lest your true love may seem false in this,
That you for love speak well of me untrue,
My name be buried where my body is,
And live no more to shame nor me nor you.
For I am shamed by that which I bring forth,
And so should you, to love things nothing worth.

LXXIII.

That time of year thou mayst in me behold
When yellow leaves, or none, or few, do hang
Upon those boughs which shake against the cold,
Bare ruin'd choirs, where late the sweet birds sang.
In me thou seest the twilight of such day
As after sunset fadeth in the west,
Which by and by black night doth take away,
Death's second self, that seals up all in rest.
In me thou see'st the glowing of such fire
That on the ashes of his youth doth lie,
As the death-bed whereon it must expire
Consumed with that which it was nourish'd by.
This thou perceivest, which makes thy love more strong,
To love that well which thou must leave ere long.

LXXIV.

But be contented: when that fell arrest
Without all bail shall carry me away,
My life hath in this line some interest,
Which for memorial still with thee shall stay.
When thou reviewest this, thou dost review
The very part was consecrate to thee:
The earth can have but earth, which is his due;
My spirit is thine, the better part of me:
So then thou hast but lost the dregs of life,
The prey of worms, my body being dead,
The coward conquest of a wretch's knife,
Too base of thee to be remembered.
The worth of that is that which it contains,
And that is this, and this with thee remains.

LXXV.

So are you to my thoughts as food to life,
Or as sweet-season'd showers are to the ground;
And for the peace of you I hold such strife
As 'twixt a miser and his wealth is found;
Now proud as an enjoyer and anon
Doubting the filching age will steal his treasure,
Now counting best to be with you alone,
Then better'd that the world may see my pleasure;
Sometime all full with feasting on your sight
And by and by clean starved for a look;
Possessing or pursuing no delight,
Save what is had or must from you be took.
Thus do I pine and surfeit day by day,
Or gluttoning on all, or all away.

LXXVI.

Why is my verse so barren of new pride,
So far from variation or quick change?
Why with the time do I not glance aside
To new-found methods and to compounds strange?
Why write I still all one, ever the same,
And keep invention in a noted weed,
That every word doth almost tell my name,
Showing their birth and where they did proceed?
O, know, sweet love, I always write of you,
And you and love are still my argument;
So all my best is dressing old words new,
Spending again what is already spent:
For as the sun is daily new and old,
So is my love still telling what is told.

LXXVII.

Thy glass will show thee how thy beauties wear,
Thy dial how thy precious minutes waste;
The vacant leaves thy mind's imprint will bear,
And of this book this learning mayst thou taste.
The wrinkles which thy glass will truly show
Of mouthed graves will give thee memory;
Thou by thy dial's shady stealth mayst know
Time's thievish progress to eternity.
Look, what thy memory can not contain
Commit to these waste blanks, and thou shalt find
Those children nursed, deliver'd from thy brain,
To take a new acquaintance of thy mind.
These offices, so oft as thou wilt look,
Shall profit thee and much enrich thy book.

LXXVIII.

So oft have I invoked thee for my Muse
And found such fair assistance in my verse
As every alien pen hath got my use
And under thee their poesy disperse.
Thine eyes that taught the dumb on high to sing
And heavy ignorance aloft to fly
Have added feathers to the learned's wing
And given grace a double majesty.
Yet be most proud of that which I compile,
Whose influence is thine and born of thee:
In others' works thou dost but mend the style,
And arts with thy sweet graces graced be;
But thou art all my art and dost advance
As high as learning my rude ignorance.

LXXIX.

Whilst I alone did call upon thy aid,
My verse alone had all thy gentle grace,
But now my gracious numbers are decay'd
And my sick Muse doth give another place.
I grant, sweet love, thy lovely argument
Deserves the travail of a worthier pen,
Yet what of thee thy poet doth invent
He robs thee of and pays it thee again.
He lends thee virtue and he stole that word
From thy behavior; beauty doth he give
And found it in thy cheek; he can afford
No praise to thee but what in thee doth live.
Then thank him not for that which he doth say,
Since what he owes thee thou thyself dost pay.

LXXX.

O, how I faint when I of you do write,
Knowing a better spirit doth use your name,
And in the praise thereof spends all his might,
To make me tongue-tied, speaking of your fame!
But since your worth, wide as the ocean is,
The humble as the proudest sail doth bear,
My saucy bark inferior far to his
On your broad main doth wilfully appear.
Your shallowest help will hold me up afloat,
Whilst he upon your soundless deep doth ride;
Or being wreck'd, I am a worthless boat,
He of tall building and of goodly pride:
Then if he thrive and I be cast away,
The worst was this; my love was my decay.

LXXXI.

Or I shall live your epitaph to make,
Or you survive when I in earth am rotten;
From hence your memory death cannot take,
Although in me each part will be forgotten.
Your name from hence immortal life shall have,
Though I, once gone, to all the world must die:
The earth can yield me but a common grave,
When you entombed in men's eyes shall lie.
Your monument shall be my gentle verse,
Which eyes not yet created shall o'er-read,
And tongues to be your being shall rehearse
When all the breathers of this world are dead;
You still shall live—such virtue hath my pen—
Where breath most breathes, even in the mouths of men.

LXXXII.

I grant thou wert not married to my Muse
And therefore mayst without attaint o'erlook
The dedicated words which writers use
Of their fair subject, blessing every book
Thou art as fair in knowledge as in hue,
Finding thy worth a limit past my praise,
And therefore art enforced to seek anew
Some fresher stamp of the time-bettering days
And do so, love; yet when they have devised
What strained touches rhetoric can lend,
Thou truly fair wert truly sympathized
In true plain words by thy true-telling friend;
And their gross painting might be better used
Where cheeks need blood; in thee it is abused.

LXXXIII.

I never saw that you did painting need
And therefore to your fair no painting set;
I found, or thought I found, you did exceed
The barren tender of a poet's debt;
And therefore have I slept in your report,
That you yourself being extant well might show
How far a modern quill doth come too short,
Speaking of worth, what worth in you doth grow.
This silence for my sin you did impute,
Which shall be most my glory, being dumb;
For I impair not beauty being mute,
When others would give life and bring a tomb.
There lives more life in one of your fair eyes
Than both your poets can in praise devise.

LXXXIV.

Who is it that says most? which can say more
Than this rich praise, that you alone are you?
In whose confine immured is the store
Which should example where your equal grew.
Lean penury within that pen doth dwell
That to his subject lends not some small glory;
But he that writes of you, if he can tell
That you are you, so dignifies his story,
Let him but copy what in you is writ,
Not making worse what nature made so clear,
And such a counterpart shall fame his wit,
Making his style admired every where.
You to your beauteous blessings add a curse,
Being fond on praise, which makes your praises worse.

LXXXV.

My tongue-tied Muse in manners holds her still,
While comments of your praise, richly compiled,
Reserve their character with golden quill
And precious phrase by all the Muses filed.
I think good thoughts whilst other write good words,
And like unletter'd clerk still cry 'Amen'
To every hymn that able spirit affords
In polish'd form of well-refined pen.
Hearing you praised, I say "Tis so, 'tis true,'
And to the most of praise add something more;
But that is in my thought, whose love to you,
Though words come hindmost, holds his rank before.
Then others for the breath of words respect,
Me for my dumb thoughts, speaking in effect.

LXXXVI.

Was it the proud full sail of his great verse,
Bound for the prize of all too precious you,
That did my ripe thoughts in my brain inhearse,
Making their tomb the womb wherein they grew?
Was it his spirit, by spirits taught to write
Above a mortal pitch, that struck me dead?
No, neither he, nor his compeers by night
Giving him aid, my verse astonished.
He, nor that affable familiar ghost
Which nightly gulls him with intelligence
As victors of my silence cannot boast;
I was not sick of any fear from thence:
But when your countenance fill'd up his line,
Then lack'd I matter; that enfeebled mine.

LXXXVII.

Farewell! thou art too dear for my possessing,
And like enough thou know'st thy estimate:
The charter of thy worth gives thee releasing;
My bonds in thee are all determinate.
For how do I hold thee but by thy granting?
And for that riches where is my deserving?
The cause of this fair gift in me is wanting,
And so my patent back again is swerving.
Thyself thou gavest, thy own worth then not knowing,
Or me, to whom thou gavest it, else mistaking;
So thy great gift, upon misprision growing,
Comes home again, on better judgment making.
Thus have I had thee, as a dream doth flatter,
In sleep a king, but waking no such matter.

LXXXVIII.

When thou shalt be disposed to set me light,
And place my merit in the eye of scorn,
Upon thy side against myself I'll fight,
And prove thee virtuous, though thou art forsworn.
With mine own weakness being best acquainted,
Upon thy part I can set down a story
Of faults conceal'd, wherein I am attainted,
That thou in losing me shalt win much glory:
And I by this will be a gainer too;
For bending all my loving thoughts on thee,
The injuries that to myself I do,
Doing thee vantage, double-vantage me.
Such is my love, to thee I so belong,
That for thy right myself will bear all wrong.

LXXXIX.

Say that thou didst forsake me for some fault,
And I will comment upon that offence;
Speak of my lameness, and I straight will halt,
Against thy reasons making no defence.
Thou canst not, love, disgrace me half so ill,
To set a form upon desired change,
As I'll myself disgrace: knowing thy will,
I will acquaintance strangle and look strange,
Be absent from thy walks, and in my tongue
Thy sweet beloved name no more shall dwell,
Lest I, too much profane, should do it wrong
And haply of our old acquaintance tell.
For thee against myself I'll vow debate,
For I must ne'er love him whom thou dost hate.

XC.

Then hate me when thou wilt; if ever, now;
Now, while the world is bent my deeds to cross,
Join with the spite of fortune, make me bow,
And do not drop in for an after-loss:
Ah, do not, when my heart hath 'scoped this sorrow,
Come in the rearward of a conquer'd woe;
Give not a windy night a rainy morrow,
To linger out a purposed overthrow.
If thou wilt leave me, do not leave me last,
When other petty griefs have done their spite
But in the onset come; so shall I taste
At first the very worst of fortune's might,
And other strains of woe, which now seem woe,
Compared with loss of thee will not seem so.

XCI.

Some glory in their birth, some in their skill,
Some in their wealth, some in their bodies' force,
Some in their garments, though new-fangled ill,
Some in their hawks and hounds, some in their horse;
And every humour hath his adjunct pleasure,
Wherein it finds a joy above the rest:
But these particulars are not my measure;
All these I better in one general best.
Thy love is better than high birth to me,
Richer than wealth, prouder than garments' cost,
Of more delight than hawks or horses be;
And having thee, of all men's pride I boast:
Wretched in this alone, that thou mayst take
All this away and me most wretched make.

XCII.

But do thy worst to steal thyself away,
For term of life thou art assured mine,
And life no longer than thy love will stay,
For it depends upon that love of thine.
Then need I not to fear the worst of wrongs,
When in the least of them my life hath end.
I see a better state to me belongs
Than that which on thy humour doth depend;
Thou canst not vex me with inconstant mind,
Since that my life on thy revolt doth lie.
O, what a happy title do I find,
Happy to have thy love, happy to die!
But what's so blessed-fair that fears no blot?
Thou mayst be false, and yet I know it not.

XCIII.

So shall I live, supposing thou art true,
Like a deceived husband; so love's face
May still seem love to me, though alter'd new;
Thy looks with me, thy heart in other place:
For there can live no hatred in thine eye,
Therefore in that I cannot know thy change.
In many's looks the false heart's history
Is writ in moods and frowns and wrinkles strange,
But heaven in thy creation did decree
That in thy face sweet love should ever dwell;
Whate'er thy thoughts or thy heart's workings be,
Thy looks should nothing thence but sweetness tell.
How like Eve's apple doth thy beauty grow,
if thy sweet virtue answer not thy show!

XCIV.

They that have power to hurt and will do none,
That do not do the thing they most do show,
Who, moving others, are themselves as stone,
Unmoved, cold, and to temptation slow,
They rightly do inherit heaven's graces
And husband nature's riches from expense;
They are the lords and owners of their faces,
Others but stewards of their excellence.
The summer's flower is to the summer sweet,
Though to itself it only live and die,
But if that flower with base infection meet,
The basest weed outbraves his dignity:
For sweetest things turn sourest by their deeds;
Lilies that fester smell far worse than weeds.

XCV.

How sweet and lovely dost thou make the shame
Which, like a canker in the fragrant rose,
Doth spot the beauty of thy budding name!
O, in what sweets dost thou thy sins enclose!
That tongue that tells the story of thy days,
Making lascivious comments on thy sport,
Cannot dispraise but in a kind of praise;
Naming thy name blesses an ill report.
O, what a mansion have those vices got
Which for their habitation chose out thee,
Where beauty's veil doth cover every blot,
And all things turn to fair that eyes can see!
Take heed, dear heart, of this large privilege;
The hardest knife ill-used doth lose his edge.

XCVI.

Some say thy fault is youth, some wantonness;
Some say thy grace is youth and gentle sport;
Both grace and faults are loved of more and less;
Thou makest faults graces that to thee resort.
As on the finger of a throned queen
The basest jewel will be well esteem'd,
So are those errors that in thee are seen
To truths translated and for true things deem'd.
How many lambs might the stern wolf betray,
If like a lamb he could his looks translate!
How many gazers mightst thou lead away,
If thou wouldst use the strength of all thy state!
But do not so; I love thee in such sort
As, thou being mine, mine is thy good report.

XCVII.

How like a winter hath my absence been
From thee, the pleasure of the fleeting year!
What freezings have I felt, what dark days seen!
What old December's bareness every where!
And yet this time removed was summer's time,
The teeming autumn, big with rich increase,
Bearing the wanton burden of the prime,
Like widow'd wombs after their lords' decease:
Yet this abundant issue seem'd to me
But hope of orphans and unfather'd fruit;
For summer and his pleasures wait on thee,
And, thou away, the very birds are mute;
Or, if they sing, 'tis with so dull a cheer
That leaves look pale, dreading the winter's near.

XCVIII.

From you have I been absent in the spring,
When proud-pied April dress'd in all his trim
Hath put a spirit of youth in every thing,
That heavy Saturn laugh'd and leap'd with him.
Yet nor the lays of birds nor the sweet smell
Of different flowers in odour and in hue
Could make me any summer's story tell,
Or from their proud lap pluck them where they grew;
Nor did I wonder at the lily's white,
Nor praise the deep vermilion in the rose;
They were but sweet, but figures of delight,
Drawn after you, you pattern of all those.
Yet seem'd it winter still, and, you away,
As with your shadow I with these did play.

XCIX.

The forward violet thus did I chide:
Sweet thief, whence didst thou steal thy sweet that smells,
If not from my love's breath? The purple pride
Which on thy soft cheek for complexion dwells
In my love's veins thou hast too grossly dyed.
The lily I condemned for thy hand,
And buds of marjoram had stol'n thy hair:
The roses fearfully on thorns did stand,
One blushing shame, another white despair;
A third, nor red nor white, had stol'n of both
And to his robbery had annex'd thy breath;
But, for his theft, in pride of all his growth
A vengeful canker eat him up to death.
More flowers I noted, yet I none could see
But sweet or colour it had stol'n from thee.

C.

Where art thou, Muse, that thou forget'st so long
To speak of that which gives thee all thy might?
Spend'st thou thy fury on some worthless song,
Darkening thy power to lend base subjects light?
Return, forgetful Muse, and straight redeem
In gentle numbers time so idly spent;
Sing to the ear that doth thy lays esteem
And gives thy pen both skill and argument.
Rise, resty Muse, my love's sweet face survey,
If Time have any wrinkle graven there;
If any, be a satire to decay,
And make Time's spoils despised every where.
Give my love fame faster than Time wastes life;
So thou prevent'st his scythe and crooked knife.

CI.

O truant Muse, what shall be thy amends
For thy neglect of truth in beauty dyed?
Both truth and beauty on my love depends;
So dost thou too, and therein dignified.
Make answer, Muse: wilt thou not haply say
'Truth needs no colour, with his colour fix'd;
Beauty no pencil, beauty's truth to lay;
But best is best, if never intermix'd?'
Because he needs no praise, wilt thou be dumb?
Excuse not silence so; for't lies in thee
To make him much outlive a gilded tomb,
And to be praised of ages yet to be.
Then do thy office, Muse; I teach thee how
To make him seem long hence as he shows now.

CII.

My love is strengthen'd, though more weak in seeming;
I love not less, though less the show appear:
That love is merchandized whose rich esteeming
The owner's tongue doth publish every where.
Our love was new and then but in the spring
When I was wont to greet it with my lays,
As Philomel in summer's front doth sing
And stops her pipe in growth of riper days:
Not that the summer is less pleasant now
Than when her mournful hymns did hush the night,
But that wild music burthens every bough
And sweets grown common lose their dear delight.
Therefore like her I sometime hold my tongue,
Because I would not dull you with my song.

CIII.

Alack, what poverty my Muse brings forth,
That having such a scope to show her pride,
The argument all bare is of more worth
Than when it hath my added praise beside!
O, blame me not, if I no more can write!
Look in your glass, and there appears a face
That over-goes my blunt invention quite,
Dulling my lines and doing me disgrace.
Were it not sinful then, striving to mend,
To mar the subject that before was well?
For to no other pass my verses tend
Than of your graces and your gifts to tell;
And more, much more, than in my verse can sit
Your own glass shows you when you look in it.

CIV.

To me, fair friend, you never can be old,
For as you were when first your eye I eyed,
Such seems your beauty still. Three winters cold
Have from the forests shook three summers' pride,
Three beauteous springs to yellow autumn turn'd
In process of the seasons have I seen,
Three April perfumes in three hot Junes burn'd,
Since first I saw you fresh, which yet are green.
Ah! yet doth beauty, like a dial-hand,
Steal from his figure and no pace perceived;
So your sweet hue, which methinks still doth stand,
Hath motion and mine eye may be deceived:
For fear of which, hear this, thou age unbred;
Ere you were born was beauty's summer dead.

CV.

Let not my love be call'd idolatry,
Nor my beloved as an idol show,
Since all alike my songs and praises be
To one, of one, still such, and ever so.
Kind is my love to-day, to-morrow kind,
Still constant in a wondrous excellence;
Therefore my verse to constancy confined,
One thing expressing, leaves out difference.
'Fair, kind and true' is all my argument,
'Fair, kind, and true' varying to other words;
And in this change is my invention spent,
Three themes in one, which wondrous scope affords.
'Fair, kind, and true,' have often lived alone,
Which three till now never kept seat in one.

CVI.

When in the chronicle of wasted time
I see descriptions of the fairest wights,
And beauty making beautiful old rhyme
In praise of ladies dead and lovely knights,
Then, in the blazon of sweet beauty's best,
Of hand, of foot, of lip, of eye, of brow,
I see their antique pen would have express'd
Even such a beauty as you master now.
So all their praises are but prophecies
Of this our time, all you prefiguring;
And, for they look'd but with divining eyes,
They had not skill enough your worth to sing:
For we, which now behold these present days,
Had eyes to wonder, but lack tongues to praise.

CVII.

Not mine own fears, nor the prophetic soul
Of the wide world dreaming on things to come,
Can yet the lease of my true love control,
Supposed as forfeit to a confined doom.
The mortal moon hath her eclipse endured
And the sad augurs mock their own presage;
Incertainties now crown themselves assured
And peace proclaims olives of endless age.
Now with the drops of this most balmy time
My love looks fresh, and death to me subscribes,
Since, spite of him, I'll live in this poor rhyme,
While he insults o'er dull and speechless tribes:
And thou in this shalt find thy monument,
When tyrants' crests and tombs of brass are spent.

CVIII.

What's in the brain that ink may character
Which hath not figured to thee my true spirit?
What's new to speak, what new to register,
That may express my love or thy dear merit?
Nothing, sweet boy; but yet, like prayers divine,
I must, each day say o'er the very same,
Counting no old thing old, thou mine, I thine,
Even as when first I hallow'd thy fair name.
So that eternal love in love's fresh case
Weighs not the dust and injury of age,
Nor gives to necessary wrinkles place,
But makes antiquity for aye his page,
Finding the first conceit of love there bred
Where time and outward form would show it dead.

CIX.

O, never say that I was false of heart,
Though absence seem'd my flame to qualify.
As easy might I from myself depart
As from my soul, which in thy breast doth lie:
That is my home of love: if I have ranged,
Like him that travels I return again,
Just to the time, not with the time exchanged,
So that myself bring water for my stain.
Never believe, though in my nature reign'd
All frailties that besiege all kinds of blood,
That it could so preposterously be stain'd,
To leave for nothing all thy sum of good;
For nothing this wide universe I call,
Save thou, my rose; in it thou art my all.

CX.

Alas, 'tis true I have gone here and there
And made myself a motley to the view,
Gored mine own thoughts, sold cheap what is most dear,
Made old offences of affections new;
Most true it is that I have look'd on truth
Askance and strangely: but, by all above,
These blenches gave my heart another youth,
And worse essays proved thee my best of love.
Now all is done, have what shall have no end:
Mine appetite I never more will grind
On newer proof, to try an older friend,
A god in love, to whom I am confined.
Then give me welcome, next my heaven the best,
Even to thy pure and most most loving breast.

CXI.

O, for my sake do you with Fortune chide,
The guilty goddess of my harmful deeds,
That did not better for my life provide
Than public means which public manners breeds.
Thence comes it that my name receives a brand,
And almost thence my nature is subdued
To what it works in, like the dyer's hand:
Pity me then and wish I were renew'd;
Whilst, like a willing patient, I will drink
Potions of eisel 'gainst my strong infection
No bitterness that I will bitter think,
Nor double penance, to correct correction.
Pity me then, dear friend, and I assure ye
Even that your pity is enough to cure me.

CXII.

Your love and pity doth the impression fill
Which vulgar scandal stamp'd upon my brow;
For what care I who calls me well or ill,
So you o'er-green my bad, my good allow?
You are my all the world, and I must strive
To know my shames and praises from your tongue:
None else to me, nor I to none alive,
That my steel'd sense or changes right or wrong.
In so profound abysm I throw all care
Of others' voices, that my adder's sense
To critic and to flatterer stopped are.
Mark how with my neglect I do dispense:
You are so strongly in my purpose bred
That all the world besides methinks are dead.

CXIII.

Since I left you, mine eye is in my mind;
And that which governs me to go about
Doth part his function and is partly blind,
Seems seeing, but effectually is out;
For it no form delivers to the heart
Of bird, of flower, or shape, which it doth latch:
Of his quick objects hath the mind no part,
Nor his own vision holds what it doth catch:
For if it see the rudest or gentlest sight,
The most sweet favour or deformed'st creature,
The mountain or the sea, the day or night,
The crow or dove, it shapes them to your feature:
Incapable of more, replete with you,
My most true mind thus makes mine eye untrue.

CXIV.

Or whether doth my mind, being crown'd with you,
Drink up the monarch's plague, this flattery?
Or whether shall I say, mine eye saith true,
And that your love taught it this alchemy,
To make of monsters and things indigest
Such cherubins as your sweet self resemble,
Creating every bad a perfect best,
As fast as objects to his beams assemble?
O, 'tis the first; 'tis flattery in my seeing,
And my great mind most kingly drinks it up:
Mine eye well knows what with his gust is 'greeing,
And to his palate doth prepare the cup:
If it be poison'd, 'tis the lesser sin
That mine eye loves it and doth first begin.

CXV.

Those lines that I before have writ do lie,
Even those that said I could not love you dearer:
Yet then my judgment knew no reason why
My most full flame should afterwards burn clearer.
But reckoning time, whose million'd accidents
Creep in 'twixt vows and change decrees of kings,
Tan sacred beauty, blunt the sharp'st intents,
Divert strong minds to the course of altering things;
Alas, why, fearing of time's tyranny,
Might I not then say 'Now I love you best,'
When I was certain o'er incertainty,
Crowning the present, doubting of the rest?
Love is a babe; then might I not say so,
To give full growth to that which still doth grow?

CXVI.

Let me not to the marriage of true minds
Admit impediments. Love is not love
Which alters when it alteration finds,
Or bends with the remover to remove:
O no! it is an ever-fixed mark
That looks on tempests and is never shaken;
It is the star to every wandering bark,
Whose worth's unknown, although his height be taken.
Love's not Time's fool, though rosy lips and cheeks
Within his bending sickle's compass come:
Love alters not with his brief hours and weeks,
But bears it out even to the edge of doom.
If this be error and upon me proved,
I never writ, nor no man ever loved.

CXVII.

Accuse me thus: that I have scanted all
Wherein I should your great deserts repay,
Forgot upon your dearest love to call,
Whereto all bonds do tie me day by day;
That I have frequent been with unknown minds
And given to time your own dear-purchased right
That I have hoisted sail to all the winds
Which should transport me farthest from your sight.
Book both my wilfulness and errors down
And on just proof surmise accumulate;
Bring me within the level of your frown,
But shoot not at me in your waken'd hate;
Since my appeal says I did strive to prove
The constancy and virtue of your love.

CXVIII.

Like as, to make our appetites more keen,
With eager compounds we our palate urge,
As, to prevent our maladies unseen,
We sicken to shun sickness when we purge,
Even so, being full of your ne'er-cloying sweetness,
To bitter sauces did I frame my feeding
And, sick of welfare, found a kind of meetness
To be diseased ere that there was true needing.
Thus policy in love, to anticipate
The ills that were not, grew to faults assured
And brought to medicine a healthful state
Which, rank of goodness, would by ill be cured:
But thence I learn, and find the lesson true,
Drugs poison him that so fell sick of you.

CXIX.

What potions have I drunk of Siren tears,
Distill'd from limbecks foul as hell within,
Applying fears to hopes and hopes to fears,
Still losing when I saw myself to win!
What wretched errors hath my heart committed,
Whilst it hath thought itself so blessed never!
How have mine eyes out of their spheres been fitted
In the distraction of this madding fever!
O benefit of ill! now I find true
That better is by evil still made better;
And ruin'd love, when it is built anew,
Grows fairer than at first, more strong, far greater.
So I return rebuked to my content
And gain by ill thrice more than I have spent.

CXX.

That you were once unkind befriends me now,
And for that sorrow which I then did feel
Needs must I under my transgression bow,
Unless my nerves were brass or hammer'd steel.
For if you were by my unkindness shaken
As I by yours, you've pass'd a hell of time,
And I, a tyrant, have no leisure taken
To weigh how once I suffered in your crime.
O, that our night of woe might have remember'd
My deepest sense, how hard true sorrow hits,
And soon to you, as you to me, then tender'd
The humble salve which wounded bosoms fits!
But that your trespass now becomes a fee;
Mine ransoms yours, and yours must ransom me.

CXXI.

'Tis better to be vile than vile esteem'd,
When not to be receives reproach of being,
And the just pleasure lost which is so deem'd
Not by our feeling but by others' seeing:
For why should others false adulterate eyes
Give salutation to my sportive blood?
Or on my frailties why are frailer spies,
Which in their wills count bad what I think good?
No, I am that I am, and they that level
At my abuses reckon up their own:
I may be straight, though they themselves be bevel;
By their rank thoughts my deeds must not be shown;
Unless this general evil they maintain,
All men are bad, and in their badness reign.

CXXII.

Thy gift, thy tables, are within my brain
Full character'd with lasting memory,
Which shall above that idle rank remain
Beyond all date, even to eternity;
Or at the least, so long as brain and heart
Have faculty by nature to subsist;
Till each to razed oblivion yield his part
Of thee, thy record never can be miss'd.
That poor retention could not so much hold,
Nor need I tallies thy dear love to score;
Therefore to give them from me was I bold,
To trust those tables that receive thee more:
To keep an adjunct to remember thee
Were to import forgetfulness in me.

CXXIII.

No, Time, thou shalt not boast that I do change:
Thy pyramids built up with newer might
To me are nothing novel, nothing strange;
They are but dressings of a former sight.
Our dates are brief, and therefore we admire
What thou dost foist upon us that is old,
And rather make them born to our desire
Than think that we before have heard them told.
Thy registers and thee I both defy,
Not wondering at the present nor the past,
For thy records and what we see doth lie,
Made more or less by thy continual haste.
This I do vow and this shall ever be;
I will be true, despite thy scythe and thee.

CXXIV.

If my dear love were but the child of state,
It might for Fortune's bastard be unfather'd'
As subject to Time's love or to Time's hate,
Weeds among weeds, or flowers with flowers gather'd.
No, it was builded far from accident;
It suffers not in smiling pomp, nor falls
Under the blow of thralled discontent,
Whereto the inviting time our fashion calls:
It fears not policy, that heretic,
Which works on leases of short-number'd hours,
But all alone stands hugely politic,
That it nor grows with heat nor drowns with showers.
To this I witness call the fools of time,
Which die for goodness, who have lived for crime.

CXXV.

Were 't aught to me I bore the canopy,
With my extern the outward honouring,
Or laid great bases for eternity,
Which prove more short than waste or ruining?
Have I not seen dwellers on form and favour
Lose all, and more, by paying too much rent,
For compound sweet forgoing simple savour,
Pitiful thrivers, in their gazing spent?
No, let me be obsequious in thy heart,
And take thou my oblation, poor but free,
Which is not mix'd with seconds, knows no art,
But mutual render, only me for thee.
Hence, thou suborn'd informer! a true soul
When most impeach'd stands least in thy control.

CXXVI.

O thou, my lovely boy, who in thy power
Dost hold Time's fickle glass, his sickle, hour;
Who hast by waning grown, and therein show'st
Thy lovers withering as thy sweet self grow'st;
If Nature, sovereign mistress over wrack,
As thou goest onwards, still will pluck thee back,
She keeps thee to this purpose, that her skill
May time disgrace and wretched minutes kill.
Yet fear her, O thou minion of her pleasure!
She may detain, but not still keep, her treasure:
Her audit, though delay'd, answer'd must be,
And her quietus is to render thee.

The "Dark Lady" Sonnets (CXXVII–CLII)

CXXVII.

In the old age black was not counted fair,
Or if it were, it bore not beauty's name;
But now is black beauty's successive heir,
And beauty slander'd with a bastard shame:
For since each hand hath put on nature's power,
Fairing the foul with art's false borrow'd face,
Sweet beauty hath no name, no holy bower,
But is profaned, if not lives in disgrace.
Therefore my mistress' brows are raven black,
Her eyes so suited, and they mourners seem
At such who, not born fair, no beauty lack,
Slandering creation with a false esteem:
Yet so they mourn, becoming of their woe,
That every tongue says beauty should look so.

CXXVIII.

How oft, when thou, my music, music play'st,
Upon that blessed wood whose motion sounds
With thy sweet fingers, when thou gently sway'st
The wiry concord that mine ear confounds,
Do I envy those jacks that nimble leap
To kiss the tender inward of thy hand,
Whilst my poor lips, which should that harvest reap,
At the wood's boldness by thee blushing stand!
To be so tickled, they would change their state
And situation with those dancing chips,
O'er whom thy fingers walk with gentle gait,
Making dead wood more blest than living lips.
Since saucy jacks so happy are in this,
Give them thy fingers, me thy lips to kiss.

CXXIX.

The expense of spirit in a waste of shame
Is lust in action; and till action, lust
Is perjured, murderous, bloody, full of blame,
Savage, extreme, rude, cruel, not to trust,
Enjoy'd no sooner but despised straight,
Past reason hunted, and no sooner had
Past reason hated, as a swallow'd bait
On purpose laid to make the taker mad;
Mad in pursuit and in possession so;
Had, having, and in quest to have, extreme;
A bliss in proof, and proved, a very woe;
Before, a joy proposed; behind, a dream.
All this the world well knows; yet none knows well
To shun the heaven that leads men to this hell.

CXXX.

My mistress' eyes are nothing like the sun;
Coral is far more red than her lips' red;
If snow be white, why then her breasts are dun;
If hairs be wires, black wires grow on her head.
I have seen roses damask'd, red and white,
But no such roses see I in her cheeks;
And in some perfumes is there more delight
Than in the breath that from my mistress reeks.
I love to hear her speak, yet well I know
That music hath a far more pleasing sound;
I grant I never saw a goddess go;
My mistress, when she walks, treads on the ground:
And yet, by heaven, I think my love as rare
As any she belied with false compare.

CXXXI.

Thou art as tyrannous, so as thou art,
As those whose beauties proudly make them cruel;
For well thou know'st to my dear doting heart
Thou art the fairest and most precious jewel.
Yet, in good faith, some say that thee behold
Thy face hath not the power to make love groan:
To say they err I dare not be so bold,
Although I swear it to myself alone.
And, to be sure that is not false I swear,
A thousand groans, but thinking on thy face,
One on another's neck, do witness bear
Thy black is fairest in my judgment's place.
In nothing art thou black save in thy deeds,
And thence this slander, as I think, proceeds.

CXXXII.

Thine eyes I love, and they, as pitying me,
Knowing thy heart torments me with disdain,
Have put on black and loving mourners be,
Looking with pretty ruth upon my pain.
And truly not the morning sun of heaven
Better becomes the grey cheeks of the east,
Nor that full star that ushers in the even
Doth half that glory to the sober west,
As those two mourning eyes become thy face:
O, let it then as well beseem thy heart
To mourn for me, since mourning doth thee grace,
And suit thy pity like in every part.
  Then will I swear beauty herself is black
  And all they foul that thy complexion lack.

CXXXIII.

Beshrew that heart that makes my heart to groan
For that deep wound it gives my friend and me!
Is't not enough to torture me alone,
But slave to slavery my sweet'st friend must be?
Me from myself thy cruel eye hath taken,
And my next self thou harder hast engross'd:
Of him, myself, and thee, I am forsaken;
A torment thrice threefold thus to be cross'd.
Prison my heart in thy steel bosom's ward,
But then my friend's heart let my poor heart bail;
Whoe'er keeps me, let my heart be his guard;
Thou canst not then use rigor in my gaol:
  And yet thou wilt; for I, being pent in thee,
  Perforce am thine, and all that is in me.

CXXXIV.

So, now I have confess'd that he is thine,
And I myself am mortgaged to thy will,
Myself I'll forfeit, so that other mine
Thou wilt restore, to be my comfort still:
But thou wilt not, nor he will not be free,
For thou art covetous and he is kind;
He learn'd but surety-like to write for me
Under that bond that him as fast doth bind.
The statute of thy beauty thou wilt take,
Thou usurer, that put'st forth all to use,
And sue a friend came debtor for my sake;
So him I lose through my unkind abuse.
  Him have I lost; thou hast both him and me:
  He pays the whole, and yet am I not free.

CXXXV.

Whoever hath her wish, thou hast thy 'Will,'
And 'Will' to boot, and 'Will' in overplus;
More than enough am I that vex thee still,
To thy sweet will making addition thus.
Wilt thou, whose will is large and spacious,
Not once vouchsafe to hide my will in thine?
Shall will in others seem right gracious,
And in my will no fair acceptance shine?
The sea all water, yet receives rain still
And in abundance addeth to his store;
So thou, being rich in 'Will,' add to thy 'Will'
One will of mine, to make thy large 'Will' more.
  Let no unkind, no fair beseechers kill;
  Think all but one, and me in that one 'Will.'

CXXXVI.

If thy soul check thee that I come so near,
Swear to thy blind soul that I was thy 'Will,'
And will, thy soul knows, is admitted there;
Thus far for love my love-suit, sweet, fulfil.
'Will' will fulfil the treasure of thy love,
Ay, fill it full with wills, and my will one.
In things of great receipt with ease we prove
Among a number one is reckon'd none:
Then in the number let me pass untold,
Though in thy stores' account I one must be;
For nothing hold me, so it please thee hold
That nothing me, a something sweet to thee:
  Make but my name thy love, and love that still,
  And then thou lovest me, for my name is 'Will.'

CXXXVII.

Thou blind fool, Love, what dost thou to mine eyes,
That they behold, and see not what they see?
They know what beauty is, see where it lies,
Yet what the best is take the worst to be.
If eyes corrupt by over-partial looks
Be anchor'd in the bay where all men ride,
Why of eyes' falsehood hast thou forged hooks,
Whereto the judgment of my heart is tied?
Why should my heart think that a several plot
Which my heart knows the wide world's common place?
Or mine eyes seeing this, say this is not,
To put fair truth upon so foul a face?
  In things right true my heart and eyes have erred,
  And to this false plague are they now transferr'd.

CXXXVIII.

When my love swears that she is made of truth
I do believe her, though I know she lies,
That she might think me some untutor'd youth,
Unlearned in the world's false subtleties.
Thus vainly thinking that she thinks me young,
Although she knows my days are past the best,
Simply I credit her false speaking tongue:
On both sides thus is simple truth suppress'd.
But wherefore says she not she is unjust?
And wherefore say not I that I am old?
O, love's best habit is in seeming trust,
And age in love loves not to have years told:
Therefore I lie with her and she with me,
And in our faults by lies we flatter'd be.

CXXXIX.

O, call not me to justify the wrong
That thy unkindness lays upon my heart;
Wound me not with thine eye but with thy tongue;
Use power with power and slay me not by art.
Tell me thou lovest elsewhere, but in my sight,
Dear heart, forbear to glance thine eye aside:
What need'st thou wound with cunning when thy might
Is more than my o'er-press'd defense can bide?
Let me excuse thee: ah! my love well knows
Her pretty looks have been mine enemies,
And therefore from my face she turns my foes,
That they elsewhere might dart their injuries:
Yet do not so; but since I am near slain,
Kill me outright with looks and rid my pain.

CXL.

Be wise as thou art cruel; do not press
My tongue-tied patience with too much disdain;
Lest sorrow lend me words and words express
The manner of my pity-wanting pain.
If I might teach thee wit, better it were,
Though not to love, yet, love, to tell me so;
As testy sick men, when their deaths be near,
No news but health from their physicians know;
For if I should despair, I should grow mad,
And in my madness might speak ill of thee:
Now this ill-wresting world is grown so bad,
Mad slanderers by mad ears believed be,
That I may not be so, nor thou belied,
Bear thine eyes straight, though thy proud heart go wide.

CXLI.

In faith, I do not love thee with mine eyes,
For they in thee a thousand errors note;
But 'tis my heart that loves what they despise,
Who in despite of view is pleased to dote;
Nor are mine ears with thy tongue's tune delighted,
Nor tender feeling, to base touches prone,
Nor taste, nor smell, desire to be invited
To any sensual feast with thee alone:
But my five wits nor my five senses can
Dissuade one foolish heart from serving thee,
Who leaves unsway'd the likeness of a man,
Thy proud hearts slave and vassal wretch to be:
Only my plague thus far I count my gain,
That she that makes me sin awards me pain.

CXLII.

Love is my sin and thy dear virtue hate,
Hate of my sin, grounded on sinful loving:
O, but with mine compare thou thine own state,
And thou shalt find it merits not reproving;
Or, if it do, not from those lips of thine,
That have profaned their scarlet ornaments
And seal'd false bonds of love as oft as mine,
Robb'd others' beds' revenues of their rents.
Be it lawful I love thee, as thou lovest those
Whom thine eyes woo as mine importune thee:
Root pity in thy heart, that when it grows
Thy pity may deserve to pitied be.
If thou dost seek to have what thou dost hide,
By self-example mayst thou be denied!

CXLIII.

Lo! as a careful housewife runs to catch
One of her feather'd creatures broke away,
Sets down her babe and makes an swift dispatch
In pursuit of the thing she would have stay,
Whilst her neglected child holds her in chase,
Cries to catch her whose busy care is bent
To follow that which flies before her face,
Not prizing her poor infant's discontent;
So runn'st thou after that which flies from thee,
Whilst I thy babe chase thee afar behind;
But if thou catch thy hope, turn back to me,
And play the mother's part, kiss me, be kind:
So will I pray that thou mayst have thy 'Will,'
If thou turn back, and my loud crying still.

CXLIV.

Two loves I have of comfort and despair,
Which like two spirits do suggest me still:
The better angel is a man right fair,
The worser spirit a woman colour'd ill.
To win me soon to hell, my female evil
Tempteth my better angel from my side,
And would corrupt my saint to be a devil,
Wooing his purity with her foul pride.
And whether that my angel be turn'd fiend
Suspect I may, but not directly tell;
But being both from me, both to each friend,
I guess one angel in another's hell:
Yet this shall I ne'er know, but live in doubt,
Till my bad angel fire my good one out.

CXLV.

Those lips that Love's own hand did make
Breathed forth the sound that said 'I hate'
To me that languish'd for her sake;
But when she saw my woeful state,
Straight in her heart did mercy come,
Chiding that tongue that ever sweet
Was used in giving gentle doom,
And taught it thus anew to greet:
'I hate' she alter'd with an end,
That follow'd it as gentle day
Doth follow night, who like a fiend
From heaven to hell is flown away;
'I hate' from hate away she threw,
And saved my life, saying 'not you.'

CXLVI.

Poor soul, the centre of my sinful earth,
[ ] these rebel powers that thee array;
Why dost thou pine within and suffer dearth,
Painting thy outward walls so costly gay?
Why so large cost, having so short a lease,
Dost thou upon thy fading mansion spend?
Shall worms, inheritors of this excess,
Eat up thy charge? is this thy body's end?
Then soul, live thou upon thy servant's loss,
And let that pine to aggravate thy store;
Buy terms divine in selling hours of dross;
Within be fed, without be rich no more:
So shalt thou feed on Death, that feeds on men,
And Death once dead, there's no more dying then.

CXLVII.

My love is as a fever, longing still
For that which longer nurseth the disease,
Feeding on that which doth preserve the ill,
The uncertain sickly appetite to please.
My reason, the physician to my love,
Angry that his prescriptions are not kept,
Hath left me, and I desperate now approve
Desire is death, which physic did except.
Past cure I am, now reason is past care,
And frantic-mad with evermore unrest;
My thoughts and my discourse as madmen's are,
At random from the truth vainly express'd;
For I have sworn thee fair and thought thee bright,
Who art as black as hell, as dark as night.

CXLVIII.

O me, what eyes hath Love put in my head,
Which have no correspondence with true sight!
Or, if they have, where is my judgment fled,
That censures falsely what they see aright?
If that be fair whereon my false eyes dote,
What means the world to say it is not so?
If it be not, then love doth well denote
Love's eye is not so true as all men's 'No.'
How can it? O, how can Love's eye be true,
That is so vex'd with watching and with tears?
No marvel then, though I mistake my view;
The sun itself sees not till heaven clears.
O cunning Love! with tears thou keep'st me blind,
Lest eyes well-seeing thy foul faults should find.

CXLIX.

Canst thou, O cruel! say I love thee not,
When I against myself with thee partake?
Do I not think on thee, when I forgot
Am of myself, all tyrant, for thy sake?
Who hateth thee that I do call my friend?
On whom frown'st thou that I do fawn upon?
Nay, if thou lour'st on me, do I not spend
Revenge upon myself with present moan?
What merit do I in myself respect,
That is so proud thy service to despise,
When all my best doth worship thy defect,
Commanded by the motion of thine eyes?
But, love, hate on, for now I know thy mind;
Those that can see thou lovest, and I am blind.

CL.

O, from what power hast thou this powerful might
With insufficiency my heart to sway?
To make me give the lie to my true sight,
And swear that brightness doth not grace the day?
Whence hast thou this becoming of things ill,
That in the very refuse of thy deeds
There is such strength and warrantize of skill
That, in my mind, thy worst all best exceeds?
Who taught thee how to make me love thee more
The more I hear and see just cause of hate?
O, though I love what others do abhor,
With others thou shouldst not abhor my state:
If thy unworthiness raised love in me,
More worthy I to be beloved of thee.

CLI.

Love is too young to know what conscience is;
Yet who knows not conscience is born of love?
Then, gentle cheater, urge not my amiss,
Lest guilty of my faults thy sweet self prove:
For, thou betraying me, I do betray
My nobler part to my gross body's treason;
My soul doth tell my body that he may
Triumph in love; flesh stays no father reason;
But, rising at thy name, doth point out thee
As his triumphant prize. Proud of this pride,
He is contented thy poor drudge to be,
To stand in thy affairs, fall by thy side.
No want of conscience hold it that I call
Her love for whose dear love I rise and fall.

CLII.

In loving thee thou know'st I am forsworn,
But thou art twice forsworn, to me love swearing,
In act thy bed-vow broke and new faith torn,
In vowing new hate after new love bearing.
But why of two oaths' breach do I accuse thee,
When I break twenty? I am perjured most;
For all my vows are oaths but to misuse thee
And all my honest faith in thee is lost,
For I have sworn deep oaths of thy deep kindness,
Oaths of thy love, thy truth, thy constancy,
And, to enlighten thee, gave eyes to blindness,
Or made them swear against the thing they see;
For I have sworn thee fair; more perjured eye,
To swear against the truth so foul a lie!

The "Cupid" Sonnets (CLIII–CLIV)

CLIII.

Cupid laid by his brand, and fell asleep:
A maid of Dian's this advantage found,
And his love-kindling fire did quickly steep
In a cold valley-fountain of that ground;
Which borrow'd from this holy fire of Love
A dateless lively heat, still to endure,
And grew a seething bath, which yet men prove
Against strange maladies a sovereign cure.
But at my mistress' eye Love's brand new-fired,
The boy for trial needs would touch my breast;
I, sick withal, the help of bath desired,
And thither hied, a sad distemper'd guest,
But found no cure: the bath for my help lies
Where Cupid got new fire—my mistress' eyes.

CLIV.

The little Love-god lying once asleep
Laid by his side his heart-inflaming brand,
Whilst many nymphs that vow'd chaste life to keep
Came tripping by; but in her maiden hand
The fairest votary took up that fire
Which many legions of true hearts had warm'd;
And so the general of hot desire
Was sleeping by a virgin hand disarm'd.
This brand she quenched in a cool well by,
Which from Love's fire took heat perpetual,
Growing a bath and healthful remedy
For men diseased; but I, my mistress' thrall,
Came there for cure, and this by that I prove,
Love's fire heats water, water cools not love.

INDEX